THE SMYTHSON CIRCLE

By the same author and available from Peter Owen

Bess of Hardwick: Portrait of an Elizabethan Dynast

THE SMYTHSON CIRCLE

THE STORY OF SIX GREAT ENGLISH HOUSES

DAVID N. DURANT

Peter Owen
London and Chicago

PETER OWEN PUBLISHERS

20 Holland Park Avenue, London W11 3QU

Peter Owen books are distributed in the USA and Canada by
Independent Publishers Group
814 North Franklin Street, Chicago, IL 60610, USA

First published in Great Britain 2011 by
Peter Owen Publishers

ISBN 978-0-7206-1344-5

A catalogue record for this book is available from the British Library

Printed and bound in Great Britain by
Windsor, Tonbridge, Kent

This book is dedicated to the loving memory of our son Nicholas and to our two youngest grandchildren Jack and Lillie.

ACKNOWLEDGEMENTS

I am grateful to Dr Richard Sheppard and David Knight of the Trent and Peak Archaeological Unit of the University of Nottingham who generously made available to me the unpublished reports on surveys and excavations carried out at Old Hardwick Hall. In this respect an archaeological survey at the Old Hall is well overdue, but I have been unable to prevail on English Heritage to commission such a programme. Dr Jennnifer S. Alexander, who has undertaken a considerable amount of research into the masons' marks at Apethorpe Hall, Northamptonshire, gave me a very interesting afternoon at Old Hardwick Hall, and I am grateful to her for sharing her knowledge of the subject. Dr Kate Harris, archivist at Longleat, helped me negotiate the research I needed for that remarkable building. Victoria Perry, archivist at Hatfield Hall, helpfully dug the floor plan of Longleat out for me. Andrew Peppitt and Charles Noble, joint keepers of the archives at Chatsworth, were unstinting in their labours in locating the items I needed. It is some thirty years since I was last intimate with the invaluable Devonshire archives, and there have inevitably been necessary changes. Dr Malcolm Airs very generously made available to me his Longleat research notes. Dr Lucy Worsley, who was at one time English Heritage's custodian of Bolsover Castle, very generously gave me valuable information on that extraordinary building and allowed me to use her unpublished papers as well as her published articles on Bolsover. Grateful thanks to Andrew Barber, curator for the National Trust, Hardwick Hall, who generously gave me access to New Hardwick, and to Nigel Wright, the Hardwick Hall House and Collections

Manager, for accompanying me on several 'closed-day' visits to Hardwick to take photographs. In particular, I am grateful to Rodney Melville of Rodney Melville and Partners, the architect responsible for the structure and fabric of Hardwick, whom I first met forty years ago and who, although now retired, still cares for the building; his knowledge is unrivalled. His confirmation of my theories on the structure of Hardwick was reassuring, and his additional information was fascinating. My sincere thanks to Jayne Amat of the Manuscripts and Special Collections, University of Nottingham, who unfailingly had ready for me the manuscripts I needed. I am grateful to Mrs Jean Roberts for a large file formerly belonging to the late F.W.C. Gregory, FRIBA, a Nottingham architect who did a great deal of research on Bolsover Castle. The file will be deposited with the Nottingham Local Studies Library.

This book could never have been written without the considerable research by an old friend, Dr Mark Girouard, in his two books *Robert Smythson and the Architecture of the Elizabethan Era* (1966) and *Robert Smythson and the Elizabethan Country House* (1983), and more recently his magisterial volume *Elizabethan Architecture* published in 2009. I am more grateful than I can say to my friend and neighbour, Allan Joyce of Allan Joyce Architects, Nottingham, who rescued me and drew all the essential floor plans of the six buildings of this book.

Also I have been continually grateful to an old and dear friend, Dr Rosalys Coope, who was responsible for establishing the iconography of the decoration in Bolsover Castle. She has lent her notes and a great deal else to me and has been an invaluable listener. At the same time my grateful thanks are due to Dr Maurice Howard, who provided invaluable information concerning *Logis Domestique*.

A good editor can vastly improve a book, and I have been very lucky to have the inspired team at Peter Owen under the Editorial Director, Antonia Owen. Charles Phillips proved to be a very good copy-editor and saved me from solecisms and other traps. Simon Smith, Peter Owen's in-house editor, has also been a source of inspiration and encouragement. Nick

Pearson, who has controlled my illustrations when restraint is needed – I wanted many more – has proved a further inspiration, and to him is due the jacket, which, in a single detail of a turret, sums up the contents of this book. The staff of Southwell Public Library deserve my thanks; they have obtained for me the research volumes I have asked for, no matter how obscure – even in one case an unpublished thesis – without a single complaint.

It is customary to thank one's wife for her patience and forbearance during the writing of a book. In her case she has proved to be a careful editor, for which I am grateful, as I am also for her in letting me fill our dining-room with card indexes, research papers and countless files. By the time this book is published Christabel will have got her dining-room back!

CONTENTS

A NOTE ON SPELLINGS

Elizabethan spelling was phonetic – Dr Johnson had not yet written his dictionary – and at times one can almost hear the local accent of the writer or speaker. In this present book, where I am quoting from an original document, I have used the original spelling; otherwise, in my own text, I have standardized with modern spelling. Names are spelled variously: Hardwick is sometimes Hardwicke – the final 'e' serving to accentuate the 'k' – Ward is often rendered as Warde, Ashmoor as Ashmore, Accres as Acres. Furthermore, as the majority of Elizabethans could neither read nor write, legal documents, such as those reprinted in the appendices here, were signed simply with a person's mark. I have not attempted to transcribe these 'signatures' but simply put '[his mark]'.

ILLUSTRATIONS

INTRODUCTION

Robert Smythson was the foremost architect of the sixteenth century. This is the story of six great houses that he designed or worked on or with which his main craftsmen were involved: Longleat in Wiltshire, where Smythson worked from 1568 until he moved to the second great house he worked on, Wollaton Hall in Nottinghamshire, in the 1580s; the Elizabethan Chatsworth in Derbyshire; Old Hardwick Hall and New Hardwick Hall in Derbyshire; and Bolsover Castle, also in Derbyshire. There are several connecting links: three houses were designed by Robert Smythson; three were built by Elizabeth Talbot, from 1568 Countess of Shrewsbury and known as Bess of Hardwick; five are within a thirty-mile (fifty-kilometre) radius of each other, and by great good fortune the building accounts survive in part for all six of the buildings, a rarity for the period. Four of the houses still stand, but one (Old Hardwick) is a ruin, and in one case (Chatsworth) the Elizabethan house was rebuilt, beginning in the late seventeenth century, on the foundations of the old building. Of Bess's work the Elizabethan cellars may survive, but I have been unable to examine them because of the work going on there; the Hunting Tower and Queen Mary's Bower are the only certain survivals from her building. Longleat (except for the interior), Wollaton Hall (except for the interior), New Hardwick Hall and Bolsover Castle remain much as they were built.

All are houses on which skilled craftsmen were employed creating Smythson's architecture, and these men provide a common thread running through the buildings. From the evidence of the surviving building accounts, some master craftsmen are traced from Longleat to Wollaton or from Chatsworth to Wollaton and then to Hardwick. Working with these men were teams of lesser craftsmen, such as the masons who were employed in cutting stone blocks, jambs and lintels for doors and windows; their names are seldom known and can be identified only by the marks they cut into the stones they worked. They made these marks so that the head mason could see who had done what and pay them accordingly from the payments he had received from the clerk of the works. By the marks we can follow them from building to building, with two exceptions: at Longleat and Wollaton Hall masons were paid by the day and so had no need to mark their work. The work of one craftsman, Thomas Accres, was never marked because he was paid an annual wage by Bess of Hardwick. Accres was a genius in modelling plaster and sculpting stone but was called a mason. He had an apprentice named Luke Dolphin working with him and by 1600 another named Miles Padley.

The magnet for these craftsmen was Robert Smythson, the first in England to be called an architect. He is first mentioned in 1568 when he was working as head mason at the final building of Longleat, in Wiltshire, where Sir John Thynne's building works lasted for thirty-three years until his death in 1580. Smythson arrived at Longleat in March 1568 with a letter of recommendation from Humphrey Lovell, the queen's master mason; he was taken on at 16d. a day and so became the highest paid of the Longleat craftsmen. He brought with him John Hills (a mason), Richard Crispin (a carpenter) and, from 1571, Christopher Lovell (a mason, like his father Humphrey). These three left Wiltshire for Nottingham when Sir Francis Willoughby began Wollaton in 1580, the year Thynne died. Smythson took charge of the building at Wollaton, a significant promotion.

In about 1670 an English statesman named Sir William Coventry wrote that few building craftsmen 'rely on their Trade as not to have a small Farm, the Rent of which they are the more able to pay by gains of their Trade'. Sir William's meaning was that, when unemployed, craftsmen survived from the produce of a small farm or smallholding. This may have been so in the late seventeenth century, when he was writing, but it will be seen that it was only the lucky few who gained a farm a century earlier. Sir William was underlining the irregular employment of building craftsmen – and this was as true in his time as it had been a century earlier. Of those we shall follow, Smythson settled in Wollaton, where his plaque survives on the wall of the church, and became a bailiff collecting rent for Sir Francis Willoughby; meanwhile, Thomas Accres, Abraham Smith and John Painter (whose surname is often recorded as Balechous – see paragraph below) all settled on rent-free farms near Hardwick, and Painter built his own pub, the Hardwick Inn, at the gates of Hardwick in 1609, the year after Bess of Hardwick's death.

The spelling of many of the craftsmen's names in the original documents is variable and phonetic. John Rhodes, for example, was variously known as Roods, Rodes or Roads; I have stuck to Rhodes. When it comes to John Painter I have used the spelling Balechous, which is the name his family members used at the Hardwick Inn. Mark Girouard has suggested that Balechous was northern European, a name too difficult for English speakers, and he was called Painter because that was his skill.

Over the fifty-odd years of building activity covered by this book the wages paid to the craftsmen remained static: at Longleat in 1560 masons were paid 10–12d. a day, the same rate paid at Bolsover Castle in 1612–14. Head masons, such as Smythson at Longleat, were paid 12–16d. a day, the same rate that the Rhodes brothers were paid at Wollaton in the 1580s. When the Rhodes moved to New Hardwick they were paid on piecework for the building of the walls. This was a huge job, and there is no means of establishing what the Rhodes as individuals were paid, because the sums given to them included payment of the masons working under them. For example, from 11 December 1691 to 23 December 1692, while working on New Hardwick, Rhodes received in cash the sum of £138. 8s. 3d., which covered his charges and those of his team of 'fellows'. The average annual expenditure on building work at Hardwick over eleven years from 1587 onwards was £340; clearly Rhodes had a very responsible job.[1] A further problem in making payment comparisons is the way in which the building accounts were kept and the work was organized. For example, at Wollaton the payments were made weekly for days worked at an already agreed rate – craftsmen were simply paid for working, not on defined piecework or by contract. At Wollaton there are no recognizable masons' marks from this period, for there was no point in making them – the craftsmen were paid by the day not by the job; what marks there are come from the alterations made in *c.* 1801–4 when the building was significantly altered by the architect Jeffry Wyatville.

Hardwick MS 6 is the most detailed of all the account books. It contains more than six hundred pages and covers both Old Hardwick Hall and New Hardwick Hall. Some of the craftsmen were paid on agreed 'bargains-in-great'. These were written contracts detailing the work to be done, with payments at stated intervals: for example, at the start, at halfway and at completion (see Appendix III for examples of two bargains-in-great). A head mason such as John Rhodes had a team working for him whose members were paid by him from the payments he received from the clerk of the works. Bargains-in-great are recorded for the building of both Old and New Hardwick Halls. At Bolsover Castle the method of payment differed again: masons were paid for piecework – for example, so much for so many feet of cornice. Nevertheless, it is possible to get a good idea of the rates in order to make a comparison.

At the lowest level were the labourers who, over the period covered by this book, were paid 6d. a day with milk and bread. At Wadham College, Oxford, in the 1550s, by way of comparison, labourers were paid between 8d. and 12d. a day but had to feed themselves – the difference, of course, being that the six buildings discussed here were in the countryside and there was little chance of labourers going home at the end of the working day.

It is notoriously difficult to make comparisons with the present-day value of money; for the purpose of this book I have taken a mason's daily wage to be 10d. a day. A mason worked six days a week and, according to the Wollaton accounts, took twenty-five saints' days off in a year, leaving 288 working days, provided that he was fully employed; this gave him £12 a year. A labourer on 6d. a day would for the same 288 days earn £7. 4s.

Work followed a seasonal rhythm. The best weather for building was usually in the summer months from May to the end of August, yet this coincided with the busiest period for farm labourers. The agricultural year should logically have taken precedence, but this was not the case – at Longleat and at Hardwick the number of labourers increased for those three months in the years 1589 and 1591. At Wollaton workers were required to provide free labour as part of their feudal rent. The seasonal rhythm can be followed in the labour accounts in Part 1 of *The Building of Hardwick Hall* (Durant and Riden), pp. xxxvii–xlii (see Bibliography).

The working week was six days with Sunday a day of rest, but occasionally the men were paid extra to work over a holiday. It was gruelling work. Women were also employed. Bess of Hardwick employed women only for light work in her gardens. However, at Wollaton Hall they were employed in carrying limestone for the kilns, while at Bolsover, built by Bess's youngest son Sir Charles Cavendish, twenty-four women were employed at 3d. or 4d. a day and six girls at 2d. a day, mainly on light work such as carrying sand or collecting bracken to protect the walls against frost.

Members of the labour force were lucky if they had a caring patron; of all those considered here, Bess of Hardwick was certainly the most. There were probably few cases in which a band of united friends moved on from one site to the next; this must have happened occasionally, but there is no hint of it in these six building accounts. What is surprising at first sight is the lack of reported accidents in what is, even today, an accident-prone industry – the only one reported (aside from a single minor injury at New Hardwick) was at Oldcotes, where a great beam fell, bringing down two others, but no one was hurt.[2] Oldcotes, sometimes called Owlcotes, was a house three miles (five kilometres) north-west of Hardwick built by Bess for her son William, begun in 1593 on land bought by Bess earlier that same year (see the bargain-in-great in Appendix III). However, the lack of reported accidents is explained by the fact that payment for injuries would appear not in the building accounts but in the household accounts. Of the building accounts considered there is only one clear run of coinciding household accounts, Hardwick MS 7 (1591–7); in these accounts, while there are many anonymous payments to workmen that may cover payments for injuries, there is only one specific mention of an injury – 'to Hollingworth 1s. and when he was hurt 2s. 6d.'[3] There is also evidence of Bess's concern for her workforce: a note on 7 December 1596 records 'Geven to Clarkson when he was robbed, ten shillings'.[4] Clarkson was a labourer and stone-breaker working in the quarry on 6d. a day.

In 1681 Sir Christopher Wren explained to the Bishop of Oxford: 'There are 3 ways of working: by the Day, by Measure, and by Great.'[5] By 'measure' he meant piecework and by 'great' a bargain-in-great. Professor Malcolm Airs has explained that 'by the day' was most often used when building smaller country houses;[6] Sir Francis Willoughby, contrary as ever and building a very large house, paid his craftsmen 'by the day', except for the Rhodes brothers, masons, who were paid 'in taske' (by piecework). Longleat and Bolsover used 'by the measure', and at New Hardwick the craftsmen were paid both by 'measure' and by 'great'. We shall have the chance to compare the three different methods of working in each chapter. Some trades did not lend themselves to working 'by great' – for example, glaziers could not be paid in this way because the size of a window was not measured for payment until the glass was in place. Carpenters were usually paid 'by measure': for example, carpenters at Hardwick were paid for felling and squaring trees ready for transporting to Hardwick for the joiners to make into panelling and doors. Sometimes the same man was both carpenter and joiner; carpenters were the better paid, supposedly because the job was more arduous.

Ideally, construction was supervised by the surveyor who worked under the architect, although that term did not exist until the beginning of the seventeenth century. Someone was needed to see that materials arrived at the right time and to the right place – that charcoal, or coal in the seventeenth century, was in place for the lime kilns and that limestone was available at the same time. This was the surveyor's main job. However, each of the six houses discussed here is a different case. Each was built by successful patrons who knew what they wanted and saw that they got it. At Longleat Sir John Thynne acted as his own surveyor; he was completely out of politics and consequently had the time. Given his wealth he was able to hire the best craftsmen to work under him and even act in part as his own architect.

At Chatsworth Bess was building the Elizabethan Chatsworth over many years: in late 1551 a 'platt' (plan) was provided by Roger Worthe for Sir William Cavendish, her husband. This was common practice, and, like Smythson providing the plans for New Hardwick, Worthe had no more to do with the building. Sir William, using a surveyor, was building Chatsworth until his death in 1557. Bess certainly knew what she wanted and was keen to see that she got what she paid for. As in all these building projects the wages were paid by a clerk of the works who – in Bess's case at Hardwick – was the family chaplain, the Revd Henry Jenkinson; as a cleric he took the honorary title 'Sir', although he was not a knight.

Wollaton Hall is another unique case: on his tomb Robert Smythson is called 'Architector and survayor unto yee most worthye house of Wollaton'. There he was combining two jobs: certainly he provided the plans and detail, but his patron, Sir Francis Willoughby, had a considerable hand in the design of his great house. Smythson ceased to be called a mason after Longleat and is referred to in the Wollaton building accounts occasionally as 'Mr'. He spent time at the stone quarry forty miles (sixty-four kilometres) from Wollaton and so could not supervise the building all the time; he brought with him from Longleat a few skilled craftsmen on whom he could rely and must have been happy to leave them to carry out his directions to the letter, no doubt with Sir Frances Willoughby keeping a close eye on the work.

Old Chatsworth was built in two stages. The first, begun in the 1550s, was completed as a two-storey courtyard house by 1564. This house was suitable for the widow of a knight, as Bess was by that date. However, Bess's marriage to the 6th Earl of Shrewsbury in 1568 and the necessity of providing accommodation for Mary, Queen of Scots (a state prisoner, intermittently, at Chatsworth from 1568) made the addition of a third storey essential. The visit of the Earl of Leicester in 1577 was a further spur to extending the accommodation. As noted above, little remains of Old Chatsworth: it was rebuilt by the 1st Duke of Devonshire on the old foundations over several years, starting in 1686; the Hunting Tower, Queen Mary's Bower and possibly part of the cellars are all that survive of Bess's Chatsworth.

Old Hardwick Hall was a piecemeal building operation. The surviving accounts open in 1587, but work may have been begun in 1568, and the building continued to evolve until the outer walls were completed in 1589. The main building work was carried out by a rough-waller, Thomas Hollingworth, with men working under him whom he paid out of the money given to him fortnightly by the clerk of the works, the Revd Henry Jenkinson. There was no architect, but the surveyor was John Painter, of whom more later. However, it was Bess who was holding the reins. The Old Hall was still being completed in 1598.[7]

New Hardwick Hall was designed by Robert Smythson, and John Painter moved to the new building acting as surveyor and consultant. Bess, as usual, knew what she wanted and kept a firm hand on expenditure. She secured the services of John Rhodes, a mason who had worked at Wollaton under Smythson. He and his 'fellows' erected all the outer and inner walls of the new house; John Painter could rely on him absolutely.

A vast amount of water was needed in the building of these houses, not just for the actual building but also to supply an army of workmen; only Bolsover Castle had no handy source on the site. At Longleat there was a reported flow beneath the building; at Chatsworth the River Derwent flowed past the front door.

Wollaton had a convenient underground spring some two hundred feet (sixty metres) to the north of the main building, and the house was connected to it by a brick-lined tunnel. 'Water-leders' were employed to carry water to where it was needed when the building was going up; today the spring is still there and known as 'the Admiral's bath' and the 'caves system'. At the foot of the stairs leading to the caves system is a small spring-fed well more conveniently placed for supplying the household.

At Hardwick there was a deep well, positioned south of the Old Hall. The well-head, built in the style of a small classical temple, is still there; originally this construction had a lead tank placed high in its roof and water was pumped up by a horse-wheel working in a wooden structure. There is still a buried lead pipe leading to the kitchens, a supply supplemented by a downpipe from the roof bringing soft water to a stone trough in the north wall of the kitchen.

Bolsover Castle had no convenient supply, although it stood on the site of a Norman castle and there must originally have been a well. Water for the household was brought in by way of pipes passing through four conduit houses (called 'cundy' houses, these were small buildings with covered access to the supply pipe) built in 1622: these still exist. The small buildings provided access for cleaning the supply. The fountain in the garden had its own supply and was serviced by a long siphon pipe from a 'cundy house' on the same level as the castle, running under a valley and arriving in the cistern house in the south-east corner of the fountain garden. The cistern was in the bottom of the cistern house and water was pumped – perhaps by a treadmill – to an upper tank to give sufficient gravity to feed the fountain, which, of course, could perform only for short, but impressive, periods. There was another source of water called 'the dark well' at the bottom of the hill on which the building stands; this was developed when the building work began – '20 February 1612. Pd Jo. Spittlehouse (labourer) for 8 days at the spring against the Castle 6s. 4d.'[8]

In all these buildings, as was the practice at the royal courts, there was a formal route worked out in the plan for the use of apartments of state – rooms to impress and intimidate visitors. The state apartments, usually on the second storey, were open to visitors of equal or higher rank to that of the host. They consisted of a great chamber, a withdrawing chamber, a bedchamber with an inner chamber and a long gallery. The formal route can best be followed in the state apartments at New Hardwick. One arrives, somewhat breathless from climbing many stairs, before the high great chamber. Here the door is flung open, and even today the reaction is amazement: at the far end of this huge space two chairs of state are set beneath a canopy where once the host would have been seated ready to greet the visitor. The effect was intentionally overwhelming: there could be no doubting the rank, wealth and power of the host. In building New Hardwick, Bess was providing a power base for her dynasty, which in the future might be required to entertain the monarch; all the accommodation necessary for entertaining the royal court had to be provided in case of a possible visit.

In addition to receiving important visitors, the high great chamber (so called in the 1601 inventory) was also used for formal meals; consequently the assembled visitors would leave the chamber for the withdrawing room while the chamber was set up for a meal. After the meal the party retired to small banqueting houses for the serving of cordials and sweetmeats. At New Hardwick there is one of these banqueting houses on the roof in the south tower, another on the ground floor and more set in the walls surrounding the garden. Leading from the withdrawing room are two state bedchambers for important visitors such as a monarch, prince, duke or earl – ranks equal to and superior to that of a countess. Visitors of lower rank would get no further than the withdrawing chamber, which had the effect of underlining the importance of the principal guest.

The sequence of rooms described above is found in all the buildings discussed in this book, although in the case of the ruins of Old Hardwick the route is speculative because the hall was no longer being used for the reception of important guests when the first inventory was made in 1601, and the grandest rooms have vanished. A great chamber was part of a sequence of rooms of reception; only a very eccentric builder would create a great chamber in isolation, and Bess was far from being eccentric.

A building of influence in the Midlands was Worksop Manor in Nottinghamshire, built by Bess's fourth husband, George Talbot, 6th Earl of Shrewsbury; a letter to Bess dated 10 October 1580 has written across the cover: 'I pray you send me Acres [*sic*] so sone as you can for I maye spare him no longer.'[9] It is clear from this that Accres was Shrewsbury's mason and not, as he became after Shrewsbury's death in 1590, Bess's employee. Moreover, in a letter of 5 August 1577 to Lord Burghley (builder of Burghley House in Lincolnshire and Theobalds in Hertfordshire), Shrewsbury wrote: 'I have sent Greves [Greaves] a platte [elevation] of a front of a lodge I am building.' There was building work at Sheffield Lodge in 1574, but Shrewsbury could have been referring to Handsworth, which he was building at Sheffield, or Worksop Manor.[10] Greaves, a mason, was working at Worksop in 1585 when the long gallery had been added, and he carved the chimney-piece with the date 1585, later seen by George Vertue, a writer, when he visited the manor with Lord Oxford in 1727.[11] Moreover, Mary Queen of Scots stayed at Worksop Manor in June 1583; security would have been impossible if the manor were still being worked on.[12] For Worksop to have been sufficiently complete by 1583 to accommodate Mary, work on it may have been started as early as 1577 when Smythson was still working at Longleat – in which case some other 'architector' must have been involved. There was sufficient accommodation at Worksop to lodge the earl in January 1581 when Lord Talbot heard that his father was staying there.[13] Shrewsbury was extending upwards on an earlier narrow hunting lodge started by the 4th Earl of Shrewsbury, and curtailed by the 4th Earl's death in 1538.[14] From a building one room deep it became necessary to build high to fit in the accommodation. Robert Smythson was probably his later architect, from the evidence of a drawing of a hall screen for Worksop Manor in the collection of Smythson drawings in the Royal Institute of British Architects library, although the measurements indicated it could not have fitted the hall and was, therefore, never executed;[15] Smythson may have been responsible for work at the manor, including the top-storey long gallery.

Quite why Shrewsbury felt the need to build the manor in the 1580s is not known, because he was if anything 'over-housed': he had Sheffield Castle (his principal residence), Sheffield Manor, Sheffield Lodge, Rufford Abbey in Nottinghamshire, Tutbury and Pontefract castles – and the use of his wife's properties. Perhaps the reason was that Shrewsbury – a man acutely aware of his position and concerned for his honour – felt that the glory of Chatsworth and the splendour of Wollaton Hall demanded a riposte.

His building work attracted skilled men to the area and the work of these men is described in the following pages. Shrewsbury was a builder and built more houses than his wife. On a lighter note, at Worksop Manor thirty orange trees were planted, which must have made it quite a garden in 1584. However, of these (his bailiff reported) all but two had died by the following spring![16]

In correspondence the manor is sometimes referred to as Worksop Lodge, but what is now known as Worksop Manor Lodge – a hunting lodge, not far from the manor – was not completed until 1595.[17] The manor was burnt down in 1761, and only a few unsatisfactory prints remain of the south front, together with a ground-floor plan by Smythson (see page 27). There are no surviving building accounts.

In the Smythson drawings in the Royal Institute of British Architects library are a ground-floor plan of Worksop Manor by Robert Smythson's son, John, probably a survey plan, and a design for a screen for Worksop Manor by Robert Smythson. It can be seen from the plan that it was a narrow site and that the only way to increase accommodation was considered to be upwards. From the illustration of the south front of the manor (see page 27), the hall (to the left of the entrance) extended through two floors, and this is likely to have been the height of the building when Mary, Queen of Scots was moved there. This was just about sufficient accommodation but not enough for an earl and his countess as well. Therefore Smythson was called to add another floor in 1584–6. The new floor included one of the most spectacular long galleries of the time.[18]

Mention must be made here of Basil Stallybrass in connection with both the Old and New Halls at Hardwick. Basil Stallybrass was an architect for the Society for the Preservation of Ancient Buildings (SPAB) which had been founded by William Morris in 1877. In 1911 he was engaged by the 7th Duke of Devonshire to repair and make safe the ruined Old Hall for the sum of £500. By the time the work was finished it had cost the duke £2,042. 0s. 5d.[19] Stallybrass attempted to identify some of the rooms in an article in 1913.[20] His findings have not been examined seriously since, but some of the assumptions he made concerning the identification of certain rooms on his floor plan have been proved incorrect. This is not surprising, as he published his findings nearly one hundred years ago, and, while he made a very good job of it, later research has shown up differences.

One of the principles of the SPAB was that a replacement must be

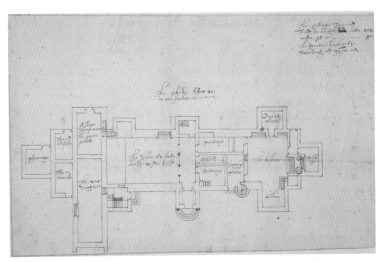

Survey plan of Worksop Manor by John Smythson, which clearly shows how narrow the building was. Because it was necessary to build on top of what was already there, the state apartments are in the uppermost storeys.

Print of Worksop Manor, from *England Display'd Being a New, Complete, and Accurate Survey and Description of the Kingdom of England, and Principality of Wales . . . The Particulars respecting England, revised, corrected, and improved, By P. Russell, Esq.; and those relating to Wales, By Mr. Owen Price* (1796)

obvious and not a fake copy of what had been lost. Consequently, tiles were placed edge outwards when replacing perished stonework. The restorations did not entirely stand the test of time: some of the experimental methods of preservation did not work, and English Heritage has spent money making the ruins safe and sealing them against the weather.

The final building in this sextet is Bolsover Castle, situated only four miles (six kilometres) north of Hardwick and begun by Bess's youngest son, Sir Charles Cavendish, in 1612. It is a fantasy castle, reminding one of jousting knights; it was never meant to be continuously lived in. It is best approached from the M1, and the first view is breathtaking: the house stands on a high ridge of rock that dominates the valley below. Sir Charles, whose main house (Welbeck Abbey) is only six miles (ten kilometres) distant, intended his castle for the entertainment and relaxation of his family and guests. However, he died in 1617 before his castle was complete; moreover, his architect Robert Smythson had also died – in 1614 – and the house's completion was left to their sons, William Cavendish (who became Duke of Newcastle in 1665) and John Smythson, the eldest son of Robert. The duke's abiding passion was the schooling of horses, and he added a riding school to his father's plans at Bolsover. Although only thirty-two pages of the building accounts survive, running for fifteenth months from November 1612 to March 1614, that is enough to be able to follow some of the workforce. The rest of the building history of this small but fascinating castle has to be found elsewhere.

Obviously sons followed fathers in their trade, but two men with the same surname are not necessarily related – and we are left to guess. Bolsover has few recognizable masons' marks; this is because the masons were paid for piecework and the clerk was concerned with paying only for completed work. The term 'freemason' (used only in two of the six building accounts) is ambiguous but seems to mean a mason who is free of his apprenticeship. The term is never used at Longleat, Chatsworth or either of the Hardwick Halls, Old and New. However, in the Wollaton accounts the term is used for all masons, from the lowest paid (Kindersley at 9d. a day) to the highest paid (the Rhodes brothers and Accres at 14d. a day). At Bolsover the term 'free masons at Shutelwod quarry' is used in reference to that quarry only, and the term is also used in the phrases 'free masons and layers at the walls' or 'foundations' and 'free masons at setting of the walls'; otherwise masons are simply referred to as 'masons'. The word 'freemason' seemingly meant what the clerk of works wanted it to mean. In these pages I have taken the term to mean a qualified mason. The terms 'head mason' and 'under-mason' are my own and used only for clarity.

As already explained, the purpose of masons' marks was to account for work done by under-masons working for a head mason who, on receiving payments from the clerk of works, paid under-masons responsible for the work they had achieved. Finished stonework was laid by layers, and their skill was valued as nearly equal to that of masons: at Wollaton the stoneworkers were paid 10d. a day and at Bolsover 12d. a day for the top craftsmen. No layers are listed in the Hardwick accounts, probably because Rhodes included them with 'his men' working for him. In the Bolsover building accounts payment is made on 29 May 1613: 'Pd Goodwin [and] Baram [masons] and their fellows . . . for 7 arch stones for the pastrie range at 8d. the stone 4s. 8d.'.[21] Several other payments for piecework are included with the entry: the seven arch stones can be counted and, unusually, are still there; three marked with a double-X mark. This suggests that Goodwin or Baram hewed four of the arch stones, but one of 'his fellows' hewed three and was paid for them. This mason remains nameless.

Wills can be a very useful source for research, but the craftsman has to have been successful enough to have acquired sufficient assets to leave – and that is rare. The wills so far discovered relating to the properties discussed in this book are reprinted in Appendix II. They are all from the Midlands, where Bess of Hardwick, Sir Francis Willoughby and the 6th Earl of Shrewsbury were building what have been called 'prodigy houses', houses large enough to entertain the monarch and court. The wills show that some of the craftsmen were taken into the service of their patrons, given farms and settled in the area. Longleat in Wiltshire proved a disappointment: a search in the probate index for the diocese of Salisbury produced nothing. It is a matter of luck when anything at all survives the passage of time.

In the absence of Worksop Manor as an example of Shrewsbury–Smythson architecture, Worksop Manor Lodge survives as an instance of the 7th Earl's architecture, attributed to Robert Smythson by Girouard.[22] The lodge is not open to the public.

This substantial building, cruciform in plan with a short but wide cross-bar containing a great hall and great chamber, is built of rough local skerry and is of five storeys; it originally had a further storey – perhaps two storeys if John Holland's *History of Worksop* is correct.[23] It is described in the Shrews-bury Papers (correspondence held in the College of Arms – see list of Manuscript Sources) as 'Mr Portyngton's newe lodge in worsopp' and as having been nearing completion in August 1595 – a dendrochronogical dating gives 1593. At all events it was a tall building of at least six storeys with perhaps a roof walk. Roger Portington was one of the 7th Earl of Shrewsbury's circle and described as Shrewsbury's 'very good frende'. The lodge was built at Shrewsbury's expense for Portington on Shrewsbury's land and only three-quarters of a mile (just over a kilometre) from his Worksop Manor. Thomas Coke, writing to the Countess of Shrewsbury from Florence in 1609 told her: 'I saw the Duke's house in Pratolino 5 miles from this town. The house is in show much what about the show of R. Port-ington's lodge in Worksop Park, and the chambers in it very like to those.' He goes on to describe terraces, a grotto and waterworks. No doubt Coke was stretching his imagination, but his note is sufficient to indicate that in its time the lodge was worth commenting on.

The lodge was probably intended as a retreat from the very formal life required of an earl at the manor – as was Wothorpe Lodge, built by Lord Exeter one mile (1.6 kilometres) from Burleigh House. Worksop Lodge was originally entered from the south by a flight of steps leading into the double height of the great hall on the second storey, above a service basement at ground level. A parlour was to one side on the east and the main staircase to the west led to the great chamber above the hall on the fourth storey; this was lit by huge Hardwick-type eighteen-light windows at both ends and reached up through two floors. A withdrawing room, also of double height, was situated off the great chamber in the west wing. The vanished sixth storey above would have been the long gallery. A curious feature is the array of chimney stacks corbelled out at second-storey level, which also contained garderobes for adjacent bed-chambers. The building was catered for by close-stools and chamber pots.

Richard Mason, seemingly a stonemason in charge of building a 'lodge', asked the earl for money in March 1595; by the date it seems likely he was referring to the Worksop Manor Lodge.[24] There are masons' marks, the majority of which repeat from Hardwick Hall, while others also appear at Bolsover Castle, Derbyshire, and Shireoaks Hall, Notting-hamshire; all these are buildings attributed to Smythson. The detail of the windows and door cases is plain, with simple unmoulded chamfers. In the roof the main staircase is cut off at the newel, indicating the loss of at least one further storey. On the 7th Earl's death in 1616 the title was in abeyance; the estate devolved upon one of his three daughters and by marriage to the Dukes of Norfolk in 1652; by then the lodge had become a farmhouse – the hearth tax of 1664 shows just eight hearths. The 1692 window tax would have been responsible for the blocking of so many original windows, giving the building a depressing 'blind' appearance.

Finally, I touch on sewage disposal in each of these houses. Longleat and Wollaton Hall each had interior garderobe chutes, which were no more than a continuation of the medieval garderobes that were by then old-fashioned. Smythson did not repeat the experiment in his later houses – most likely his patrons did not want him to; they used the more convenient chamber pots, supplemented by close-stools, which in Bess's case was luxuriously 'covered with blewe cloth stitcht with white with red and black silk frenge' carefully listed in the 1601 inventory of the contents of New Hardwick Hall. With any system, until the introduction of the wash-down closet in the nineteenth century, servants were called upon to take the close-stool pans and chamber pots to be emptied in the privies outside, preferably to the north of the house. There was a row of privies at the New Hardwick just about where the public toilets are today. It was an awfully long walk from Bess's close-stool to the privies, but it was then the only solution.

Sir John Harrington, a godson of Elizabeth I, built a valve water closet with an overhead cistern at Kelston near Bath in 1596 and published full illustrations and estimated cost – the cistern was depicted with fish in it to indicate that it contained water. Queen Elizabeth had one installed at Richmond Palace, but it never caught the public fancy. The invention was ahead of its time: plumbing had not been invented; it was not until the late eighteenth century that a WC was installed at Hardwick Hall!

To sum up, the book will look closely at the two buildings on which Robert Smythson worked, Longleat, Wiltshire, and Wollaton Hall, Nottinghamshire. Also Elizabethan Chatsworth will be discussed because some of the craftsmen in the Smythson circle worked there and at Old Hardwick Hall, which was built without the aid of an architect. New Hardwick Hall, for which Smythson certainly provided floor plans and, presumably, elevations and other details, has the most complete set of building accounts from which it can be seen how the plan changed during the course of the building. Bess's insistence on having large windows caused a design fault, and Smythson must, against his better judgement, have been overruled by his patroness; he faced the same problem at Wollaton. The Little Castle at Bolsover has been attributed to Smythson, but he died in 1614, the first year of the short run of surviving building accounts, and it was left to his son John to complete the building and to add a terrace range before the Civil War closed down the building work and the Earl of Newcastle, for whom Bolsover was built, fled the country for self-imposed exile.

1

ROBERT SMYTHSON

The first surviving reference to Robert Smythson is in the letter he brought to Longleat in March 1568 from Humphrey Lovell, the queen's master mason. The letter was addressed to Sir John Thynne, who had just embarked on his third attempt to build Longleat House after a devastating fire the previous year.

Smythson was then thirty-three years old. He brought with him super-lative references, and Sir John Thynne took him on together with his team of skilled masons – in all, five men. Mark Girouard has pointed out that, as Smythson had recently been working for the queen's cousin, her vice-chamberlain, Sir Francis Knollys, he probably came to Longleat from Caversham near Reading, where Sir Francis was building his great house.[1]

Nothing is known about Smythson's early life or where he was born. In a two-part article in *Country Life* in 1991 Adrian Woodhouse suggested that Smythson came from a family of the same name living in the parish of Crosby Ravensworth, Cumberland. This is an interesting hypothesis, but there are no firm facts linking Robert Smythson with the Westmoreland/Cumberland Smythsons. However, one guess is as good as another, and Woodhouse may be right.[2]

Smythson's epitaph on his wall plaque in Wollaton Church makes it completely clear that he was responsible for Wollaton Hall; it describes him as 'Architector and Survayor unto yee most worthy house of Wollaton and divers others of great account'. This was the first time that the word 'architector' had been used to indicate a profession.

Documented building work by Smythson includes Longleat (Wiltshire), Wardour Castle (Wiltshire), Worksop Manor (Nottinghamshire), Welbeck Abbey (Nottinghamshire) and Wollaton Hall (Nottinghamshire). He is also associated with Corsham Court (Wiltshire), Barlbrorough Hall (Derbyshire), Manor Lodge (Nottinghamshire), Shireoaks Hall (Nottinghamshire), Doddington Hall (Lincolnshire), Hardwick Hall (Derbyshire), Normanby Hall (Lincolnshire), Oldcotes (Derbyshire), Pontefract Castle (West Yorkshire), Caverswell Castle (Staffordshire), Fountains Abbey (North Yorkshire), Wooton Lodge (Staffordshire) and the little castle at Bolsover (Derbyshire). This makes a total of eighteen buildings. In addition, Smythson had possible connections with Heath Old Hall (Yorkshire), Gawthorpe Hall (Lancashire), Bradford-on-Avon Hall (Wiltshire), Lulworth Castle (Dorset) and Shaw House (Buckinghamshire). The list indicates a concentration of works in the Midlands based on Wollaton, where he lived, and in the area surrounding Longleat in Wiltshire, where he was based before he moved to Wollaton, where he is first recorded in 1583.

When Smythson arrived at Longleat with a team of five skilled masons he was clearly a very experienced mason. Where did he learn his trade? He would have worked as 'a boy' (an apprentice) to a mason; there are several examples in the following chapters of other masons employing a boy. This position served as an apprenticeship in which necessary practical skills were learned. One of the mysteries arising, however, is how such skills as vaulting were learned when church building was rare – vaulting was erected at Bolsover Castle. From this apprenticeship Smythson would have progressed to being a member of a team under a head mason.

He picked up the skills necessary to build in brick as well as in stone. Although Smythson's career before Longleat is not documented, Caversham, the building on which he had probably been working immediately before coming to Longleat, was 'fairly built of brick'.[2] At both Longleat and Wollaton Hall Smythson worked primarily in stone, but he also used brick in the construction of such structures as relieving arches over doors and windows at Wollaton and in interior walls at Longleat. Another of the houses with which he is associated, Doddington Hall in Lincolnshire, is built of brick with stone trim. However, by that time Smythson earned his living as a bailiff for the Willoughbys at Wollaton: he had ceased to work as a mason and become what amounted to being a consulting architect – he provided plans and designs.

At Longleat Smythson would have learned a great deal from his colleague Alan Maynard. Maynard was a French mason and sculptor who preceded Smythson at Longleat. He was well versed in the classical styles of French architecture. Smythson understood the classical orders and when using them put them in their strict sequence, but that knowledge could easily have come from books such as John Shute's *The First and Chief Groundes of Architecture*, published in 1563 and based on the Roman author Vitruvius's *Ten Books of Architecture*. Both these volumes might have been in Knollys's or Thynne's libraries and were certainly in Willoughby's library at Wollaton. The only thing that can be said with certainty, however, is that by the time Smythson left Longleat, aged forty-five in 1580, he was fully conversant with the latest trends, a highly skilled mason and fully capable of organizing a large labour force of the kind required for building a great house.

Many architects down the centuries have suffered from difficult patrons. Sir John Thynne at Longleat was certainly awkward, but Smythson had a supporting ally in Maynard, and with patience he survived for twelve years. Sir Francis Willoughby at Wollaton may have been his most demanding patron; the prospect room at Wollaton was built with a wooden floor that was doomed to fail because it was originally designed for a smaller area in which it might have worked; it was a type of grid illustrated by Italian architect Sebastiano Serlio and used to support a ceiling, but at Wollaton it had to support the floor above it. Almost certainly Smythson must have pointed out tactfully that the proposed grid would be unstable, but, like so many architects, he had to bend to his patron's demands.

Again, at Hardwick Hall Bess of Hardwick's demand was for large windows, but they weakened the walls in which they were set. Smythson understood this fault and supported the main walls with buttress turrets, but these in turn had a structural fault because of the large windows in the turrets, and that was left for succeeding generations to correct at great expense. Of course both buildings outlasted their reasonable lifespan, and no doubt neither Bess nor Willoughby would have expected their houses still to be standing in the twenty-first century.

By a fluke of history some of Smythson's architectural drawings survive in the Smythson drawings in the Royal Institute of British Architects library. This collection contains the work not only of Robert Smythson but also that of his son John and perhaps additionally of Robert's grandson – also called John. These give us a significant insight into Robert's professional development: the drawings range from plans and elevations to designs for screens, chimney-pieces, panelling, windows and tombs. Surprisingly, the collection also contains three late medieval architectural drawings by an unidentified hand, which includes Bishop Fox's Chantry in Winchester Cathedral. (When Fox died in 1528, his chantry was already built.) The Gothic style was unfashionable at the time, but knowledge of it proved useful to Smythson in his attempt to solve structural problems such as the large areas of glass at New Hardwick. Medieval church builders had solved this same problem with buttresses, and this was the solution attempted by Smythson at Hardwick.

Smythson may have been the first in England to draw a perspective elevation: one of his drawings for Wollaton shows the entrance front in perspective. His plans show courtyard houses, H-plan and rectangular, and houses with basement services; the latter was a continental importation used at Wollaton and in part at Longleat and Hardwick Hall. Smythson was innovative, but his problem must have been to sell innovation to a conservative clientele: the royal court was organized around an old-fashioned ritual that required a great hall, a great chamber, a withdrawing chamber and a long gallery, most of which no longer served on the Continent. Consequently, the new plans developed in France and Italy simply could not be adapted to English usage.

Smythson used the cross-hall only twice, at Worksop Manor Lodge and at Hardwick. The idea had already been worked out by Bess in the Old Hall, where buildings already on the site had prevented the extension of her father's hall east to west, and so, in order to accommodate the retinue of a countess, the hall had been extended north to south. For her the arrangement had worked, and there was no reason not to have a similar layout in her New Hall. Intriguingly, two other Smythson drawings show a cross-hall in houses that were never built; seemingly, other patrons were not prepared to make the leap. Although Worksop Manor Lodge in Nottinghamshire, completed by 1595 for the 7th Earl of Shrewsbury, has a second-storey transverse hall, Oldcotes, the building put up by Bess of Hardwick in 1593, might also be added to the list.

On his retirement from active stonemasonry with the completion of Wollaton Hall in 1588, Smythson, by then aged fifty-three, acted as bailiff for the Willoughby estates – he lived in the village of Wollaton at the hall's gates. His only son, John, appeared as a freemason for the first time very late in the Wollaton accounts in March 1588, paid 10d. a day. In the Wollaton accounts, where the term freemason is used, it means a mason free of serving his apprenticeship; a qualified mason. Girouard suggests that in the 1590s, when John was still living in Wollaton, he was working as his father's assistant.[3] John's life in the employment of William Cavendish, 1st Earl of Newcastle, led him to a career similar to that of his father.

Robert Smythson's wall plaque in the little church at Wollaton records his death on 15 October 1614, when Bolsover Castle was being built. The identity of his wife is not known – by the time he made his will (see Appendix II) in August 1614 she was already dead; there is no mention of her, although a slim clue is that his eldest daughter was christened Mary and it was common at that time for the first-born daughter to take her mother's name. His modest plaque carries a mason's mark. Was the plaque carved devotedly by John as a tribute to his father?

An aerial view of Longleat House, Wiltshire, viewed from the north

2

LONGLEAT HOUSE
THE HOME OF THE 7TH MARQUESS OF BATH

The exterior of Longleat remains largely as it was when completed after Sir John Thynne's death in 1580. The gestation had been very long: started by Thynne in 1547, the house was built over a period of thirty-three years until his death. Then it was left to his heirs to complete. The interior was unfortunately modernized by Jeffry Wyatville in 1801–11, but he left the great hall much as it was; he followed the same formula at Wollaton, where he worked at the same time. A further attack on the house was carried out, by J.D. Crace, an interior decorator, in the 1870s. Some of the original chimney-pieces were moved, but three survive intact.

John Thynne was born *c.* 1513 at Church Stretton in Shropshire. He prospered under the wing of Edward Seymour, 1st Duke of Somerset and Lord Protector of the kingdom in 1547–9; Thynne was knighted by Somerset after victory over the Scots in the Battle of Pinkie Cleuch in 1547. Sir John Thynne married well. He married his first wife, Christian (the daughter of Sir Richard Gresham, Lord Mayor of London), in 1549. They had three sons and six daughters. Christian died *c.* 1566. His second wife was Dorothy, a daughter of Sir William Wroughton, and they had five sons. She outlived her husband.

Thynne was already a wealthy man when, in 1540, he bought the former Carthusian priory of Longleat from Sir John Horsey, which Sir John had bought in 1539 following the Dissolution of the Monasteries Later he was the Lord Protector's steward in London when Somerset House was being built in the Strand, starting in 1547. Somerset's enthusiasm for architecture was infectious. In addition to Thynne, others among Somerset's protégés went on to build their own houses: Sir William Sharington in 1539 bought the convent of Laycock Abbey in Wiltshire and tinkered about adding and altering the building until his death in 1553; Sir Thomas Smith built Hill Hall, Essex, starting before 1557; and the greatest of them, Sir William Cecil (Lord Burghley after 1571), built Burghley House in Lincolnshire, starting in the 1570s, and Theobalds in Hertfordshire, beginning in 1564 – both houses big enough to entertain Queen Elizabeth I's court.

Somerset was an ambitious man and brother of King Henry VIII's third wife, Jane Seymour, the mother of Henry's heir (later King Edward VI). The prince was only nine years old when his father died in 1547. Somerset suppressed the details of Henry's will, an act of treason, and took over as Protector of his nephew. However, Somerset was outwitted by his enemies, charged with treason and executed in 1552. Thynne, whose support of Somerset was undoubted, spent ten months in the Tower, from October 1549 to the following August, and was fined £6,000, the equivalent today of several millions. This was the end of Thynne's political life. Nevertheless, he managed to hold on to some of his wealth and retired to Longleat to devote himself to restoring his fortune and building his house. Thynne was not a sympathetic character; letters to his family show no sign of compassion, and he comes across as an Elizabethan whose childhood was devoid of affection – compare the case of Sir Francis Willoughby in Chapter 4.

Between 1547 and 1552 Thynne began what in essence was an adaptation of the monastic buildings. This was the start of a programme of building and rebuilding lasting thirty-three years. At the beginning, Thynne, detained in the Tower, wrote to his steward John Dodd very often, sometimes twice a day. Dodd was in essence taking the place of Thynne, although the supervision of the building work at Longleat was in the hands of Thomas Berryman whom Thynne appointed as surveyor and head mason. But because Thynne was in the Tower Berryman could refer back to his employer only by the slow process of writing and receiving letters. Dodd had more authority over the building than did Berryman, and when Berryman was summoned to London by Thynne in May 1547 he was not paid his expenses until Thynne's return to Longleat.[1] Thynne's purpose was to 'show him my pleasur' (a consultation) as he would have done had he been at Longleat. Shortly after Dodd was told: 'when Beryman may have tyme I would be glad to have the plat (plan) of myn outhouses and the rest set forth as heretofore I did appoint to be sent unto me.'[2] From this it is apparent that Thynne was keeping as close an eye on the work as his circumstances allowed and that during his visit Berryman had promised to send the plans, but a month later had not sent them. After Thynne returned to Longleat in 1554 he acted as his own surveyor.

The second Longleat was more ambitious: a new wing was added to the older house between 1554 and 1558 with, in 1559, grand rooms added to the east and north. However, Thynne suffered a setback: he employed a mason, a local man, William Spicer, who worked at Longeat from 1555 to 1563. Spicer was given the contract to build a wing of grand rooms, and Thynne made him bailiff and rent-collector of the manor of Lullington. Their relationship over the next four years deteriorated, and in 1563 after some serious rows Spicer left, together with £34 of Lullington rent money and an uncompleted contract. He also left the new building with an unfinished interior. One would expect a sticky end for Spicer, but he flourished and ended up surveyor of the royal works in London. The impression is that Thynne had met his match.

For this second Longleat Thynne took on John Chapman in 1553 at 10d. a day. Chapman was a skilled stone-carver, who was responsible for some of the finest carving at Lacock Abbey and who had worked for King Henry VIII. Berryman's work had been acceptable when he was adding to the monastic buildings, but the second Longleat was grander, and Thynne rightly calculated that Chapman was the better mason. Berryman, on 8d. a day, had to play second fiddle to Chapman, on 10d. a day, for six years before he left around 1559; Chapman stayed on until 1567. Thynne found that as his ambitions for Longleat expanded he had to entice skilled crafts-men at higher rates of pay. William Love, the first head mason in 1547, had been paid 6d. a day; Berryman began on 8d. a day, but his fee was raised to 10d. a day. After Berryman came William Spicer, head mason from 1560 to 1563, who had started on 6d. a day but changed to taking on a bargain-in-great some time before his hurried departure, which may have been caused by Spicer's dissatisfaction with his rewards. To find a succes-sor to Spicer, Thynne had to pay more. The costs of building were rising.

Thynne was left with a problem. To resolve it he took on two skilled craftsmen, sculptor and mason Alan Maynard and joiner Adrian Gaunt, together with the men these two brought with them. This was a happy choice. The two new arrivals were French, with a wide experience of Renaissance architecture; Maynard had a significant influence on the interior at Longleat. However, fate had not finished with Thynne. In April 1567 the house was largely destroyed in a fire, and Thynne was forced to move to another property on his estate. However, he did not give up and started again on his third Longleat.

In March the following year Robert Smythson arrived with a letter of high recommendation from Humphrey Lovell, the queen's master mason:

> Accordenge to my promes I have sent unto yowe this bearer Robert Smyth-son freemason, who of laytt was with Master Vice Chamberlaine, not dowting hem but to be a man fett for your worshepe, and with these covenantes: first he to have XVId a daye holle, that is to say VIIIs a weke and a nage [nag, or horse] kept in your worshepes charges, and whiles they are in cominge and the carriage of their towels (tools) paid for. Hemselfe ys contented to stand to your worshepes benevolence trowsting you well conseder of hem.[3]

Smythson was on a daily wage of 16d., which was maintained for four years. He and his wife rented the parsonage of Monkton Deverill from

Print showing Longleat House from the north. Detail from from *Britannia Illustrata*, by Leonard Knyff and Jan Kip, 1707

Thynne and he commuted six miles (ten kilometres) to work at Longleat on the 'nage', taking about thirty minutes. Maynard rented a property from Thynne at Woodlands on the edge of the park.

Maynard did not witness the fire; he had left Longleat at the end of 1566 but returned again about the same time that Smythson arrived in 1568. As joint head mason with Smythson, Maynard was paid 14d. a day, while Smythson received the promised 16d. a day; how Maynard took to the arrival of a new craftsman who was treated as superior to himself (at least as far as payment was concerned) is not recorded. What is clear is that Thynne was not by then paying his craftsmen by bargains-in-great or by piecework but by the day; later this arrangement was changed to payment by task or piecework. This made sense in view of the work to be done, which could not be assessed beforehand and consisted of repairing the fire damage.

Thynne was gathering a strong and talented team for his renewed attempt to provide himself and his heirs with a suitably grand house. From 1552 the head carpenter was John Lewis at 12d. a day. Lewis had worked for the Duke of Somerset, probably at Syon House.[4] Under him was Richard Crispin at 10d. a day: he would go on to Wollaton, where he would be paid 14d. a day. The head joiner was still the capable Adrian Gaunt on 12d. a day. Working under Smythson were several men who had arrived at Longleat with him: Edward and Valentine Mercer, John King, John Hodgkyn and John Hills from Maidstone. (Hills's will is reproduced in Appendix II; he apparently worked for the Duke of Somerset at Brentford before going to Longleat in 1568; he stayed with Smythson, following him to Wollaton and from there to Hardwick.) In 1571 Christopher Lovell, Humphrey's son, joined the team, and he, too, went on to Wollaton.[5]

There were approximately one hundred masons working at Longleat over the time it was being built. We know frustratingly little of their working careers. John Chapman, the mason who received the substantial payment of 10d. a day, was at Longleat from 1553 to 1567. Earlier, Chapman was working at Lacock Abbey for Sir William Sharrington and while there, in 1552, the Duke of Northumberland had ordered from Chapman a chimney-piece for Dudley Castle in Staffordshire; the chimney-piece was dispatched by cart the following year.[6] William Spicer was originally a local man from Nunnery in Somerset. Other names we know are Thomas Phillips, who possibly came from Bristol, and John Symmons, who later lived in Berkshire. Richard Crispin was a carpenter at Longleat from 1554 to 1580 before moving to Wollaton. In the main, the skilled craftsmen did not travel far. There was plenty of work at Longleat: ten masons worked there for twelve or more years, while Robert Fosbery was there for twenty-two years; Richard Jarvis, a bricklayer, was there for nineteen years, and Alan Maynard (head mason from 1563) clocked up twenty years. Richard Crispin became joint head carpenter with John Lewis, and they worked at Longleat for twenty-six and twenty-nine years respectively. William Brown, another carpenter, was there for twenty-seven years. One of the sawyers, John Williams (on 6d. a day), also worked there for twenty-seven years. These, apart from Crispin, might be said to have made Longleat their career.[7]

The year 1568 saw the high point of employment: fifty-eight masons and sixteen bricklayers, mostly for that one year. By the following year the number of masons was down to twenty-two, and bricklayers to only two, a number maintained through to 1575. The high number of masons and bricklayers were needed in 1568 to demolish and rebuild unsound walls after the fire of 1567. In May that year a steward wrote to Thynne reporting progress: 'The west side of Longleat ys almost taken down to the corbel.' By September, Robert Fosbery, a mason, had been paid for demolishing thirty gable ends, the 'pediements' of two windows, the hall porch and ten chimney-pieces.[8] This explains that the roof and attic floors of the west wing were taken down 'to the corbel'; by 'corbel' he meant the corbel table, a series of external projections immediately below the eaves.

Smythson and Maynard evidently had few or no differences and worked well together, Smythson gaining much from his association with Maynard. Maynard's experience came at first hand from France, but Thynne had his ideas as well. It is clear that the long façades of Longleat buttressed by bays at either end were based on the appearance of Somerset House in London (1547–52), but at Longleat that design was subtly improved. Smythson skilfully drew a two-storey bay (see page 51) that shares features of the three-storey bays at Longleat; it was perhaps drawn before the third storey was added by Thynne or his son.

The exterior of the third Longleat was probably finished in early 1570;[9] a very indistinct drawing by Maynard of the façade of Longleat survives, and what can be seen of the roof has a very French appearance – the drawing has oval dormers that Thynne obviously rejected in practice. Thynne wanted a roof on which to promenade, and with its turreted stairwells, classical chimney stacks and banqueting houses the roof resembles a small village and commands fantastic views. Banqueting houses were a feature of sixteenth-century social life; we shall encounter them at Wollaton and at New Hardwick. In this period banquets meant something different to our modern understanding of the term – they consisted of a dessert course of fruit, sweetmeats and wine, served after the main meal was over.

In 1572 Thynne began yet another reconstruction, the fourth and final Longleat, in which the house took the form we largely see today. The building of Longleat extended over thirty-three years, and the plan of the final fourth house was nothing like that of the first, which had been constructed around the priory. The plan of the fourth house, in fact, was never completed. Thynne died in 1580 leaving many rooms unfinished: the proposed long gallery and the rooms beneath it were not built until Wyatville's time in the early nineteenth century, and the apartments of state were left uncompleted. As the plan evolved over the years, the building grew around a large west courtyard and, to the east, two small courtyards, with the great hall in the south wing. The great hall was completed and left intact by Wyatville; the upper part of the hammer-beam roof, attributed to John Lewis, head carpenter,[10] was covered over when a ceiling was inserted below the hammer-beams in the 1690s but was copied by Smythson at Wollaton, and three chimney-pieces attributed to Maynard survive. These demonstrate his great skill as a sculptor. The screen is by Adrian Gaunt, the French joiner who was paid by bargain-in-great the total of £13. 6s. 8d. 'uppon ye workinge of the Scrynes' in November 1578,[11] when he had previously been paid 1s. a day.

By good luck a contemporary plan of Longleat exists. It was probably supplied by Thynne to Sir William Cecil, Lord Burghley, in the 1570s; the plan (see page 53) is kept at Hatfield House, which belonged to Burghley's son Robert Cecil, 1st Earl of Salisbury, and clearly shows the outlines of rooms but not their purpose. It also shows a completed north wing, which was not built until 1801–11 (by Wyatville). Although the Hatfield plan does not indicate the purpose of the rooms – most were not even finished by the 1570s – it is possible to identify their intended use in some cases: the great hall, centre bottom of the ground-floor plan, is obvious with its distinctive screen passage leading off to stairs to the kitchens and services. In this area the plan becomes confusing because it shows the kitchen at the same floor level as the hall, while in reality the kitchen was partly sunk into a basement; the plan shows the ground-floor level and not how the stairs entered the kitchen at a lower level. Which spaces were intended to be the buttery and pantry is anyone's guess. To the east of the great hall in the south-east bay is the parlour, an informal room used much as a college common room is used today.

The upper-floor plan is less confusing: the great chamber, where formal meals were taken, occupied the space in the south-east corner over the parlour; from there the route through the formal rooms proceeded through a lobby to the withdrawing chamber, where the party withdrew after the meal, and to a bedchamber, which – according to an inventory of 1639 – was the 'Redd Bedchamber'. An essential part of any set of formal rooms was the long gallery: in the plan of Longleat it stretches along the north side of the building, but it was not built until the extensive work of 1801–11. What Thynne's intentions were for the spaces north of the withdrawing room cannot be known; if the Red Bedchamber was intended to be a state bedchamber then it was badly placed – it was in the way *en route* to the gallery. The space in the north-east corner should have been a secondary bedchamber off the state bedchamber, suitable for occupation by a royal consort, but on the plan it has no direct access from the Red Bedchamber. We shall never know what Thynne's intentions were or where his own apartments lay; the plan may have been as puzzling to Sir William Cecil as it is to us.

Where the plan differs from previous buildings in England is that it represents a house standing above a partly below-ground basement lit by small ground-level windows. The house is raised on a podium that contains cellars, service rooms and the lower part of the kitchen, which otherwise would have reached up partly through the second storey. This made for a neater plan and one that Smythson used at Wollaton and, in a smaller way, at New Hardwick, where the basement is occupied by the beer and wine cellars lit by ground-level windows, and the kitchens' floor level is three feet (one metre) lower than the rest of the ground floor. The arrangement found at Longleat was common in France at the time, and Thynne, who visited that country in the 1540s, would have been aware of its popularity there. However, at Longleat the arrangement proved inconvenient for those who worked in it, for it looked out into a small, dark interior courtyard and ventilation must have been difficult.

Another continental innovation was the provision of twelve interior garderobes, which can be counted on the Hatfield plan. Garderobes were medieval in conception and were designed to discharge into a moat. In France, where they were known as 'lieux', their use survived. Problems arose when there was no convenient moat – as, for example, at the Archbishop's Palace at Southwell in Nottinghamshire, where a fourteenth-century circular multi-garderobe that survives at second-storey level has four outward-facing seats served by shafts that were cleaned out at ground level. The same system was used at Haddon Hall in Derbyshire, where the early-sixteenth-century garderobes in the lower court discharge into shafts that again were accessed for cleaning by small doors at ground level. At Longleat the problem was perhaps solved in better fashion: the garderobe shafts, one of which survives but which has never been examined, may have connected to a drainage system, as at Wollaton – according to Girouard 'the gurgling of a culvert flowing underneath the house can still be heard in certain parts of the basement', suggesting a more advanced system than the dry channels at Wollaton.[12]

Who, then, was responsible for the plan of the final Longleat? The only certainty is that Thynne himself had a considerable hand in it. Thynne had some experience of drawing plans and designs: with Spicer he had made and signed the design for part of the second Longleat; he had even designed his own tomb.[13] Moreover, he had his experience under the 1st Duke of Somerset in London to draw on, and with Humphrey Lovell, the queen's mason (who had written the letter of recommendation for Smythson), he had drawn up a design for a house for Lord Hertford,

Somerset's son. At other times in their careers Lovell, Spicer and Adrian Gaunt were unable to achieve anything with the coherence and boldness of the final Longleat; the design was probably made by Maynard but with valuable input from Smythson. Thynne, while having the ability to draw up a plan, would have relied on his two experts for practical advice on construction and style.

Apart from being driven by his desire to build, Thynne also had a flair for making money, which comes out in his dealings with his workforce; it has already been seen that by attempting to reduce rates paid to Spicer he lost the services of a master craftsman. When Smythson came to Longleat his letter from Lovell to Thynne stated his terms of employment: 16d. a day, making him the highest-paid of all the craftsmen. Four years later, in 1572, the arrangement had changed to task or piecework, by which Smythson was paid for work done. Maynard's terms at 14d. a day were similarly changed. Between them, together with their teams of masons, Smythson and Maynard were responsible for the new façades of the fourth Longleat.

The accounts show no payments to Smythson between 1574 and 1575, so during this period he was probably absent. On his return the relationship between Maynard and Thynne deteriorated – it seems to be a mirror image of the Spicer episode. The cause of the dispute may have been that Thynne – in a money-saving move – had changed their contract from payment by the day to task or piecework. Then Thynne had one of the big windows bays made not by Maynard (the obvious choice), but by three under-masons – two, King and Mercer, from Smythson's team and another, named Vincent, who was a long way down the hierarchy of masons. Since they were paid at a lower rate, this saved money and Maynard and Smythson were shut out. However, the three produced unsatisfactory work on the capitals and were never paid for them. Thynne's action throughout this dispute demonstrates his ruthless character. Unlike Spicer, who decamped with £34 of Thynne's money to see him through the time before he found another job, Smythson and Maynard had only their savings to live on, and although Thynne owed them money there was no alternative job to go to. They held out as long as their savings allowed before caving in and accepting a lower rate of payment.[14] Together they wrote a grovelling undated letter[15] offering to do the work at a lower price than anyone else. This episode does not show Thynne in a good light but indicates the roots of his success.

Where was Smythson between 1574 and 1575 when his patron, as it were, 'stabbed him in the back'? He was working at Wardour Old Castle, Wiltshire, in 1576 until its completion in 1578. Judging by the style of the buildings and the fact that only Smythson had the required skills, Mark Girouard links Smythson with Corsham Court, Wiltshire, and possibly Shaw House, near Newbury in Berkshire; both were started in the mid 1570s.[16] To determine Smythson's whereabouts, these two buildings, neither on the grand scale of Longleat, might suggest an answer. Smythson was apparently taking work on when it was offered; what Thynne thought of this is unknown. But because Smythson was paid either by the day or by task, when he was not at Longleat he was not being paid – and this may have suited Thynne.

At Longleat Thynne, in effect, became his own surveyor, which was unusual in a building of this size. Taking on this role gave him complete control, and this suited a man who knew what he wanted and usually got it. The supply of good-quality stone was a problem; the first three Longleats used a local quarry, but for the fourth Longleat Thynne wanted something better. He bought a quarry near Box in Wiltshire, a distance of twenty-five miles (forty kilometres) from Longleat. The stone, already worked 'square at the quarry'[17] or prepared, was expensively dragged on sledges by oxen, not in horse panniers as at Wollaton or by the 'carriage' used at Hardwick for heavy loads. Wood in quantity was taken locally from Thynne's estate, and slate was imported from Wales. The accounts also show payments for large quantities of bricks; in contrast to Wollaton, where brick walls were faced with Ancaster stone, at Longleat the interior walls only were built of brick.

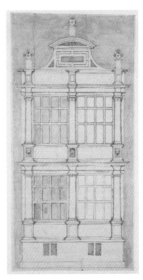

Above: A chimney-piece at Longleat attributed to
Alan Maynard, the French mason and sculptor,
from a 1537 design by Sebastiano Serlio

Right: A drawing by Robert Smythson of a
two-storey bay window associated
with Longleat, which has three-storey
bays with similar details

What was the cost? Since the accounts are incomplete the grand total
will never be known, but from 1568 to 1577 the average yearly expenditure
was £732, making a total for those years of £7,320; the following two years,
up to Thynne's death in 1580, are incomplete, but the expenditure for 1580
was £491.18 The earlier years, beginning in 1547, when Thynne was building a smaller Longleat, would have been less costly, but if at a guess it was
£400 per year the total estimated figure comes out at a staggering £15,000,
worth many millions at today's values. Thynne was certainly a man who
got what he wanted – and to that can be added, no matter what cost.

As most of the interior decoration at Longleat has been destroyed it was
brave of Anthony Wells-Cole in his book *Art and Decoration in Elizabethan
and Jacobean England* to attempt an appraisal of the sources used. He pro-
vides a very convincing assessment. Taking the three original surviving
chimney-pieces attributed to Alan Maynard as a starting point, Wells-
Cole correctly identifies the architrave of the chimney-piece decorated with
scrolls as being from a design by Sebastiano Serlio of a window plinth

from a woodcut in his Book IV of *L'Architettura* (published in 1537).[18] A second chimney-piece has detail from the same source, and the third, in the great hall, has detail adapted either from Italian architect Andrea Palladio's *I Quattro Libri dell'Architettura* (*The Four Books of Architecture*; published in 1570) or, more likely, from French architect Philibert de l'Orme's two books on architecture, *Nouvelles Inventions pour Bien Bastir et à Petits Frais* (*New Developments for Good Building at a Low Cost*; 1561) and *Le Premier Tome d'Architecture* (*The First Volume of Architecture*; 1567). The screen in the great hall made by Adrian Gaunt uses motifs derived from a set of cartouches published in 1555 in *Multiarum Variarum'que* by the Dutch architect Hans Vredeman de Vries.[19] Someone working at Longleat clearly had access to these important publications; the probability is that Thynne owned them and that Alan Maynard used them.

With the death of Thynne in 1580 the building work stopped. However, two masons, Maynard and Hilliar, stayed on until 1582; carpenters Nutall and Brown remained until 1581; a sawyer named Ward and his man stayed on until 1582; a glazier named Palmer and a brickmaker, Beron, remained until 1581. These men would have been engaged in finishing off uncompleted work – the roof was on, and the building was weathertight. Smythson took off in 1583 for Wollaton Hall, which was begun in 1580, and took with him only one of the men he had brought with him to Longleat, John Hills, together with Richard Crispin, the skilled carpenter who had worked at Longleat since 1554. Of those we can be certain. Others we cannot be sure of are men with surnames familiar from Longleat who turn up in the Wollaton accounts, which do not list Christian names; among these, two masons named Vincent were at Longleat and one at Wollaton, while two Gregorys, also masons, were at Longleat and one worked at Wollaton.

Masons' marks suggest that more masons migrated between building projects than are shown in the accounts. Of the masons' marks surviving at Longleat, four repeat at New Hardwick, two are found at Bolsover in Derbyshire and one at Worksop Manor Lodge in Nottinghamshire.

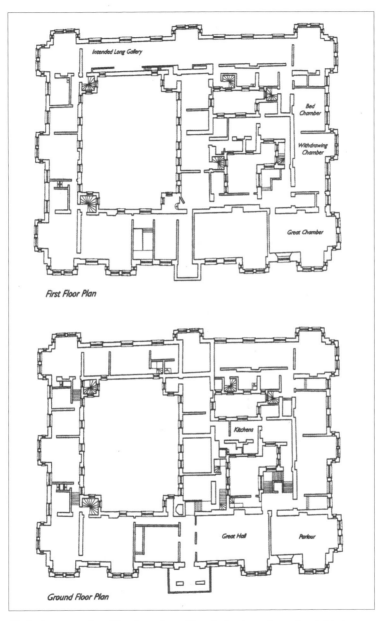

Elizabethan ground- and first-floor plans of Longleat redrawn from plans held at Hatfield House, Hertfordshire (Marquess of Salisbury), no doubt sent to Sir William Cecil (created Lord Burghley in 1571) by Sir John Thynne, the builder of Longleat House

A print from *Britannia Illustrata* by Leonard Knyff and Jan Kip, 1707, of Chatsworth looking
north, with the old Elizabethan front on the left of the house

3

CHATSWORTH HOUSE
THE HOME OF THE 12TH DUKE OF DEVONSHIRE

Today Chatsworth House in Derbyshire is very much changed from the house Bess of Hardwick began building there in 1552. This is because Bess's house was rebuilt, on the same foundations and beginning in 1687, by William Cavendish the 4th Earl (created 1st Duke of Devonshire in 1694). Furthermore, a new wing was added to the north of the house in the nineteenth century by William Cavendish, 6th Duke of Devonshire. Of the Elizabethan building, as we have seen, only the Hunting Tower, Queen Mary's Bower and perhaps part of the cellars remain.

Bess of Hardwick's early life is described in Chapter 5, which discusses Old Hardwick Hall in Derbyshire, where Bess was probably born, in 1527. In this period it was customary for the children of the gentry to be sent to serve in the households of socially more elevated families, where they would learn elevated manners and how such a superior household was run. Bess was sent to the Zouche family at Codnor Castle, Derbyshire – Lady Zouche was a distant cousin of the Hardwicks. We do not know exactly when Bess was sent, but – according to custom – she would have been no younger than ten years old. By 1543 she had left the Zouche household, and she married for the first time in that year, when she was not yet sixteen years old; her husband, Robert Barley, was aged only thirteen but died the following year, leaving his widow with an annual income of £8. 13s.

Bess then became a lady-in-waiting to a distant kinswoman, Lady

Frances Grey, wife of Henry Grey, Marquess of Dorset, and lived at Bradgate Park near Leicester. Lady Grey was the daughter of King Henry VIII's younger sister, Princess Mary, and Charles Brandon, Duke of Suffolk. The appointment followed within a year of Bess becoming a widow; she would have been well able to fill the post from her experience with the Zouche family. It gave her access to the court of King Henry VIII, since the Greys' royal connection made court attendance unavoidable. It would have been obvious to Bess that she would have to marry again. She met and, in 1547, married Sir William Cavendish, a widower with three daughters and at forty years old just more than twice Bess's age.

Sir William Cavendish came from a successful Suffolk family. He was a younger son and had had to make own way in the world. His father, Thomas Cavendish (who died in 1524), had been secretary to the treasurer of the king's exchequer in King Henry VII's reign and therefore had useful contacts at court. We know nothing of William until 1530 when he was in the service of Thomas Cromwell.

Cromwell took advantage of Cardinal Wolsey's rapid fall from grace in 1530. Wolsey had been a loyal servant of the king and virtually ran the country between 1516 and 1529. Made a cardinal in 1515, he fell foul of Henry's desire to divorce Catherine of Aragon in 1529 when, notwithstanding his close relationship with the pope, he was unable to secure Henry's divorce. Wolsey had failed his master: he was stripped of his office and property and after being accused of treason fell ill and died on 29 November 1530. Cromwell, who had been in Wolsey's service, moved into his late master's shoes. By 1536 he had become chancellor of the exchequer, principal secretary of state, master of the rolls and lord privy seal.

Cromwell recognized ability in Cavendish, who had an accountant's tidy mind, and appointed him an auditor sent to value religious houses during the Dissolution of the Monasteries. In 1531 Cavendish accepted the surrender of Sheen Abbey, while the following year he audited the possessions of the hugely wealthy St Albans Abbey. Cavendish was an ambitious man on the make. In 1534 the abbot of St Albans offered him the lease of the manor of

Northaw at a very reasonable rent; the abbot was hoping to buy the good will of Cavendish and his master Cromwell. However, the abbot had misjudged his man; by March 1535 Sir William received an outright grant from the king of the lands and manor of Northaw. A busy period followed: in one year, 1546, Cavendish was appointed treasurer of the king's chamber and treasurer to the court of general surveyors and was made a privy counsellor.

Cromwell, like his late master Wolsey, lost his position through difficulties arising from Henry's divorces and marriages. For political reasons Cromwell needed Henry to marry German noblewoman Anne of Cleves, but Henry, after meeting her, realized that in marrying her he was making a mistake. Although the marriage went ahead on 6 January 1540, it spelled the end of Cromwell's career. He was arrested on 23 May, an act of attainder was passed and on the very day that Henry separated from Anne, 23 July 1540, Cromwell was given the privilege of a private execution in the Tower of London; he was beheaded with what has been called barbarous cruelty. To make the matter public, his severed head was boiled and set up on a pike.

Through this turmoil William Cavendish survived, and in 1546 he was knighted. Clearly Sir William was a survivor. When the old king died in January the next year Sir William, already twice widowed and with three surviving daughters, had the leisure to marry again – this time to Bess, a widow of little wealth, at Bradgate Manor on 20 August 1547.

Sir William by then had possession of a scattered estate of church lands. Bess and he began rationalizing the holdings by selling off lands in Hertfordshire. Meanwhile, in Derbyshire Francis Leche – who was married to Bess's youngest sister, Alice – had sold Chatsworth and its lands to Francis Agard; in late June 1549, after Agard overreached himself, he sold Chatsworth to Bess and Sir William Cavendish for £600. In 1552 by a complicated deal with the Crown they swapped their lands in Cardigan, Hertfordshire and oddments of old church lands in Lincolnshire for lands at Doveridge some thirty miles (fifty kilometres) from Chatsworth. It made good sense for the Cavendishes.

Bess, although she married four times, had all her eight children by Sir William. They were Frances (born 1548), Temperance (born 1549 and died young), Henry (born 1550), William (born 1551), Charles (born 1553), Elizabeth (born 1554), Lucretia (born 1557 and died young) and Mary (born 1556). The two girls who died at an early age are remembered at Hardwick as the subjects of hangings that were formerly at Chatsworth.

It is known that in December 1551 repairs had been carried out on the building already at Chatsworth: records dated 17 December state that a 'goodman bisseter' (a carpenter) and his man had worked for seventy days on repairs costing £3. 10s. 8d., a considerable sum. Then on Christmas Eve that year a payment was recorded for drawing a plan for a new house at Chatsworth: 'Item geven to Roger Worthe my Mrs [Master's] mason for drawing my Mrs Platt 20s.'[1] The individual concerned may well be the Roger Worthe (or Warde), a mason who worked for Sir William Cecil at Burghley (by 1556 Burghley House was up to roof level and so must have been started about the time of Worthe's visit to Chatsworth). That Warde was something considerably more than a mere mason is shown in a letter he wrote to Sir William Cecil asking him to 'drawe a tryke [sketch] of the upryght for youre Lucan [dormer] Wyndow and the gabylle end over hytt . . . '[2]

Bess and her husband were planning to build a grand Chatsworth – when eventually complete in the late 1570s, the house was a four-storey building with an internal courtyard. However, the project was interrupted when Sir William died suddenly in October 1557, leaving Bess a widow for the third time. There were probing questions about £5,000 missing from the accounts, and the £5,000 debt was transferred to Bess. With this and with other additional debts she was facing a difficult future, and it can be assumed that any building work at Chatsworth was stopped following Sir William's death.

Two years later Bess married a wealthy courtier, Sir William St Loe, using his money to finance the building of Chatsworth and pay off her debts. St Loe must have been a patient man; tied to his court life, he had little time to get up to Chatsworth, where Bess was fully occupied with her building and bringing up her six surviving children. However, he was seemingly happy for Bess to spend his money.

According to Chatsworth MS 2, a record of building expenditure for the twelve months from October 1559 to October 1560, the craftsmen were paid by the day. Although the record gives no indication as to how far the building had progressed, the details are instructive. On 18 May 1560, following the winter shutdown of building work, William Galle, a mason, was paid 2s. 6d. for five days at 6d. a day; and John Colleshaw, a less skilled mason, was paid at a daily rate of 4d. Carpenters at 8d. a day and joiners at 6d. a day were the highest-paid of the craftsmen. Plasterers came in lower at 4d. a day and at the same rate as stone-breakers and plasterers; labourers were paid 2d. a day.[3] On 13 April 1560 MS 2 records an increase in the wage account at Chatsworth: limestone for making mortar and plaster was paid for, as well as charcoal to fire the lime kilns. A page in the accounts for April is headed: 'payde to the workemen that hathe wrought on the work about the newe byledng'. On 25 April Bess wrote to Sir John Thynne, then trying to complete his first rebuilding of Longleat, asking for the speedy loan of the plasterer who had created floral decoration for his hall. In signing the letter she mistakenly wrote 'Elizabeth Cavendish', then – remembering – crossed through 'Cavendish' and substituted 'Sayntlo'.

The sudden restarting of building at Chatsworth was the direct result of her marriage to Sir William St Loe: she was able to use the money that he had inherited on his father's death just twelve months earlier. New but unspecified work was undertaken. Bess was building a house of magnificence suitable to the dynasty she was intent on founding. However, not all Bess's energy was spent at Chatsworth, for she made time to support her new husband at court. During her absences from Chatsworth James

Cromp, her servant from the time she was married to Cavendish, was left in charge. Frequent instructions were sent to Cromp on how the work was to be carried out, where masons were to be found, and so on. When Cromp was away from Chatsworth on other business another old Cavendish servant, Francis Whitfield, took over his responsibilities. Whitfield was instructed that the porch should be finished before the battlements were started and the crest was to be the same colour as the porch.[4] In Bess's letters these instructions were interspersed with messages to her children and to her aunt, Marcella Linaker, who was living at Chatsworth. Marcella was told to make a little garden beside the new house and was sent bundles of garden seed. In December 1560 a grill and knocker 'for the great gate at Chattesworth' costing 12s. were sent up from London.[5]

By the end of October 1564 the new Chatsworth was complete. William St Loe, a relative of Bess's husband, wrote from London – where he had been doing some business for her. He declared himself glad that she was in good health and expressed the wish that the sight of her newly finished building would sustain her; then he added that Sir William St Loe must stay there.[6]

Sir William St Loe died in 1565. Fortunately he had made his estates over to Bess, who was now a wealthy widow. By this time Chatsworth comprised a compact two-storey building, with Bess's chambers on the second storey on the cold north-west corner. Her withdrawing room opened into the matted gallery (called matted because the floor, likely to be made of lime ash cement, was covered with woven reed matting), and the formal route followed on into the apartments of state: the low great chamber, the tymes chamber (actually a withdrawing chamber), the nobleman's chamber (the state bedchamber) and an inner chamber. For a knight's widow, as Bess was, these rooms were sufficient; guests of higher rank would use the superior state apartments.

Two years after the death of St Loe Bess married George Talbot, 6th Earl of Shrewsbury. She was now a countess. A year later, in 1568, Mary, Queen of Scots was sent to Shrewsbury and Bess as a state prisoner requiring accommodation – hardly a good start for a newly married couple. There are no accounts for 1568, but it seems that when Mary stayed at Chatsworth her apartments must have been completed and the workmen discharged. Yet when the Earl of Leicester stayed there in the summer of 1577 we know that there was a rush to complete his apartments. It may have been that at the time of St Loe's death Chatsworth was finished, but that after Bess's marriage additions had to be made because a countess required a larger household than a knight's lady, and that with the arrival of Mary, Queen of Scots in 1568 a third storey was added. Chatsworth may have become a tall house by circumstances forced on Bess, rather than by design.

By January 1577, when Chatsworth was again nearing completion, George Hickette, freemason, was paid 6d. a day, but some bargains-in-great were taken: 'Itm Payd to John Shute [a mason] the 18 of April [1579] in full payment of his bargayne for the chemnye[piece] in the Purple Chamber measured by Roberts [head mason] 10/6d.'[7] By the time of an inventory taken in 1601 the Purple Chamber was situated on the second storey next to 'Hellens Chamber' on the north-west corner. Roberts was Thomas Roberts – see his will in Appendix II; he was a mason on 6d. a day at Chatsworth and from 1582 to 1588 at Wollaton, where he was paid 12d. a day.

Thomas Accres, the gifted mason, made his first appearance at Chatsworth on 4 February 1577 and again on 21 June that year. He was initially paid 5d. a day,[8] although by May 1578 he was the highest-paid mason at 7d. a day. The date of Accres's arrival is significant because at this time the Earl of Leicester, who planned to visit Buxton's baths for his health, accepted Bess's invitation to go on to Chatsworth in June and July. The building was incomplete. Three rooms of the earl's apartments – including those called 'The Withdrawing Chamber in the Earl of Leicester's Chamber' and 'The Earl of Leicester's Chamber' in the 1601 inventory – were yet to be finished. There was a burst of work: hair was ordered for plasterers together with glovers' patches 'for ye paynters', and from January 1577 plasterers and glaziers were busily employed. Blackstone for Accres's chimney-pieces was quarried at

Ashford-in-the-Water, five miles (eight kilometres) west of Chatsworth. On 21 June 1579: 'Itm geven by yo la. Commandment to Thoms Roberts xijd. To Thoms Accres xvjd to Nicholas Laverok xijd. For working one Sunday and on [one] night at the coing [coming] of the Earl of Leicester.'[9] Bess even sent for two plasterers from Kenilworth, Leicester's home. Sawyers cut timber for wainscoting and doors, while wallers and masons completed what seems to have been a courtyard or garden walls. This was not in any way a major building operation but, rather, work necessary to complete what had previously been unfinished. In May Shrewsbury had petitioned Queen Elizabeth to move Mary, Queen of Scots (then held at Sheffield Castle) to Chatsworth for three weeks while Sheffield Castle was spring-cleaned. Bess was having none of that: with workmen coming and going security would be impossible. She wrote to Shrewsbury pointing out that since he had sent no provisions it was impossible to accommodate their prisoner at Chatsworth.

Even after Leicester left the work continued. An entry for 17 March 17 1578 reads: 'Payd Ambrose Russell [a mason] upon a reckonying of his bargain of the skrine [screen] as appeareth by his bill xxs.'[10] This was a stone screen replacing what was probably a wooden one.

There are only two views surviving of the old Chatsworth: a needlework (see page 63) and an oil painting attributed to Welsh landscape artist Richard Wilson (see page 67), both now at Chatsworth. A 1699 view of Chatsworth by Dutch draughtsmen Leonard Knyff and Jan Kip (see page 63) shows the house halfway through the 1st Duke of Devonshire's rebuilding: a view of the old west front and main entrance of the Elizabethan Chatsworth a year before that front was demolished and replaced with what is there today. By this date, already, there is very little left of Bess's great house.

The rebuilding begun in 1687 by William Cavendish, the 4th Earl of Devonshire (1st Duke of Devonshire from 1694), involved taking down and

A detail from *Britannia Illustrata* by Leonard Knyff and Jan Kip, 1707, showing Chatsworth as it was before 1699, partly rebuilt. The east and south fronts have been rebuilt in the baroque style we see today, but the west front, the old Elizabethan entrance front, remains together with the original north front.

A needlework cushion cover of the west entrance front of Chatsworth as it was when completed by 1580; through the entrance arch a fountain plays in the open courtyard around which the house was built.

then rebuilding the house in piecemeal fashion, one side at a time. It is likely that the cellars beneath Chatsworth date back to the original house; however, they are currently closed for the removal of asbestos, and consequently I have not been able to examine them. A more certain survival from Bess's house are the Hunting Tower and the moated structure adjacent to the present main drive known as Queen Mary's Bower.

The Hunting Tower, so called because it was used as a place from which to watch hunting, was built *c.* 1580. Abraham Smith is mentioned in a bargain-in-great in April 1581 for making wooden moulds for a plasterer, James Both (Booth): 'Both hath taken by great the frise and cornish of the four turrets uppo the monte to be cast in such a mould as Habraham shal mak for the same . . .'[11] The 1601 inventory refers to 'a turret in the mount' and to 'the Stand' (a turret from which to view hunting) as two different buildings. It is a challenge to make sense of these references. The present Hunting Tower has four turrets and has cornices but no friezes. If we examine its surviving plasterwork we find deep-cut reliefs of non-repeating leafed branches with Tudor rose flowers. The moulds must have been very difficult to make because the ceilings are small domes with no flat surfaces; Smith and Booth must have been highly skilled to produce this work in such a small space. As a footnote, although the Stand has gone, the wood immediately adjoining the east side of Chatsworth garden is known as Stand Wood.

The Hunting Tower may have been built by Smythson, who possibly did other work that was destroyed in the 1st Duke's rebuilding.[12] This rebuilding was curious in that the duke tended to keep to the same room plan as the Elizabethan house; the chapel on the ground floor remained in the same space, the space of the Elizabethan high great chamber on the third storey became the great dining chamber, while on the floor below the Elizabethan low great chamber is a space now occupied by the family dining-room. The principal rooms of reception remained on the top floor. In Bess's building, as we have seen, this arrangement may have been dictated by the need to add a third storey in order to accommodate Mary, Queen of Scots and the Earl of Leicester.

There are several fine examples at Chatsworth of inlaid marquetry panelling in coloured woods. According to the 1601 inventory, Bess's withdrawing chamber was, 'verie fayre waynscotted deep French panel markentryie', while her bedchamber was 'verie fayre waynscotted to the height [to the cornice] with coulored woods'. The upper floor of one of the turrets was 'verie fayre waynscotted & with alabaster black stone and other carving'; it was a very grand space, probably a banqueting house giving on to the roof. Another turret was 'fayre waynscotted with Coulored woods and pyramids'. Yet, strangely, there was no panelling in the 'Nobleman's Chamber', a grand room splendidly furnished on the second storey, or in the 'Tymes Chamber' and the 'Low Great Chamber.' The 'Matted Gallery', which took up almost the complete length of the east side of the second storey, was 'fayre waynscotted to the height markentrie with portals'. The identity of the skilled craftsman or craftsmen who made the inlay is not known, but the building accounts for 9 December 1577[13] gives a clue: 'Payd to Tayler the inlayer aforhand V Li [£5] toward the payment of VIII Li [£8] for tow [two] years wadge to begin at candlemas contwilvmonth [come twelvemonth] which shall be in XXI reg years.' (The final phrase means the twenty-first year of the queen's reign, so February 1579.) That is the only mention by name of an inlayer in the incomplete accounts. He was paid a high annual wage and thus was valued by Bess; but for what inlaid work was he responsible?

There is not a great deal of inlaid marquetry panelling mentioned in the 1601 Chatsworth inventory. On the ground floor only the parlour contains inlaid panelling; on the second storey 'My Ladys Bedchamber' and the long matted gallery are the only rooms with inlaid panelling, and that completes the first Chatsworth. On the top storey there is mention of 'The Fynishers Chamber', 'the Worme Chamber', the high great chamber and the unidentified 'high gatehouse', which would not have been a big chamber. Panelling is easily put up, taken down and moved about, and it is speculation to suggest that the inlaid work on the ground floor and second storey was original in the 1601 inventory, but it is a start. On the third storey there are only four chambers with inlaid panelling; could 'Tayler the inlayer' and his supposed team have completed these four chambers in the 1570s? I think it very possible.

Tayler may have had a team of inlayers working for him. He and his men may well have made the four inlaid panels that are today hanging on the first flight of back stairs at New Hardwick. If so, these were probably originally made for Chatsworth because there is no inlaid work at Hardwick original to the building. The date is right: one panel is dated 1576, a year when Tayler may have been working at Chatsworth, and the date of the print from which one is derived (Frankfurt, 1564[14]) gives ample time for a copy to have arrived at Chatsworth by 1576. Tayler is not recorded in any of the fuller building accounts for Hardwick – he vanished from Bess's accounts. Inlaid panels of a seaweed design and pilasters surrounding three sides of the altar in the Upper Chapel at New Hardwick are further remnants of inlaid work from the first or second Chatsworth.

Bess's heir, her eldest son, Henry, failed her dynastic ambitions. He married Shrewsbury's daughter Grace in 1568 when he was eighteen and Grace a mere child and was immediately sent on an extended Grand Tour to Constantinople for two years until his bride should be old enough for child-bearing – at about the age of fifteen. Their arranged marriage was not a success: Henry and Grace were expected to produce a male heir, but they had no legitimate children. Henry's male heir was his illegitimate son Henry (from whom were descended the lords Waterpark), and he had numerous other children; one hundred years after his death he was still remembered as 'the ram of Derbyshire and Staffordshire'. Dynastically, Henry was useless as far as Bess was concerned: she called him 'my bad son Henry', and William her second son became her heir. However, Chatsworth, by his father's will, was entailed on Henry with use to Bess during her lifetime.

The 1601 Chatsworth inventory presents us with an interior only part furnished; by this date most of the furnishings had been removed to the

A detail of the west front of Old Chatsworth, attributed to Richard Wilson (1714–82), although this is disputed; in any event, it was painted before 1676 when the 4th Earl of Devonshire began his rebuilding work, starting on the far side – the east front – which can still be seen in the painting to have its Elizabethan turrets.

Old and New Hardwick Halls, and consequently it is not possible to work out the original scheme of interior decoration at Chatsworth. Nevertheless some of the rooms in the 1601 inventory were fully furnished, such as the sumptuous nobleman's chamber containing: 'ffowre peeces of Cloth of golde and velvet hangings'. Bess's bedchamber in the north-east corner of the second storey was kept ready against her coming and fully furnished; that, too, was decorated with wainscoting 'to the height with coulored woods' and consequently had no need of hangings. The real point of the 1601 inventories of Chatsworth and Hardwick was to list exactly what was in the three houses to ensure that Henry did not get his hands on the contents and that they went to William. She could not interfere with the entail: Chatsworth went to Henry by his father's will, but she could make certain that the place was empty. As it happened William bought the unfurnished Chatsworth for £8,000 from Henry in 1609, a year after their mother's death.

Other fragments from Chatsworth at Hardwick include a superlative panel of carved alabaster of *Orpheus and the Muses* brought from Chatsworth by the 6th Duke in the nineteenth century and now the overmantel in the state withdrawing chamber at Hardwick. It is tempting to speculate that this alabaster was originally in the room called the 'Muses' Chamber'. Although mentioned in the inventory as being near the Earl of Leicester's chamber and the high great chamber, the Muses' chamber was unfurnished and unlisted and has been impossible to locate on the floor plan. The Blue Room at Hardwick has a chimney-piece with an alabaster panel of the *Marriage of Tobias and Sarah*. The faded initials beneath the cornice supporting the panel are discussed in Chapter 6 on New Hardwick Hall. The whole chimney-piece is likely to have come from Chatsworth when the house was remodelled from 1687 and would probably date to *c.* 1570; it was certainly never made for Hardwick – the entablature has been taken off to fit it into the height of the room, indicating that it is what can be called a 'made-up piece.'

A late-seventeenth-century painting of Chatsworth attributed to Richard Wilson shows the building strangely lit from the north-west by the sun, which might just be possible around midsummer (see page 67). It also shows the west front and terrace flanked on either side by two-storeyed gazebos with a round flat-topped building in front of the main entrance to the courtyard overlooking the River Derwent beneath the viewer. The inventory does not identify these detached buildings; they must have been unfurnished.

Of the masons employed at Chatsworth, Thomas Accres, Thomas Hollingworth, Thomas Outram, Abraham Smith and a plasterer, John Marker, went on to work at Hardwick; only Accres worked at Wollaton. Peter Sympson, a mason at Chatsworth from 1577, may be the same mason who worked for the Earl of Shrewsbury in 1574 (Appendix III).

Did Bess start the fashion called 'the tall house of the Midlands' that continued with Shrewesbury's Worksop Manor in Nottinghamshire? She may have, but both house were 'tall houses' forced by circumstance that became a style taken up by other builders, including Smythson.

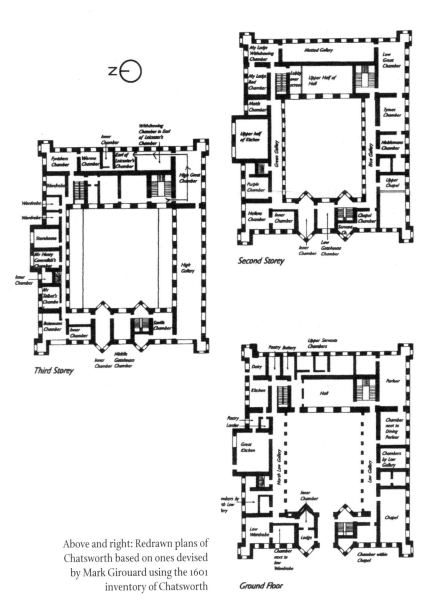

Above and right: Redrawn plans of
Chatsworth based on ones devised
by Mark Girouard using the 1601
inventory of Chatsworth

69

An aerial view of Wollaton Hall from the west

4

WOLLATON HALL
CITY OF NOTTINGHAM NATURAL HISTORY MUSEUM

Wollaton Hall, Nottingham, is by anyone's standards an extraordinary building. On a stone plaque on the south front a Latin inscription tells us 'Behold this house of Sir Francis Willoughby, built with rare art and bequeathed to the Willoughbys. Begun 1580 and finished 1588.' The 'rare art' exhibited on the building's exterior was derived from architectural pattern books compiled by Hans Vredeman de Vries, a Dutch-born painter-turned-architect who lived in Antwerp. His three pattern books, published in 1565, 1566 and 1601, had enormous influence on architecture throughout northern Europe; he promoted the northern taste for flat patterns in strapwork and for carved decoration of interlaced bands imitating cut leather. Before Wollaton Hall this had never before been attempted on any building in England on such a scale; there had never been a building quite like it and never was again. Wollaton Hall remains unique to this day, although the Victorians were strangely attracted by the house's four corner turrets and repeated them at Highclere Castle in Hampshire between 1839 and 1842 and Mentmore, Buckinghamshire, between 1850 and 1855. To understand Wollaton Hall we have to understand the man who built it.

Francis Willoughby had a very disturbed upbringing.[1] In Tudor times children were treated like small adults, and their needs were often not well understood. Some authorities say that an unloved child grows into an unloving adult, and Francis certainly found it difficult or impossible to relate to his contemporaries.

He was born into a family with substantial holdings of land in Nottinghamshire, Herefordshire, Warwickshire, Lincolnshire, Dorset, Essex and Kent. The Willoughbys had clawed their way up from the modest station of their forebear, Ralph Bugge, a thirteenth-century wool-merchant, each generation improving its situation by judicious marriage. By the sixteenth century they were established gentry of great wealth. They had the good fortune to find coal beneath their Nottinghamshire pastures and as early as the late fifteenth century had five coal pits at Wollaton producing an income of £214 out of a total of net receipts of £8,591 – an enormous income for the time. Over the twelve years from 1549 to 1561 this grew to a total of £4,636 for coal, against net receipts of £3,178 from other sources.[2]

Francis was born in 1547. His mother, Anne, died a year later, and his father, Henry Willoughby, gloriously foolish, died in 1549 leading his men against Robert Kett, a rebel camped with 19,000 men at Mousehold Heath near Norwich. (Exactly why Kett rebelled against authority has never been explained, but he became a magnet for dissidents and before long had an army of 16,000 men and had seized Norwich. The dispute was neither religious nor political, and Kett was from Norfolk gentry who had came to England with the Normans.) Willoughby had enjoyed his inheritance for only seven months and died leaving his heir Thomas (aged eight), a daughter Margaret (age unknown) and Francis (aged two). Because the heir was a child the estate fell into wardship – see Appendix I for an explantion of the laws of wardship. Henry's brother-in-law – Henry Grey, Duke of Suffolk – was a supervisor of the will and took on the profitable wardship of Thomas, the heir. The chief executor of the will, George Medley, took Francis and his sister Margaret into his own household at Tilty in Essex. Medley was a stepbrother of the orphan's mother and also of the Duke of Suffolk.

In 1550 Suffolk left the family home at Bradgate Manor, near Leicester, for London to be nearer to the levers of power; Francis and his sister were transferred to Bradgate. To be orphaned and moved from pillar to post can only have been detrimental to Francis's development, but further disturbance was in store. Suffolk, a very ambitious man, plotted to put his daughter Jane Grey on the throne to displace Mary Tudor, and both Suffolk and his daughter were beheaded for their folly. Medley was by this time living in the Minories, London, as were Francis and Margaret. Under suspicion of being involved in the plot, Medley was locked away in the Tower for a spell. These were troublesome times – a letter from Mrs Lenton, left in charge of his household in the Minories, was desperate: she wrote that she 'knows not where to place Master Francis and Mistress Margaret Willoughby now that Mr Medley's house is likely to be seised.'[3]

In 1554, when things had settled down following Queen Mary's accession to the throne, Thomas Willoughby's wardship was taken on by a Catholic peer, Lord Paget, for the profits accruing to his ward. Francis and Margaret for once fared better: with Medley they moved back to Tilty. Medley decided that it was now time: 'to put Mistress Margaret and Master Francis Willoughby to school'.[4] Medley took his responsibilities seriously; in addition to receiving private tuition, Francis was sent to schools in London, Cambridge and Saffron Walden. At such schools beating the boys was a regular event. Between the ages of six and ten Francis was put to study Hebrew, Latin, Greek and arithmetic. He was also taught to write the italic script, to dance, sing and to play on the virginals. It was the education required of a typical courtier. In later life he made donations to Jesus College, Cambridge, perhaps indicating that he had been a student there.[5] In any event, Francis Willoughby had the best classical education available in England in the 1560s. He was without doubt the most cultured of all Smythson's patrons.[6]

Francis's brother Thomas, under the wardship of Lord Paget, was married to Paget's daughter. However, Thomas died aged eighteen in 1559, apparently from overheating himself while hunting at Middleton, the Willoughbys' main family home in Warwickshire. Francis was now the heir and became the target of wardship, which was bought by Sir Francis Knollys, a cousin to the queen, in 1560. Now aged thirteen, Francis refused to marry Knollys's daughter. This may indicate strength of character or, more likely, that the executors of his father's will, becoming sick of the Willoughby estates being plundered, could see a way out of their dilemma – they bought out the wardship in 1554 for £1,500. Francis became his own master then and a very good catch in the marriage market. Margaret, his sister, was married off to Sir Matthew Arundell around 1558 with £300 for her marriage money, but no doubt her brother would have had to provide a negotiated dowry. Sir Matthew will shortly play a more important part in this account of Wollaton Hall.

By 1564 Francis had taken the matter of his marriage into his own hands and proposed to Elizabeth, daughter of Sir John Lyttleton, a Warwickshire neighbour; she brought £2,000 to the marriage. Francis's sister Margaret objected strongly, perhaps because she thought her future sister-in-law was getting her brother on the cheap, perhaps because she disapproved of Sir John. Francis on his side agreed to settle the customary one-third of his estate – excluding the coal pits – on his bride for her lifetime. Francis and Elizabeth had six daughters and a son (born in 1580, he died shortly afterwards). It was a stormy marriage.

Francis quarrelled with his daughters, his wife and his relatives as his relationships with all around him descended into chaos. He spent freely, living in the style expected of the wealthy. But all was not as it seemed: he was spending beyond his income and borrowing at 10 per cent compound interest secured on land to cover the shortfall. The Wollaton coal pits were turning in good profits: from April to October 1586 income from the pits was £276. 10s. 10d.[7] Earlier, in 1583, he had enjoyed splashing out, spending thousands of pounds on buying land.[8] However, his attempts to extend his industrial enterprises showed losses: planting forty acres (sixteen hectares) of woad in 1585 resulted in a complete loss – and the grower, by whom Francis had been taken in, was thrown into prison. Undeterred, Sir Francis forged ahead with a plan to establish blast furnaces at Oakamoor in Staffordshire and at Middleton on borrowed money. Oakamoor was near to Alton woods for fuel, and it belonged to Bess of Hardwick. Bess lent £400 to Loggin, Sir Francis's ironmaster, at the usual 10 per cent, secured on Willoughby land. Shortly afterwards, Sir Francis fell out with Loggin, who was sacked. Later, in 1591, Sir Francis negotiated a further loan of £3,000 from Bess of Hardwick – a deal that would give his heir considerable grief.

Sir Francis's frantic search for an heir brought him to select Sir Percival Willoughby, a distant relative, whom he married to his daughter Bridget in 1583. Sir Percival believed he was marrying into a wealthy and unencumbered family, a belief that was to prove a chimera, as his inheritance, burdened by debts, proved to be an ongoing worry to him. Moreover, Sir Percival fell in and out of favour with his difficult father-in-law.

Queen Elizabeth's visit to the Earl of Leicester at Kenilworth Castle, Warwickshire, in 1575 had a highly stimulating effect on the members of the Midlands gentry who attended. It was probably on this occasion that Francis was knighted. In 1575, like others of his peers, Sir Francis invited the queen to visit him at Middleton in Warwickshire or at his house in Wollaton village, but the invitation was refused because plainly neither house was big enough to accommodate the royal court. This may have been the stimulus behind the building of Wollaton Hall.

A further incentive was the possibility of having a much-needed male heir. Although by this time Sir Francis's relationship with his wife Elizabeth was severely strained – and increasingly they lived apart – they were sufficiently reconciled in 1579 for Elizabeth to become pregnant with the son born to them in 1580. By 1582, however, the marriage was seemingly at an end, and Elizabeth, having had enough of her husband, successfully petitioned the queen for a separation, formalized by an order from the queen to Sir Francis to pay an allowance of £200 a year for maintenance.[9] Extraordinarily, Elizabeth once again returned to her husband in 1588, but by the following year she was back in London claiming poor health, which she certainly suffered, and the need for treatment. She died in London in June 1595.

Before August 1595 Sir Francis married Dorothy Tamworth, a widow of twenty-nine, nineteen years younger than her new husband. This caused further dissent in the family. Sir Francis spent the early months of his marriage making efforts to reduce his debts – which now totalled more than £21,000. He sold land and reduced his total indebtedness to a more manageable £7,000 – part of which was the debt of £3,000 to Bess of Hardwick, secured on several manors.

His wife Dorothy quickly became pregnant, but Sir Francis was not to see his latest child, who was born after he died in 1596. Poison was suspected, as his death was convenient.[10] Until the birth the family held its collective breath. If the baby were a boy, he would be the heir rather than Sir Percival. There was great relief when the baby proved to be a girl.

Beginning in 1580, Sir Francis set out to build a house at Wollaton suitable for his dynasty and for entertaining the monarch. It would seem that he could have begun preparations for building the house as early as 1573. There is a curious entry in the Wollaton household accounts for 12 May 1573, to a Platt (plan) maker: 'who came from London to measure the groundes'.[11] This can be interpreted in two ways: it either relates to a plan preceding Smythson's (see page 79), or Sir Francis was simply having land surveyed. The latter is most likely.

Next he seems to have turned to Robert Smythson. In the Smythson Collection in the Royal Institute of British Architects library[12] there is a ground-floor plan for Wollaton surrounded on four sides by eight equal rectangles, with the gardens in the rectangle to the south (see page 78). To the east is a small stable block and to the west a bakehouse and brewhouse, but it is doubtful if these were ever built. The plan of the house is almost as built. There is also a drawing for the hall screen – still surviving – and what may be the earliest perspective architectural drawing by an English architect, showing the detail of one of the corner towers.[13]

The south front of Wollaton Hall today; the turreted four-bay High Hall, which, it is surmised, must have been Sir Francis Willoughby's idea, is a wasted space because the very narrow spiral stairs within prevent access for anything other than the smallest furniture.

It must have been through his sister, who was married to Sir Matthew Arundell of Wardour Castle, that Sir Francis contacted Robert Smythson. In 1576 Smythson was a mason working on Wardour Castle. The date is credible: to be able to start his new building in 1580 Sir Francis would have begun planning in the mid 1570s.

In building his new house Sir Francis was making a statement. The house is sited on top of the only hill in the area and was meant to be seen. Even now, owned by Nottingham City Council and surrounded at a distance by urban housing estates, Wollaton House cannot be ignored; its amazing silhouette dominates the horizon. But what what Sir Francis's intended statement? Like his life, the message is confused.

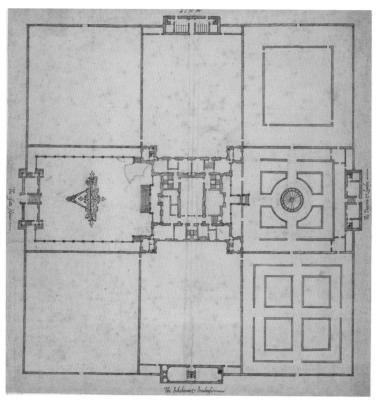

Floor plan of Wollaton Hall by Robert Smythson; it is doubtful if the outbuildings were ever built, although in the garden on the south (right-hand side of the picture) the circular feature is marked today by a fountain in a circular pond.

We know that Sir Francis had a library of the most valuable books of his time, and some of the details at Wollaton can be attributed to designs in these books. There is no inventory of Sir Francis's books although in a damaged and incomplete manuscript of *c*. 1660 his descendant and name-sake Francis Willoughby the naturalist (1635–72) attempted to draw up a list of the books at Wollaton. This list included: *I Quattro Libri dell' Architettura* (*The Four Books of Architecture*), published in 1570 by Italian architect Andrea Palladio; *L'Architettura* (*Architecture*), published in seven volumes beginning in 1537 by Italian architect Sebastiano Serlio; and *De*

Right: Drawing of the proposed screen for Wollaton; the heads of Serapis, the Graeco-Egyptian god of the underworld, were swapped for lions' heads on the actual screen as built (below).

Below: The screen at Wollaton with the lions' heads; the stone balustrade is by Wyatville.

Architectura (*On Architecture*), written by the Roman architect Vitruvius in the first century BC.

In addition, the catalogue prepared when Wollaton Hall was sold to Nottingham City Council in 1925 lists editions of the seventh book of Sebastiano Serlio's *L'Architettura* and of *Nouvelles Inventions pour Bien Bastir et à Petits Frais* (*New Ideas for Good Building at a Low Cost*), published in 1561 by the French architect Philibert de l'Orme. Furthermore there were copies of works by another French architect, Jacques Androuet du Cerceau – *Livre d'Architecture* (*Book of Architecture*), published in 1559, together with a second volume of this work published in 1561. There was also Jacques Androuet du Cerceau's most influential book, *Les Plus Excellents Bastiments de France* (*The Best Buildings of France*), published in two volumes in 1576 and 1579. *The First and Chief Groundes of Architecture*, published in 1563 by English architect John Shute, completed the list. Willoughby was certainly equipped with the best reference books obtainable in his time. Additionally, it is likely that he possessed *Architectura oder Bauung der Antiquen aus dem Vitruvius* ('Architecture of the Ancient Buildings of Vitrivius'), published in Antwerp by Hans Vredeman de Vries in 1577, three years before the building started.

In an article in *Country Life* in 1991[14] Mark Girouard argued convincingly that at Wollaton Hall Willoughby set out to recreate Solomon's Temple in Jerusalem. As Girouard points out, no one knew what the temple looked like, but this was plainly no deterrent to Sir Francis. There had been three temples on the site in Jerusalem, and a number of descriptions of the ancient building had survived. From these descriptions it was clear that there had been a sanctuary, the holy of holies, over which rose a central tower of up to three storeys in height. At Wollaton a rectangular plan with four substantial corner turrets has above it, in the centre, a clerestory to light the great hall. So far this is the kind of building one might expect Smythson to design for his patron. Placed on top of the clerestory, however, is an all-dominating and quite remarkable prospect room, with bartizan turrets – small projecting turrets – at the corners (see page 77). This was obviously Sir Francis's contribution to the design.

The earliest and the most complete inventory for Wollaton Hall is that of 1601. In this the prospect room is called the 'High Hall' and is said to contain only '1 joynd stoole' and 'certen mattes'. Clearly it was not a living space. Access by a spiral staircase made it impossible to carry substantial furnishings there, and there was no heating; but on the other hand the room commanded a breathtaking view of countryside on all sides. To an Elizabethan, the Temple in Jerusalem was probably designed by God Himself – and so possessed God-given standards of perfection. Sir Francis, as far as we know, was not inspired by God but by Friar Overton's tower at Repton, Derbyshire, which has four corner turrets, by nearby Mackworth Castle, with its bartizan towers, and by Mount Edgcumbe, Cornwall, which had a similar central hall lit from above by a raised clerestory and was built in 1546.[15] Sir Francis's sister, Margaret, was married to Sir Matthew Arundell, a member of an originally Cornish family; the builder of Mount Edgcumbe, Sir Richard Edgcumbe, married Sir Matthew Arundell's aunt. The house therefore would have been known by both Sir Francis and Smythson.

The plan, a rectangle with a square tower at each corner, is based on designs by French architect Jacques Androuet du Cerceau (*c.* 1515–90), who published his two volumes of *Les Plus Excellents Bastiments de France* in 1576 and 1579 and the first and second *Livre d'Architecture* in 1559 and 1561. In the Willoughby papers held at Wollaton Hall there is an undated plan, obviously rejected by Sir Francis because the reverse side is covered with his scribbling – he lists family members to identify a possible heir in place of his recently dead infant son.[16] The document, which shows the plan and elevation for a house with four corner turrets, as at Wollaton (see page 82), is an almost direct copy from *Les Petites Habitations* (*Modest Dwellings*), a book of *c.* 1545 attributed to du Cerceau and recently more exactly retitled *Logis Domestiques* (*Domestic Buildings*); he borrowed the designs from Italian architect Sebastiano Serlio (1475–1554), whose *L'Architectura*, the first architectural pattern book, was published (as noted above) in seven parts beginning in 1537. Today the only surviving copy of *Logis Domestiques,* lacking a title page, is held in the Bibliothèque Nationale, Paris. The given title, *Les Petites Habitations* (the original title is unknown), is a misnomer as the book contains elevations and plans of six quite grand châteaux. The late David Thomson pointed out that the plan in Willoughby's hands was ideal for a divided household, of which there were many in France: a *grande salle* (main room or hall) divides the property into two halves so that husband and wife could live separate lives without meeting each other in the building.[17] Unfortunately there is no plan of the upper floor, and we do not know if the *grande salle* extended through the upper floor. This

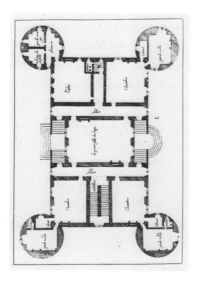
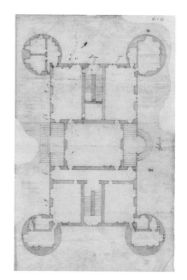

Clockwise from top left: Floor plan of a building from *Logis Domestiques* (*c.* 1545; *Domestic Buildings*), formerly called *Les Petites Habitations* (*Modest Dwellings*), a book of architectural designs by the French architect Jacques Androuet du Cerceau; a floor plan for Wollaton Hall based on the du Cerceau design and rejected by Sir Francis Willoughby; the elevation of the entrance front of the same du Cerceau plan layout must have appealed to Willoughby, although it was not nearly big enough to accommodate his large household. He was thinking of something far grander, and the final plan for Wollaton permits Willoughby and his wife to occupy quite separate apartments.

By looking at the exterior of Wollaton we can see that Sir Francis had many ideas that were skilfully controlled and utilized by Smythson. In addition to the influence of du Cerceau, there is strong evidence that many details on the exterior are taken from the *Architectura oder Bauung der Antiquen aus dem Vitruvius* of Hans Vredeman de Vries (1577), and within the house the curious windows of the prospect room (high hall), the alcoves between the pilasters and the strapworked gables crowning the turrets are from the same source (see page 85) .[18] Smythson was familiar with de Vries from his time at Longleat.

The plan from *Les Petites Habitations* deserves more attention because it contains ideas that were new at that time. For example, the kitchen and services are placed in the basement, which was an innovation in English planning and which made for a more compact arrangement. The plan also calls for the front door to lead straight into the *grande salle* – or hall, as Willoughby would have understood it – just as at Old and New Hardwick. This arrangement did not appeal to Sir Francis. The central hall at Wollaton is therefore accessed by a dog-leg route that brings the visitor past the stair to the kitchen to enter the hall beneath an elegant screen passage. The reason for this diversion was because all hall screens traditionally hid three service doors from the diners in the hall – one leading to the kitchen, one to the pantry and the third to the buttery, essential routes of supply for the formal service of meals. The dog-leg leads the visitor past the stair to the kitchen, the pantry and the buttery. Such a layout was necessary because the royal court still maintained a medieval routine; to have changed anything would have made a visit by the queen difficult to manage. For example, there was a yeoman of the pantry who required a pantry for the service at mealtimes of bread and dry foods and a yeoman of the buttery needing a buttery for the service of butter and wet foods. Eventually both jobs were conveniently amalgamated into that of the butler. On the continent, by contrast, things had moved on, and there were no great halls. The layout contained in the French plans by du Cerceau would have been useless to Sir Francis: where Sir Francis's great hall would have been, the French plans had a *grande salle de logis* ('main hall') not used like an English great hall for eating in – or else the space contained a staircase. Both were quite unsuitable for Sir Francis.

On the second storey at Wollaton Hall are two suites of state apartments – one in the south wing and a second in the north wing, the two connected by the long gallery in the west wing. These rooms provided suitable accommodation for a monarch and consort or a queen and prince – as when Queen Anne and Prince Henry stayed at Wollaton in 1603. Wollaton also had a modernized version of the medieval garderobes. In medieval buildings garderobes discharged into moats, but there was no moat at Wollaton. Instead, on the east and west sides of the building there were five interior garderobe chutes, serving seats on all three storeys, and one on the roof. These discharged into a large main drain on each side of the house that was used to clean out the system. Smythson here was drawing on his experience at Longleat, which had at least fifteen similar garderobes. It would be pleasant to report that forethought extended to a rainwater cistern on the roof for flushing down the chutes to the 'night soil men' waiting in the main sewer, but there is no evidence of such a facility.[19]

In the 1601 inventory at Wollaton we can follow the use of garderobes. The family was probably not in residence when the inventory was taken – the document records that six chamber pots were stored in the 'wardrobe'. The two state apartments in the west wing of the second storey had access to garderobes in the north-west and south-west turrets that lead off the spacious north and south state bedchambers. Additionally, each bedchamber was equipped with a chamber pot. The south bedchamber was then called 'the best bedchamber', and it was the best equipped: in the south-west turret containing the garderobe there was a leather close-stool with a pewter pan. A further garderobe on the same floor was in the gallery on the

A print taken from *Architectura oder Bauung der Antiquen aus dem Vitruvius* by Hans Vredeman de Vries (1577) – as an example of his use of the Corinthian order – in which many of the exterior details of Wollaton Hall can be found; some of these details can easily be seen in the photograph on page 77, including the windows of the High Hall, the alcoves on the third storey and the strapwork on the turret tops.

east wing, centrally placed in the inner wall. Sir Francis's important guests were assured of a comfortable night.

However, his less important guests were also well catered for. On the ground floor two 'painted chambers' – bedchambers with decorated walls and/or ceilings – in the east wing were part of secondary suites (see page 95). Originally two withdrawing rooms, each with a garderobe set in the inner walls, by 1601 these had become bedchambers. The original bedchambers in the north and south ends of this wing had garderobes in each of their attached turrets, with the addition of a chamber pot in the south turret and no fewer than three chamber pots in the north turret. These were no doubt stored there, although the inventory shows a total of only eight chamber pots, plus the six in storage. For a house of this size and grandeur, by comparison with Longleat and New Hardwick, this is a small number of chamber pots. The fifteen garderobes were clearly intended for use and took the place of the customary chamber pots and close-stools.

Of the original interior of Wollaton little remains but the great hall, the kitchen and the prospect room; there was a fire in 1642 when part of the east wing was burnt out. It was not restored until the end of the century. Wollaton suffered more serious damage still in 1801–32, when three campaigns of renovation were carried out under the architect Jeffry Wyatville who, by the time the work was finished, had been knighted. He was repeating a similar programme of 'modernizing' at Longleat in 1806–13. The huge expenditure at Wollaton in this period was directed towards making the building more habitable. Extra floors were inserted in the corner turrets, and a door was punched through the north wall of the great hall, displacing an original fireplace. Additional accommodation was created for servants and, to the west, extensive additions were made to the services. There was hardly a room that was not renovated. No doubt left over from Wyatville's depredations were four alabaster statuettes left in an attic. Mark Girouard has speculated that they could have originally been on a fireplace and that they represented the Four Seasons. They have since disappeared.[20]

Wyatville's renovations also affected the exterior of the house. Sash windows were inserted in place of casement windows with leaded lights. Extra doors were added, together with a French window in the middle of the south front. Steps were added to the north entrance, and balustraded steps were put on the south front.

Wollaton is faced with Ancaster stone on a brick core: where the inner walls have been exposed, the rear arches of all original openings are of brick.[21] Unfortunately, the first two years of the building accounts are missing: they would have shown payments for the brick construction of the sewage tunnels. In an account detailing annual expenditure for the years 1584–5 there is a payment to William Hill for 1585 of £20. 5s. 1d. for 189,000 bricks at 2s. 3d. a thousand.[22] The building accounts themselves show weekly payment to 'layers' at the high rate of 10d. a day – equal to the pay of lesser masons. These are not stone-layers – that job was essentially done by masons – but bricklayers.

The stone is Ancaster freestone, a fine oolitic limestone of even texture quarried at Ancaster in Lincolnshire, north-east of Grantham and forty miles (sixty-four kilometres) from Wollaton. Ancaster stone is grey when newly quarried but weathers to a warm buff-yellow. However, it was unadvisable to use the stone for foundations because it absorbs moisture and decays. As a consequence the foundations of Wollaton are part second-hand sandstone rescued from nearby Lenton Priory, and part Mansfield white stone, a good sandstone used in the underground courses up to the top of the plinth course. Mansfield is fourteen miles (twenty-three kilometres) north of Wollaton; Willoughby was unlucky in that there was no useful building stone within easy reach. The only mineral he had was coal, which he traded for Ancaster stone – the carriers arriving with stone had their carts and mule panniers reloaded with coal. Consequently, the stone cost him only the price of the one-way carriage and, of course, the lost sale value of the traded coal.

The building stands on Bunter sandstone. The basement, occupied by the kitchens and other services, surrounds a central block of natural sandstone

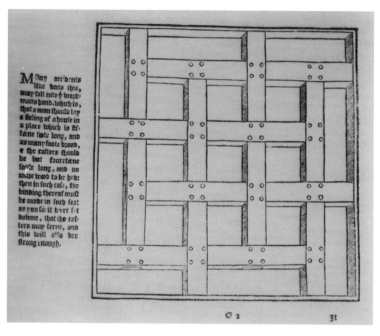

A Chinese grid taken from Sebastiano Serlio's *L'Architettura*, published in English in 1611; it was designed for a small ceiling and not to support a large floor as in the High Hall at Wollaton.

that supports the floor of the great hall. The kitchens and service rooms of the basement are arranged around the four sides of this central block of natural stone. Smythson repeated this layout in part at New Hardwick, where the great hall also stands on a natural sandstone block partly surrounded by cellars.

Pamela Marshall suggested that Smythson, a cautious builder, used excessively thick supporting walls at Wollaton.[23] It is curious, therefore, that he used a risky design in the Chinese grid, which was illustrated in the first book of Sebastiano Serlio's *L'Architettura*. In the example given by Serlio the grid was used to support only a small ceiling, but at Wollaton it had a floor laid over it. Serlio explains how to construct a fifteen-foot (5.6-metre) square ceiling using fourteen-foot (4.3-metre) timbers. The design probably worked on that basis, but the High Hall is thirty feet by

sixty feet (nine metres by eighteen metres) with false hammer-beams sus-
pended beneath it copying the real thing at Longleat – all adding to the
weight the grid was expected to support. The use of the grid at Wollaton
did not work; the weight was too great. Some writers have suggested that
shortage of timber of sufficient length was the problem, but this is unlikely:
Bess of Hardwick floored over a greater width in the high great chamber at
New Hardwick, and, in fact, Willoughby's south great chamber floor has a
span of twenty-six feet (eight metres), only three feet (one metre) less than
that of the High Hall. The problem is most likely to have been caused by
Willoughby's insistence overriding Smythson's caution. Between 1677 and
1695 attempts were made to strengthen the walls (and prevent them col-
lapsing) by inserting exterior buttresses on each corner of the prospect
room. However, the problem continued until the floor was recently
replaced. Willoughby used Serlio again as a source in his design of the surviving fireplace in the great hall, which is taken from his fourth volume of
L'Architettura (published in Venice in 1537).

Since the interior was mainly destroyed by Wyatville there is little left
to comment on. In Smythson's architectural drawings in the Royal Institute
of British Architects library there is a design for a screen similar in every
way to that in the great hall, except for the addition of a man's head
intended to represent Serapis, the Graeco-Egyptian god of the underworld (see page 79). This likeness is taken from *Heads of Gods and Godesses
from Ancient Coins* by Abraham Ortelius, which was published in Antwerp
in 1573. This may seem to be an obscure source for Smythson to use, but
after its publication the book enjoyed a wide circulation; it was quite probably in Willoughby's library.[24] For the actual screen a lion's head, also
illustrated in Smythson's drawing, was substituted.

The first surviving account book for the building at Wollaton opens for
the week ending 31 March 1583, when the best-paid of the freemasons
who had worked at Longleat were paid together at 12d. a day, with eight

others at 11d. a day, two at 10d. and two at 8d., together with five carpenters and sixteen labourers. From this list the only men to go on to Hardwick were John Rhodes and his brother Christopher, together with Lovell who shortly afterwards joined the team at Wollaton. Both Lovells then vanish from the accounts, but, as we shall see, 'Lovils Wyffe' was paid at Hardwick for polishing blackstone in May 1596 and again 6d. at Hardwick in November 1598 for no specified work. As we have seen, Lovell was an old colleague of Smythson's from their years at Longleat. Smythson was not treated as a working freemason: he had risen in the professional world and, sometimes addressed as 'Mr' in the Wollaton accounts, was paid an annual wage.

Smythson spent many working days at the Ancaster quarry where the stone was – as far as was practical – either cut to form from wood stencils or 'scappled' (rough cut) to reduce the weight on the forty-mile (64-kilometre) journey. Both Lovell and Smythson were paid on 'imprest', that is, they were paid a sum of money that they worked through until a task was completed. It is difficult, since the majority were paid for a day's work and only a few by imprest, to know what they were working on, but an entry for 9 April 1586 reads: 'To Ragge [plasterer] and his fellows for imprest upon seeling the gallery roof with lyme and heare: 40/-.'[25] Again, on 25 November 1587: 'pd to the joyner of Derby in pt pmt [part payment] for seeling the Dyning plr being 180 foote of measured weynscot at 1js. the foot: £5. Pd to him by my master at two several times for the same work £14.'[26] Judging by the high cost this panelling must have been something out of the ordinary.

Thomas Accres, the astonishingly gifted stone carver and plaster worker who worked at Chatsworth (where he is first mentioned in 1577), did not arrive at Wollaton until 1584. He was paid the high quarterly wage of £7. 10s. As he was paid a wage there is no record of what work he did – he may be responsible for the hall screen and the fireplace. He was still at Wollaton in November 1588 when the accounts end.[27]

The records give a very good idea of the fluctuating numbers of craftsmen and labourers. During the winter the labour force was reduced: for example, in 1584–5 twenty-two labourers were paid on 26 November but only five on 7 December and later that month only two, but by 22 March the following year twenty-three labourers were once again employed. This amounted to a winter shutdown; a similar practice was followed at Hardwick, where interior work only was carried out in the winter months. The number of masons at Wollaton was maintained, however, and they were kept busy cutting stone for the following season. At the end of March 1582, when the accounts open, fourteen masons were employed; at the height of the work in October 1585 thirty-nine masons were employed.[28] Thereafter the number declined until finally, at the end of building in 1588, there were only eight. Of those, only four had stayed the full course from 1582. From time to time the accounts record payments for oyster shell. This was used to level the joints of the stone ashlar – and in places can still be seen. John Smythson, Robert's son, makes his appearance as a mason from 30 March 1588 at 10d. a day.

Another important group was the joiners. None was accounted for until February 1583 when they would have been employed in roofing and laying floors. By the end of that year there were only four working; clearly not a great deal was going on. However, by November 1585 there were nine joiners, the highest number employed during the construction at Wollaton.

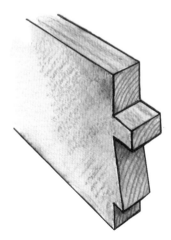

A double tusk and tenon joint as used in
the floors of the north great chamber
at Wollaton Hall and the Long
Gallery at New Harwick Hall

There was a distinct difference in pay between carpenters and joiners: carpenters earned 10–14d. a day, while joiners received 9–12d.; clearly, joinery was a lesser trade. Supporting the floor of the south great chamber are joists joined with a double tusk and tenon joint (see page 91) – a joint used when joists are deep and long and/or when the weight they carry is significant. This same joint was later used in the long gallery at Hardwick.[29]

Women were employed at 3d. a day at the lime kilns and in loading lime, a practice not found at Hardwick. A further cost in the accounts is for ironwork, particularly making iron bars used for strengthening windows. These were, and still are, used in churches, where large sheets of leaded lights can vibrate in the wind if not strengthened and supported. The purpose of the bars was to prevent that vibration. They were placed inside across the windows, and copper wires soldered into the lead of the glass were twisted around the iron bars.

A mason named Hellywell in the Wollaton accounts worked there at 12d. a day and may have been the same man as James Heliwell, a mason who worked for Shrewsbury's bailiff, William Dickenson, when he built his house at Chesterfield in 1575.[30] A bargain-in-great was made (see Appendix III) signed with two masons' marks. One of these was Heliwell. One of the marks is repeated at Shireoaks Hall, a Smythson house of 1600 in Nottinghamshire; the bargain may have been for one of Shrewsbury's houses.

What became of the craftsmen working on Wollaton? Christopher Lovell, who arrived at Longleat in 1571 with such promising credentials, does not appear in the accounts after October 1585 and more or less vanishes from the record after Wollaton. He may have returned to Wiltshire, which was perhaps his home, although there are two intriguing references at Hardwick. The first is in November 1598, 'Given to Lovils Wyffe', and the second in May 1596, 'To lovells wyff 10/- upon a reckoning of her polishing a stone; and geven to lovell his wyffe 10/-'.[31] She would have been polishing black Ashford marble from Derbyshire – and a great deal of it, too, judging by the size of the payment. Her husband may have died; at Wollaton there is a reference in May 1586 to a John Lovell as 'Old Lovell';[32] the Christian name may have been a slip of the pen for there is no other mention of any John Lovell. Finally, a slim clue: an inventory, dated 9 November 1618 and valued at £71. 2s. 4d. for Thomas Lovell of Whitchurch, is witnessed by Richard Lovell and John Painter – whom we shall meet at Hardwick. Was Thomas Lovell the son of Christopher?[33]

Thomas Accres, with his apprentice Luke Dolphin, had returned to Bess at Hardwick by December 1591 on a quarterly wage of £3. 6s. 8d. 'besides his groundes (farm) at Ashford'.[34] He was paid £7. 10s. a quarter at Wollaton, but that may have included an accommodation allowance; Dolphin was paid 25s. a quarter. Accres continued at Hardwick under Bess's heir William, Lord Cavendish, no doubt living in the area, until March 1607 when he died and an entry reads: 'Given at my Lords command at Thomas Accres burial vs.'[35]

John Hills, another valued mason who came from Longleat with Smythson, died at Worksop, Nottinghamshire, in 1592 (see Appendix II). Worksop is near Sheffield, and Hills could well have been employed by Shrewsbury on any of the houses he was building. Worksop is also relatively close to Hardwick, but Hills was never employed by Bess. Richard Crispin, the second carpenter at Longleat and head carpenter at Wollaton on 14d. a day, disappeared after Wollaton.

Robert Smythson, however, is well accounted for. At Wollaton Smythson achieved a release from masonry: in the building accounts he was acting as a bailiff for Willoughby and collecting rents as early as 1588 and later, in a law case of 1600, was classified as 'bailiff to Mr Percival Willoughby'.[36] Smythson settled in Wollaton village and made himself useful to his Willoughby patrons, so earning a very worthwhile income and leaving himself time to draw plans and elevations for other patrons without having the considerable work of supervising the actual building work. Smythson achieved the ambition of all masons of not entirely relying 'on their trade' for their income. However, it was left to others in the Smythson circle to win, in Sir William Coventry's words (see Introduction), 'a small Farm, the Rent of which they are the more able to pay by gains of their Trade'. As we shall see, Thomas Accres, Abraham Smith and John Painter did rather better than that at Hardwick.

*

By the time Wollaton Hall was complete it had cost an estimated £8,000.[37] The total is impossible to calculate exactly. Although stone that was swapped for coal was free, there was a hidden cost in the lost coal sales. Some workers provided boon work, according to the custom whereby a feudal landlord had the right over tenants to demand a number of free working days. This was mainly used at Wollaton for transport. When workers provided boon work they were being taken off other (usually agricultural) tasks – another hidden cost to Willoughby. He was spending well above his income.

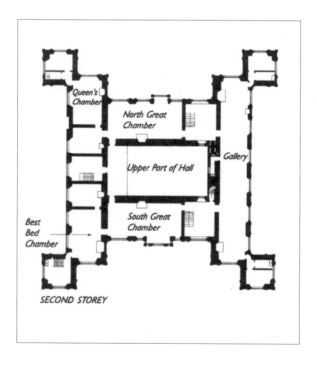

Floor plans of Wollaton Hall based on the 1609 inventory. Above: The second storey has two great chambers at top and bottom, connected by a long gallery, which were for the accommodation of high-ranking guests. Right top: The ground floor has the pantry next to the staircase. Right bottom: The basement shows, at centre, the solid rock on which the great hall stands. The kitchen, at top, is conveniently 'below stairs' – Wollaton was the first great house to introduce this arrangement.

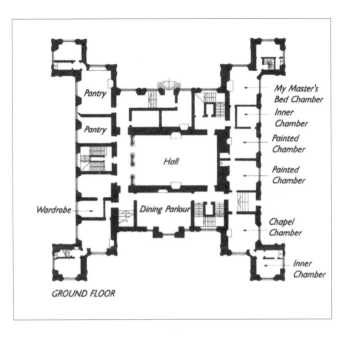

GROUND FLOOR

- Pantry
- Pantry
- Wardrobe
- Hall
- Dining Parlour
- My Master's Bed Chamber
- Inner Chamber
- Painted Chamber
- Painted Chamber
- Chapel Chamber
- Inner Chamber

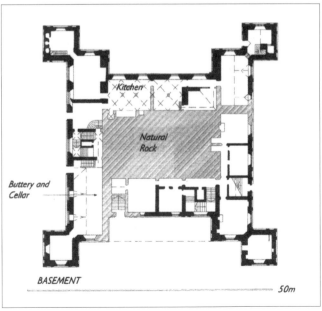

BASEMENT

- Kitchen
- Natural Rock
- Buttery and Cellar

50m

After the building's completion Bess of Hardwick visited in August 1592. She was returning from a year-long visit to London and the court of Queen Elizabeth I. The queen had been floating the idea of marrying off Bess's orphaned granddaughter, Arbella Stuart, to Rainutio, the son of the Duke of Parma, which would have ended the draining war against Spain in the Netherlands. Portrait miniatures were exchanged between the two, but it all came to nothing when Parma died in December 1592. By then Bess and Arbella had left the court. No expense had been spared to make an extravagant impression at court: Bess travelled in style; every town she passed through the church bells were rung and the poor were given 20s. to share.

Before coming to Wollaton, Bess and her large entourage spent the night with her daughter Frances, who was married to Sir Henry Pierrepont and living at Holme Pierrepont, a house four miles (six kilometres) south of Nottingham. After this Bess diverted to visit Willoughby at Wollaton Hall: she was no doubt keen to see the completed building, but more important were business arrangements entered into when Bess had loaned Willoughby £3,000 in 1591 on six manors, valued at £15,000, at 10 per cent interest a year. She must have heard rumours of his shaky finances and doubtless wanted to discuss the security of this huge loan, which represented roughly twice the total cost of building Wollaton Hall. With the marriage of Arbella a possibility, Bess had to provide her granddaughter with an income, and to this end the loan was in Arbella's name. At Wollaton in 1591 Bess, astute as ever, demanded additional manors as security. This agreement came home to roost eighteen years later, in 1609, when William Reason, Bess's old receiver of rents and surveyor, surveyed the manors.[38] Arbella foreclosed on the loan, forcing Percival Willoughby to pay up the debt, and the manors became hers.

Wollaton Hall itself continued in the possession of the Willoughbys until 1925, when the 11th Lord Middleton (Willoughby) sold the property to

Nottingham City Council to raise funds to pay death duties. From 1926 Wollaton Hall, under the ownership of the City of Nottingham, became a natural history museum and has remained so since. There is some merit in this use because Sir Francis's descendant, Francis Willoughby (1635–72), was renowned as a naturalist.

An aerial view of Old Hardwick Hall from the north-west

5

OLD HARDWICK HALL
IN THE CARE OF ENGLISH HERITAGE

Little is known of what was on the site of Old Hardwick Hall before Bess of Hardwick began building there in 1587. The house, centred on the great hall, grew haphazardly as circumstances dictated. Old Hardwick Hall had no architect and has no architectural form. This must have been a very uncomfortable building to occupy. Today, Old Hardwick is a roofless ruin.

The building of Old Hardwick Hall took place over at least four periods. The first resulted in the hall built perhaps by Bess's father or by his father, together with a series of small rooms immediately to the west: these rooms are all that remain today of the earlier house. In the second period the great hall was built: this was a building two storeys high, put up before Bess's recorded building programme started in 1587. In the third period part of the east wing – comprising two storeys of four bays – was built, before 1587. The fourth and final period comprises Bess's extensive building programme between 1587 and 1595.

Two valuable pieces of evidence have survived, apart from what remains of the building – building accounts[1] from July 1587, and an inventory[2] of the contents made in 1601 when Bess was no longer using the Old Hall as her principal residence. She had moved into New Hardwick Hall in 1597, before it was finished, and after this date the Old Hall had become an annexe to the main house and a repository for furnishings removed from Chatsworth.[3]

The rebuilding of the Old Hall was forced on Bess by her harassment at the hands of her estranged husband, George Talbot, 6th Earl of Shrewsbury. He became very unreasonable in his attitude towards his wife. Not only did he attempt to assert his ownership of Chatsworth in the summer of 1584 by riding over that July with a party of forty mounted men and forcing her out of her old home but he intercepted her bailiffs, robbing them of her rents, and stopped paying her maintenance money. Chatsworth, as we have seen, was Bess's only during her lifetime and had been entailed on her son Henry Cavendish. Old Hardwick was her only refuge, but it needed enlarging to accommodate a countess and household.

Bess was born in 1527, probably at Hardwick. She was one of five children. Her only brother, James, the heir to their father's estate, had been born in 1526. John Hardwick, their father, died in 1528 but since James was under twenty-one the estate was taken over by the Office of Wards (see Appendix I). In John's will, made in 1527, he had attempted to avert this outcome: he specified that the portions of his estate belonging to his four daughters should be forty marks each on marriage and that so long as his wife Elizabeth remained a widow she had possession of the hall and demesnes until James became twenty-one; the estate was made over to trustees – a fiction to avoid the estate being held in wardship. The ploy did not work. Two inquiries, or Inquisitions Post Mortem, were held in 1528 and the estate passed into wardship. Just under half the interest in the wardship was sold by the Crown to John Bugby, an officer of the royal pantry at court; the other part remained held by the Crown. However, the family continued to live at Hardwick, and it is likely that Elizabeth Hardwick reached an agreement to rent back the Crown's portion.[4]

James inherited Hardwick in 1547 when he was twenty-one. He died bankrupt in the Fleet Gaol in 1581, after Bess had lent him money on the security of his lands. On his death the estate was seized by the lord chancellor, and, since Bess was his main creditor, she was in a strong position. In 1583 she bought back the estate from the lord chancellor for £9,500[5] –

worth several millions in today's money, in the name of her son William and repossessed her father's estate.

What condition her father's old hall was in we simply do not know, nor exactly what buildings there were. A rent roll of 1570 begins: 'Imprimis the houses the courtes the barne yards and the dovecote yards . . . xls.'[6] The figure of forty shillings quoted here is the rental value of the main buildings. This is a very high sum for that time, suggesting that it was a property of some substance. The estate amounted to five hundred acres (two hundred hectares), the same size as it had been in 1528 at her father's death;[7] it brought in an income of £341.

Tantalizingly we know little of Bess's relationship with her only brother. She was fond of her half-sister Jane – after the death of Bess's father her mother married Ralph Leche – who married Thomas Kniveton of Mercaston, Derbyshire, and who was a lady-in-waiting to Bess for which she was paid £30 a year. She had a room in the Old Hall and another at the New Hall when the household moved in 1597. With Bess's other siblings there are no reported disagreements. James was never an entrepreneur although he tried to be one: through the 1560s he was buying, with borrowed money, land that produced a return less than the interest on the loan. Then, throughout the 1570s, he was selling land to pay off pressing debts until, inevitably, this came to an end – in 1579 he was arrested for a debt of £200 to Juliana Penne, a widow, outstanding from a loan given by 'Anthony Penne gent of London now dead'.[8] This was just one debt, and there were others – another for £600 continued unpaid. Why didn't Bess settle these tiresome debts? James's begging letters had gone on for years. Two early letters[9] to Bess survive, both written in February 1565 when she was Lady St Loe. One was from James asking for a loan, on the security of a coal-mine at Heath in Derbyshire; the second was from her mother pleading James's dire need. No doubt Bess recognized that her brother's matters had got out of hand. Moreover, James had no legitimate heir.

It is not clear what ownership Bess had in Old Hardwick before her brother's death in 1581; in the legal order of things, when she married

George Talbot, 6th Earl of Shrewsbury, in 1568, all Bess possessed became the property of her husband during his lifetime. A legal document,[10] dated 7 February 1568, was signed within a few months of their marriage specifying which of their children should marry whom and what land would be made over. This document makes it clear that Bess already possessed the manor house of Hardwick and appurtenances that on marriage passed to her husband. Later, in 1572, when Shrewsbury was pressed for money and Bess's sons were approaching the age of twenty-one, Shrewsbury saw that he could not afford to pay them their portions and passed back to Bess the lands originally hers that had come to him on their marriage.[11]

There is a strong probability, therefore, that when Bess married Shrewsbury in 1568 she had an interest in Hardwick. Her father's old hall and manor house were too small for her purpose, and she might well have planned improvements or new building. However, from the first years of her marriage Bess was fully occupied. Mary, Queen of Scots was handed to Shrewsbury to be kept safe as a prisoner the year Bess married him. From then onwards Bess had a full-time job until Mary was taken off their hands in September 1584. By this time Shrewsbury was suffering severe health problems; his fortune had been depleted by the cost of supporting Mary and her royal court, and he was behaving towards his wife as no husband should. He was a sick and exhausted man.

Despite being busy, however, Bess did find time through these years to be at Hardwick. Her daughter Elizabeth addressed a letter[12] to her mother at Hardwick Hall before her marriage to the Earl of Lennox in 1574; and Bess's husband sent timber to Hardwick in 1577.[13] What was her accommodation when she was there? On the floor plans (see pages 132 and 133) the east wing can be seen set at angle to the rest of the building; was this a separate three-bay building of two storeys set a few yards from her family's old hall to the west? Were the barn, lodgings or dovecote responsible for the angle? For a lady of Bess's social standing once she had become a countess the old accommodation would have been cramped – certainly not what she was accustomed to at Chatsworth. We know that this new building was of only two storeys because at the opening of the building accounts in July 1587 an entry records the addition of a third storey. The 1601 inventory lists 'My Ladies Old Bedchamber' with an 'Outer Chamber', the former fully panelled, and (also mentioned in the building accounts of 1588)[14] a suite in the east wing. But how long had it been since Bess had used these rooms? When the dust of expanding the Old Hall settled Bess had a full suite of bedchamber and withdrawing chamber on the cold north side of the new east wing, which she used until she moved in to the New Hardwick in 1597.

Bess already had an interest in Hardwick before she repossessed the estate. Certainly her father's house would not have accommodated a countess and her household. She had a sizeable retinue and when she visited London in 1591–2 took a retinue of forty.[15] Clearly, alterations must already have been made at Hardwick to house them all. Moreover, in the 1590s the house had also to accommodate her son William and his household. By 1586 Queen Elizabeth had enforced a reconciliation between Bess and her estranged husband – he was bound by the impossibly enormous sum of £40,000[16] to end all discord with his wife – and Bess's revenues were restored.

Knowing the state of Bess's finances is important when considering the building at Hardwick because the Old Hall shows signs of what might be considered the cutting of corners. In the first place it was built by rough-wallers, who were cheaper than masons, and then the rough-walling was rendered – a cheaper alternative to ashlar because rendering was done by plasterers. Bess's revenues were restored to her by order of a commission appointed to examine both sides of her marital argument[17] and by the queen's order made on 8 May 1586. Shrewsbury did not give up without further fighting, and it is likely that Bess had to wait for her money. There-fore, in 1587 she may well have been restricted by lack of funds. However, a more likely reason for the lack of skilled masons is that Sir Francis Willoughby was building Wollaton Hall until 1588, and Bess had lent him three of her Chatsworth masons: Thomas Accres (who did not return to her until August 1594 to the New Hardwick Hall), John Rhodes and his brother

Christopher (who did not arrive at Hardwick until 1591). Once there the Rhodes took on the immense task of building the walls of the New Hardwick – see Chapter 6.

A final piece of evidence useful in identifying what building Bess might have begun and when, is from a tree-ring analysis of the Old Hall timbers commissioned by English Heritage in 2002. This reports: 'The majority of the samples [taken] appear to have been felled over a short period in the late sixteenth century especially for the construction of the hall.' This coincides with the building accounts, which show payments for seventy-three carriages of timber dragged over from Pentridge in the dry summer season between June and October 1588. Bess's hall, which she was building over, had a span of thirty feet (nine metres) and so required huge timbers. Furthermore, she had to find timbers of an equal length to support the two floors above her hall. More interest is added by the fact that thirty-nine tree-ring samples cover a period from 1375 to 1590. The English Heritage report states: 'From the interpretation of the sapwood it would appear that some timbers used in the late sixteenth-century construction of the Old Hall were reused, having been felled in the very late fifteenth to very early sixteenth centuries. It is possible that these reused timbers were original to the earlier manor house, which is known to have existed on the site and to have been incorporated into the Old Hall.'[18]

The earliest surviving document to name Hardwick is a charter of c. 1200 by which Ralph de Sudl passes to William son of Ellis lands called 'Herdewike and Dercet': '1 virgate of land and a messuage [house with outbuildings]'.[19] More easily understood is a document dated 1391 by which William de Low grants the manor of Hardwick to Roger de Hardwick and his wife Joan.[20] This is the first mention of the Hardwicks as a family.

By the 1580s Hardwick Hall was not a cleared site but one cluttered with earlier buildings: a dovecote, a barn[21] and two six-bay half-timbered lodgings that were taken down in 1594–5 after they had been used by the masons and re-erected elsewhere on the site to make 'a hay house'.[22] Additionally, there were 'the old lodgings', which, as we shall see, were taken down to make way for a new staircase.

The living quarters were possibly two separate buildings – what is now the east wing (part-built earlier by Bess) and, near by to the west, her father's old hall. The buildings, both of two storeys, were south-facing and looked over a garden accessed by two doorways, both now blocked: one in the east wing, now part buried, must have been the main entrance to that section; the other was to the west of the great hall hearth near the entrance to what was the screens passage – the traditional screen-fixture hiding entrance to the services.[23]

Bess's father's old hall was a different building from the north–south hall which occupied part of the site. Bess built this north–south hall some time before 1587. Basil Stallybrass puts forward the persuasive hypothesis that Bess's father's hall may have been aligned east–west on the same site as the later north–south hall and stood thirty feet (nine metres) in length. According to Stallybrass, the hall door (now blocked) gave into a screens passage, with services to the west and a hearth in the centre of the south wall – as at Haddon Hall.[24] A thirty-foot (nine-metre) hall would have been perfectly adequate for a Derbyshire squire farming five hundred acres (two hundred hectares). Because of Bess's need for a much larger hall, and because of the constriction of the site, she turned the hall round to run north–south and built a great hall measuring sixty by thirty feet (eighteen by nine metres). (See the ground-floor plan on page 133.)

By 1587, therefore, Old Hardwick Hall consisted of a newly built great hall aligned north–south, sixty feet (eighteen metres) in length and two storeys in height. Adjoining it to the west were the old buttery, pantry and kitchens, while to the east were 'the old lodgings' and Bess's new two-storey block set at an angle because of (I suggest) the obstruction of some other building in the farmyard. Bess therefore had sufficient accommodation for her household to eat in the hall and a suite for herself in her new angled block. However, this outline of the buildings does not explain where her

household slept. Were the old lodgings of six bays and two storeys sufficient? Presumably they had to suffice until Bess built on to the west wing in
1588.

The Hardwick building accounts start in July 1587. Bess was living at South
Wingfield Manor that summer.[25] In the case of the Old Hall, these documents are accounts of expenditure on the workforce, which Bess signed off
fortnightly when she provided her clerk of works, David (or Davy) Flood,
with cash to pay the men. Using them for the purposes of dating and reporting on building progress may be misleading because the accounts often
record payments for work that may have been obvious at the time but
which is difficult to identify today. As we have noted, bargains-in-great
(what we would recognize as contracts) were made by the skilled workmen,
and payments were made at intervals specified in the bargains until the job
was completed. Skilled workmen employed others who mainly remain
anonymous. Accres, the gifted mason, was an exception here: we know the
names of his two apprentices, Luke Dolphin and Myles Padley. We also
know that Accres was paid a quarterly wage of £3. 6s. 8d. in Bess's household accounts, while his two apprentices were paid separately: Dolphin
received 25s. a quarter and Padley just 10s. for six months.[26]

However, for the most part, little or nothing is known of the workmen
lower in the hierarchy. We have discussed the masons' marks that were used
to distinguish the work of one under-mason from that of another and how,
to ensure fair payment, each under-mason would carve his mark on his
finished stonework. There is an interesting example of these marks at Old
Hardwick. The stone arch over the four ovens in the pastry of the old hall
has four stones marked with an R. (A pastry was usually a room where tarts
were prepared and baked, but in this case the presence of four ovens makes
it likely that the room was used for baking bread as well.) It might be tempting to attribute these marks to the only mason or under-mason known to
have been working there at the time whose name began with an R (Robert

A rubbing of the
under-mason's
mark carved into
the stone arch over
the ovens at Old
Hardwick Hall

Rothwell), but it would be wrong to do that. Rothwell would have had a
bargain-in-great specifying his work, and the stonework he made would
have been left unmarked because the clerk of works, Davy Flood, knew
what Rothwell was doing. Furthermore, in the building accounts there is
no payment for the arch, indicating that it was work included in a bargain-
in-great and either cut or laid by an anonymous under-mason using the R
mark. Another lead is from the marks on the corners of the east wing: on
the east and south faces there are quoins – dressed corner stones – with the
mark of two overlapping Vs. Thomas Hollingworth, a mason who had
worked at Chatsworth in 1577, was employed at Hardwick from June to September 1589 on piecework for which he was paid a total of £2. 18s. for
turning out seven hundred quoins when the east wing was going up. This
work is all he is recorded as having done – apart from in November 1589
when he was paid 12s. for setting three chimney shafts in the east wing
(long since demolished).[27] The double V appears again briefly in the New
Hall on the gatehouse, in Bess's withdrawing chamber on a door lintel and
jambs and again in the state withdrawing chamber on a lintel and jamb. If
this indicates work done by the same man, we can tell from the kind of
work he was carrying out that he was not a master mason; he could have
been employed briefly on the New Hall as an under-mason. (The same
mark appears at the early-seventeenth-century Quenby Hall, Leicestershire;
at Shireoaks, Nottinghamshire, built in the late sixteenth century and

attributed to Smythson; at Lyvedon New Build, Northamptonshire, which dates to the 1590s; and at Grimsthorpe Castle, Lincolnshire, where building work was also carried out in the late sixteenth century.)

Was Bess getting value for her money? She corrected the mathematical addition of her clerk of works, Davy Flood, but she did not check the actual measurements she was paying for; in March 1591 a glazier named Thomas Bracks was paid for more glass than was set in one of the payments that can still be checked – for the windows of the pantry and buttery in the Old Hall. Was Flood involved in this deception and eventually caught out? He left his position at the end of November 1591. On the other hand we also find some underpayments, such as the payment of £1. 16s. 1d. to the masons Nayll and Mallory on piecework for 156 square yards (130 square metres) at 2d. a yard for setting the hall floor in the Old Hall in October 1590;[28] the area is actually 160 square yards (134 square metres). Additionally, for flooring the serving place the masons were paid £1. 4s. 9d. for thirty-three square yards (twenty-eight square metres), which in fact is 1½ square yards (1.25 square metres) less than the floor area.

Bess would have known exactly where she was when paying out on bargains-in great, but in other cases much depended on the honesty of the clerk of works and the craftsmen themselves. Only some of the craftsmen working on the Old Hall – such as masons, rough-wallers, carpenters, joiners, sawyers and plasterers – were paid by bargains-in-great. It was comparatively easy to work out their charges but impossible to work out for glaziers and for plumbers, who were engaged to cover the flat roofs with lead sheet and install flashing at edges, downpipes for rainwater and pipes to carry water to the kitchens. These, together with the remaining skilled craftsmen, were paid by measure.

Two carpenters working at the Old Hall, brothers Thomas and John Beighton, had worked for William Dickenson in 1575 when he was building his own house at Chesterfield; Dickenson was bailiff to the Earl of Shrewsbury.[29] The brothers went on to work at New Hardwick.

*

The accounts provide a good idea of the conditions of employment. Scaffolding was provided when it was needed; bread, oatmeal, butter and milk were paid for weekly for the masons, and there were candles for evening work in the winter. Work was a six-day week, with saints' days for holidays.

Robert Rothwell, the master mason, was boarded out in 1588 at 3s. 8d. for two weeks. We don't know if he returned home on Sundays, but the overall cost was a little over 3d. a day. The same rate was paid at Longleat in the 1560s. In December 1588 Bess paid out £6. 1s. 8d. for five weeks boarding for an unknown number of wallers.[30] It was the practice during the building of both Old and New Hardwick for outside work to shut down in December and then not resume until March when the winter frosts had finished. During those winter months interior work was carried on as usual using candlelight when necessary.

Raff Smith, a carpenter, pawned his horse to Bess in December 1588 for £1. 8s.[31] It is interesting to examine what job Smith was working on. He arrived at Old Hardwick in March 1588 and took a bargain-in-great for the roof of the Forest Great Chamber. He was paid a total of £24 over March, May, August and November 1588. In March 1589 he was paid £1, and thereafter his name is not recorded again. Whether he got his horse back is not known, but he may well have cleared his debt as part of that final payment.

Payment of £1 was made on 10 December 1588 to a labourer named Burghley for 'tooe dayes worck in baringe and making cleane the worck folks chamber'. The chamber must have been in a dreadful state for it to have taken two days to clean it. We can only guess where the chamber was: perhaps it lay in what remained of the old building. Another mystery is the wine cellar. Payment was made to a mason named Robert Winchester on 22 May 1591 for: 'the hewing and working of on playne dore for the new wyne cellere hard by the dresser windoe 4s.'[32] Today the dresser window is there, but there is no sign of this new cellar. Moreover, where was the old wine cellar?

Bess drove a hard bargain but was also charitable. For example, a labourer named Henry Owthram, who was employed by her, arrived at the Old Hall at the end of October 1587 in rags and shoeless and was given 1s. 6d. to buy footwear. He worked at the Old Hall for only four weeks. An entry for 27 November reads: 'Geven to Henry Owttram over and besides his garments 5/-'.[33]

Good-quality sandstone was readily available at Hardwick, as the quarry was just below the Old Hall. Limestone for mortar and plaster exists in a ridge between Hardwick and Ault Hucknall, and there was a limestone quarry,[34] although there is no sign of it today. Lime kilns were built to roast the limestone into quicklime. Timber was transported at great cost from Pentrich wood, eight miles (thirteen kilometres) from Hardwick as the crow flies. Glass presented a problem, however: Bess's estranged husband had the monopoly of glass-making, but she was unwilling to deal with him; in any case glass does not travel easily. Consequently the Old Hall remained without glazing until the summer of 1591, by which time Bess had her own glassworks, possibly at South Wingfield, together with a blast furnace for ironwork. Both works were managed by Sylvester Smyth. Bess had passed over her own lead workings at Winster, Aldwark and Bonsall to her son William.[35]

When the surviving building accounts open in July 1587 the walls of a third storey in the east wing had been built on top of earlier two-storey walls. Wide south-facing windows required large openings that weakened the structure – see below. In that July two masons, seven wallers and six carpenters were paid for unspecified work. The employment of the carpenters indicates that the walls were up and that they were putting a roof over the space.

In November 1587 a rough-waller named Thomas Hollingworth[36] – a different man to the mason of the same name – was paid the huge sum of

£8. 15s. for work he had completed on the east wing, part of payment by measure for putting up all the rough walling of the Old Hall.[37] During the winter of 1587–8 a plasterer named James Hindle was busy in the gallery. This was the south-facing space on the new third storey above the great chamber; when a fourth storey was added in 1589, this gallery became the low dining chamber. The stairs, infilling a space to the west between the hall and the new work, were built only in 1589.[38] The neatly turned corner of the east wing can be seen from outside with alternate long and short quoins and the stairwell stonework abutting.

The building accounts for May 1591 make reference to a 'well light': 'To Robert Winchester (a mason) for the hewinge and working of 9 Foots of playne windoe stuffe for the stayres that Yearn (a mason) setts upp in the well light.'[39] This has proved something of a red herring. The words in fact refer to a window in the wall of the stairwell: there was no overhead window light and, as can be seen in the ruins, the stairs had a ceiling with an attic room above in the gable end. It is far from easy to know from the descriptions given in the accounts where these spaces were, particularly when the names changed as the building grew. Hollingworth, the rough-waller, knew his trade: all his windows have relieving arches over them, while there are none in the earlier work.

In 1588 work switched to the west of the hall. Before we investigate this, we must take note that the south and west walls of the hall up as far as the top of the first storey pre-date 1587; wherever the hall of Bess's father was situated it was not the present great hall, which at thirty feet (nine metres) wide is only slightly smaller than that of the New Hall. There are obvious alterations: to the right of the hearth is a partly blocked window in the right-hand corner – the blocking was done in the nineteenth century to keep out vandals. Also visible are the remains of the jamb of a blocked door pre-dating 1587: this originally opened through the south wall, marking the entrance to the screens passage. The windows to the right and left of the hearth are Bess's work: the hearth was moved about a foot (thirty centimetres) to the west and centred in the now solid wall – the chimney breast was widened in a wall already there when she created the huge great hall pre-1587. Bess's great hall had a wood screen at the north end and was entered by a single door in the north wall, with high windows on either side;[40] it was not then sheltered by a porch. The present remains of a porch were built later when the single entrance door and the lower part of the two windows were blocked and two smaller side-doors inserted (see the ground-floor plan on page 133). Confusion has come about because although the building accounts mention expenditure on a porch these are referring to the colonnaded portico of the New Hall.

The west wall of the hall has behind it a jumble of rooms that make no sense in their relation to the use of the great hall. This clutter of spaces housed the service rooms for the building lived in by Bess's father. They extend west to the stairs: the first flights of the stairs may well be Bess's father's stairs. Basil Stallybrass identified the small space behind the south end of this hall's west wall as the buttery – however, although it was no doubt well placed to be used in this way in Bess's father's time, it was not used as a buttery by Bess herself. Indeed, no buttery is mentioned in the Old Hall building accounts except at the end when the last of the glazing was being inserted in 1591: 'To Thomas Bracks for 55 foots and a halff of glasse for the buttery and pand pantry and for on lowppe light [borrowed light] towards the surveying place at 4½d. the foot £1. 0. 10.'[41] (The word 'pantry' after 'pand' is probably a correction by the clerk of the works.) This entry refers to the space (called the 'buttery' by Basil Stallybrass) behind the south-west corner of Bess's great hall; this space had one window and the space next to it was the pantry, which borrowed its light from the serving place leading to the kitchens. By the time of the 1601 inventory the space Stallybrass calls the buttery had become a bedchamber: a fireplace was inserted and a flue diverted from the bedchamber overhead, where the fireplace was blocked. Stallybrass was right about the use of the buttery, but he cannot have been right in his claim that the bedchamber above – the one with the blocked-in fireplace – was Bess's old bedchamber; she would never have tolerated the clatter of service immediately below her room. Actually her old bedchamber was in the quieter two-storey east wing.

Meanwhile work continued on the east wing. On 15 January 1588 a load of animal hair was delivered from Mansfield, and a second load arrived eight days later; by the end of that month ninety-three loads of hair had been paid for. The hair was mixed into the first layer of plaster to help it bind. These entries suggest that a good deal of plastering was being done in late January: a payment was also made to 'the plomer' for four and a half pounds (two kilograms) of pitch; the plumber would have been fixing lead flashing on an unspecified roof. By mid February Edward Worthington and his man, both slaters, were paid for a month's work on the roof. All this winter work was being carried out on the east wing.

Demolition of unwanted sections of Bess's father's house followed. An entry for 20 May 1588 reads: 'To Robert Ashmore [a waller] for the digging of foundacion and takinge downd the old chimney . . . 4s. 9½d.'[42] There is no possibility of establishing where this was, but at a guess it was in what is now the west wing. This was followed on 3 June: 'To Robert Hunter [a labourer] for the digging of a roode of Fowndacion nyer the kytch dresster whear the doore most be . . . 1s. 8d.'[43] A rood was a measure of area. Over the centuries its size has varied. In the collection of Smythson drawings at the Royal Institute of British Architects, John Smythson's designs for a riding house at Welbeck dated 1622 give a rood as: seven yards long by one yard high by one yard wide (6.4 by one by one metres). The work for which Robert Hunter was paid was probably digging out the space for the kitchen near the door and serving hatch. A further demolition was recorded on 19 August: 'To John Beighton [a carpenter] for one dayes work when he pulled dowe the old lodgings . . . 9d.'[44] This was demolition of the timber-frame lodgings of the old house, which may have been attached to the east end of Bess's father's hall and the newer east wing; they had to go to make way for the new staircase built the following year.

There are some expensive foundations at the base of the west wall of the kitchen consisting of masons' work in smooth ashlar standing on the natural rock – very necessary considering the weight it carries. This work is unaccounted for in the accounts. Thomas Hollingworth, the rough-waller, reappears in the accounts for May 1588 when he and his men are paid for 22 roods, at 4s. the rood, for walling over the hall – heightening the west wall by two storeys.[45]

The new west wing included a massive east–west wall containing two hearths in the kitchen and four ovens in the pastry. The higher they worked the more per rood Hollingworth and his team were paid; for the ground floor (89 roods) the rate was 2s. a rood, for the next storey (62 roods) 3s. a rood and for the third (55 roods) and fourth storeys (84 roods) 4s. a rood.[46] This is as good an example of the use of payment by measure as one can get: the work was completed in record time – the quicker Hollingworth was the more money he and his men made.

This immense job, some ninety feet (twenty-seven metres) high, was started at the latest before the end of May and was complete by mid December 1588. Hollingworth and the wallers were paid a total of £73 for 290 roods of the west wing from the ground to the top of the fourth storey – the Hill Great Chamber, so called because it overlooked the hill on which the building stands – including ovens, windows and the cost of lodgings, before the winter shutdown had overtaken them. It was a stupendous achievement. With the four walls up, the site was taken over by carpenters to roof the building and lay floors before plasterers moved in to complete the new west wing.

The following year further payments to Hollingworth indicate a new payment by measure at a lower rate. At this stage additions were being made to the east wing. An entry for 5 July 1589 reads: 'To Thomas Hollingworth for the walling of 35 roods of walle which is the whole sum from the bothome of the fundacion to the toppe of the leads . . . £4. 13s. 4d.'[47] at 2s. 8d. a rood; it refers to the new Forest Great Chamber – named after the plasterwork decoration of trees and deer – which had been added to the east wing on top of the work done earlier in 1587. Why was Hollingworth paid for walling from the bottom of the foundations when walls had already been put up in 1587? The accounts also refer to northerly extensions of this wing. Hollingworth and his team were paid a total of £34 for building 274 roods between March and October 1589. This was not as much as their work the previous year: they were adding to what was already there, and the east wall is ashlar – and so was built not by Hollingworth's team but by masons. It is not indicated how far north this wing extended, but on the east wall in the north-east corner at second-storey level there are the remains of a door jamb.

Whatever space that door led into was demolished as unsafe and rebuilt by John Painter (also known as Balechous) in 1620–1, when the door was blocked.[48] Hollingworth and his men heightened the Old Hall's east wall and were paid £5. 13s. on 2 August 1589 for '34 Roods of walle over my ladyes Chamber and the next Chamber to that at 3s. 4d. the Rood'.[49]

Bess was demanding large windows in her new Forest Great Chamber, but such windows tend to weaken the wall in which they are inserted. Because the south wall was only two feet (sixty centimetres) thick at ground level it was not strong enough to carry the weight of the high great chamber. However, whoever was in charge knew what they were doing: the problem was resolved by building two projecting bays into which the windows were inserted – a practice carried to the limit in the New Hall – leaving the heavy floor supported on a strengthened inner wall. The projecting bays acted as buttresses, giving extra strength.

With the walls of the Forest Great Chamber complete it was the turn of the joiners, carpenters and plasterers to set to work. A curious payment is recorded for 12 November 1589: 'To Beighton [a carpenter] for the makinge of 2 stepes in the midel chamber. . . . 6d.'[50] Wherever the 'midle chamber' may have been in the east wing, did it have a raised dais for a chair of state? Going by the general practice in the New Hall, where most of the flooring is lime-ash plaster, it is likely the flooring of the Old Hall was also lime-ash plaster, made from the residue of the lime kilns. However, there are no records of payments for the Old Hall flooring, either lime-ash, which would be laid by plasters, or timber.[51]

Bess now had two great chambers. When completed, the Forest Great

Chamber in the east wing had the full sequence of formal rooms: great chamber, then withdrawing chamber leading to a bedchamber. The long gallery was inconveniently placed beneath the great chamber on the third storey and beneath that was the low dining chamber. This represented the sequence of rooms required by a countess for the reception of important visitors. The kitchen was wrongly placed in the west wing: the prevailing south-west wind blew kitchen smells through the house, although the family and state apartments were far enough to the east to avoid the worst. This was not a mistake Bess made at Chatsworth: there the two-storey kitchen was placed in the north wing. The placing of the Old Hardwick kitchen was forced on her because the building could extend only one way in 1588 – to the west.

The ground floor of the east wing on the south side has in the centre a blocked entrance door and window partly buried below ground level, and to its right and left (also partly buried) blocked windows (see page 117). This indicates a change of plan in the building of the east wing. The centre door may represent an original ground-floor entrance to a pre-1587 building, which – by the time work was finished in 1587 – consisted of three rooms; above these, on the second storey, was the low dining chamber. That was the height of the building when the accounts begin in July 1587. In 1589 the long gallery was built over the Low Dining Chamber before the building stopped for winter and carpenters and slaters put a roof over the new building. The following year in 1590 the two projecting bays for windows were put in, and the Forest Great Chamber was built on top of the long gallery, making four storeys with a range of five storeys behind.

Once the central door in the south wall of the east wing had been blocked, access was gained from the interior. The plinth of the 1590s – a ground-level course of stone on which the building stands – extends across the window in the bay; this plinth is attached and not part of the load-bearing wall.

Throughout the winter of 1590 a labourer named Thomas Hollingworth (a third Thomas Hollingworth, distinct from the mason and the rough-waller already encountered) took two bargains-in-great for 'earth work'.[52] The first was worth the substantial sum of £3 for 'the earthwork at the hill side' – that

Blocked entrance door in the east wing of the south front of Old Hardwick
Hall; the plinth is attached to the base of the walls because the ground level
was raised after the ground-floor spaces were no longer important.

is, the west end of the building. The second was for 35s. and represented a
great amount of earth moved; it might account for the built-up ground level
on the south side of the east wing. More certainly, on 26 September 1594
Stephen Bell is paid 'for vj days leveling the Cunduit Court 2/-'.[53] By then any
pretence that the south court was a garden had ceased, and the well conduit
was built.

The well conduit is still there. The stone was hewn in December 1591 by
Henry Nayll (who had arrived in July 1587) and Richard Mallory (who had
arrived in February 1589). The attendant well house, a wooden structure
containing a pump powered by a horse-wheel, has gone. This was paid for
on 10 February 1593: 'Pd to Mylington [carpenter] upon a reckoning of
26/8d. that he is to have for building of the well house.'[54] Water was
pumped up to a cistern in the top of the conduit house, and from there a
lead pipe took the supply to the kitchen. This was supplemented by a soft-
water supply piped on the north side of the building by a downpipe from
the roof of the Hill Great Chamber into a cistern in the kitchen. The scar
left by the downpipe can still be seen.

*

All this construction work required large amounts of building materials. Transporting and unloading these was strenuous and expensive work that could be carried out only in the dry summer months when the ground was hard. Wains (carts) were needed to transport heavy timbers to Hardwick from Pentrich wood. Between early June and the end of August 1588, when the west wing was going up, accounts record payment for seventy-three wain and carriage journeys. Several things could go wrong: wheels often broke and had to be replaced, or the ox harnesses wore out. Worst of all was the strain on the teams of oxen, which worked six to a team and probably two abreast: black soap was used to ease shoulders blistered by the wooden yokes; in May and June 1588 five teams (totalling thirty oxen) were shod, yet by September their hooves were being treated with 'vergrease'. Young oxen up to two years old would have done a full day's work but the older oxen could manage no more than a morning's labour. One has only to walk down the steep drive that passes close to the west wing to get some idea of the toil involved: the drive, rising steeply, turns sharply at the top, making a very difficult turn just when the greatest strain was needed if hauling a weight. Today the journey ends on a flat lawn before the Old Hall gate, but at that time there was no grass, only bedrock with hollows infilled to make a hard, flat yard.[55]

Lime, for lime mortar and plaster, was baked in kilns. Limestone for one kiln cost the huge sum £4. 4s. and from March to July 1588 ten kilns were in use. This may seem a large number but is a small total when set against what was to follow when the New Hall was being built.

It is difficult to establish where many of the rooms actually where, particularly as most of the east wing is demolished. Only a few of the spaces can be identified definitively by means of the inventory and the building accounts: the Hill Great Chamber and the Forest Great Chamber (at the top of the west and east wings), the great hall, the chamber at the upper end of the hall (identified in the building accounts as the buttery), the service rooms on the ground floor of the west wing and the little gallery (so called in the building accounts and mentioned in the inventory).

In April 1589 the little gallery was being roofed by the carpenter John Beighton: 'To John Beighton upon a Recening of his last bargen of three ponds 30s of the little gallery Rooff the other 30s when yt is Fynished £1 10s.'[56] His roof timbers would have had roman numbers cut into them so he was able to assemble them in the right order. Although today one can see that there is an attic chamber above the little gallery, the space was not floored over until after the roof was on, and Beighton would have been looking down into the gallery. The long gallery, in the east wing in the third storey, was added in 1588 on top of the low dining chamber.

In addition to the few identifiable rooms listed above, we can see from the building accounts that on the north side of the east wing overlooking the court were Bess's new bedchamber on the third storey and her withdrawing chamber above on the fourth storey under an attic room in the roof – both severely cold in winter and inconveniently placed. Next to her withdrawing chamber on the north side was the great withdrawing chamber.

The progression of rooms of state, beginning with the great chamber (in this case the Forest Great Chamber) and climaxing with the state bedchamber, has already been discussed (see pages 23–4), yet there is no mention of such a sequence in the building accounts, and we have to search for it. However, as will be seen in Chapter 6, the sequence is perfectly clear in the New Hall because it is still there. The plan of the Old Hall, however, is filled with anomalies, and there is little of which we can be certain. Normally in a plan for a building of this size one could be sure that none of the important rooms or family rooms would be in the service wing because of noise and smells of cooking. Nevertheless, the remarkable plaster overmantels in the west service wing survive. They were certainly never intended for servants' quarters.

Something can be made of the procession of formal rooms from the Hill Great Chamber. From the door at the south end one would have processed over the stairs into the little gallery. Here there is a hearth nearly in the centre of the west wall, and above it is a shield with a Hardwick saltire (a cross) – Bess's family arms, supported by two stags; it is a smaller version of the overmantel in the great hall of New Hardwick. From the little gallery a door in the east wall led into a central passage, eventually arriving in the formal apartments in the east wing. This passage had on one side the withdrawing chamber that was furnished with nine tapestries, mostly nine feet (2.7 metres) high and reaching to the floor, with two windows panelled beneath their sills and a hearth. On the west wall of the great hall, high up near the top, are two fireplaces. (They are high on the wall because this is a ruin, and the floors are gone.) The southerly of these was in the withdrawing chamber, and from there the procession crossed the passage to the bedchamber. Both these rooms have gone but they were on the top floor above the great hall. Like the withdrawing chamber, the bedchamber had more than one window and was furnished with tapestries nine feet (2.7 metres) high (see the floor plan on page 132). This bedchamber was probably on the north side overlooking the court, because leading from it was a smaller, completely panelled inner chamber. This could not have been to the south of the passage because the main staircase in the east wing already occupied the space three storeys up. (See also Appendix V.)

Important rooms of reception were in the four/five storeys in the north part of the east wing, together with Bess's old bedchamber and the family rooms such as Bess's withdrawing room, which was on the top storey above her bedchamber and next to the great withdrawing chamber.[57] The latter three spaces were unquestionably in that section. There is no mention in the building accounts of her son Sir William Cavendish's bedchamber. It has always seemed unlikely that his bedchamber would be over a service space (the larder), which is where Stallybrass put it on the basis of these words in the inventory, 'In the Chamber above the Larder a bedstead'.[58] It is far more likely that Sir William's bedchamber was in the more comfortable east wing. It is included in the inventory in a section of ten rooms that appear as a consecutive listing in the east wing.

When considering the inventory it is well to notice that its making took time and would have been spread over several weeks. The wardrobe in the east wing has something like one hundred and thirty items in it, and it would have taken the clerks several days to list: the contents were hangings, curtains, carpets, rugs (some with gold thread, some with silver); the inventory details the material, such as taffeta, velvet or canvas. The items all had to be unwrapped, unfolded, examined and then folded up again. Then there was a sequence of outer room, low wardrobe with a chamber at the low wardrobe door. (At Wollaton Hall the wardrobe was on the main floor, at Chatsworth on the third storey, at Worksop Manor on the ground floor.) The clerks would then have visited the chamber at the Forest Great Chamber door, which was on the top storey, and there were the rooms that follow in the inventory, covered on different days from the wardrobe sequence.

Stallybrass may have been wrong in the placing of some of the spaces, but he was correct with the Old Gallery. There are eleven references in the building accounts to the 'Old Gallery End' of the building. One of them concerns payments to a plasterer named John Bynny in 1596:'Payd to John Binney the 13th November for shutting the walls in the half-pace at the old galarye end from the galarye dore to the lowest Lowplight [loup-light/borrowed light] in the stears in measure 99 yards at 1d. yard . . . 8s. 3d.'[59] The measurement of the walls of the 'half-pace' (the landing) down the first flight of stairs to the loup-light is a hundred square yards (eighty-four square metres). The Old Gallery, therefore, was off the east of the landing with the Hill Great Chamber to the west.

The Old Hall would have been an uncomfortable house for Bess to inhabit and difficult for her household. Nevertheless, when she returned in early August 1592 with her granddaughter Arbella Stuart from her long visit to the court in London it was to Hardwick she went. She stayed there until mid October and returned again in time for Christmas, then remained until the end of May 1593. Thereafter she stayed at Hardwick no less than seven times between May 1593 and July 1596, including one stay of ten months in 1594–5. She obviously preferred Hardwick to South Wingfield Manor, which was only six miles (ten

Top: A seventeenth-century drawing of Old Hardwick Hall seen from the north, from an album of drawings held by English Heritage at Audley End, Essex; New Hardwick Hall can be seen over the wall on the extreme left.
Above: The north front of Old Hardwick Hall today

kilometres) from Hardwick and where, although it was Shrewsbury property, she had a legal right to occupation during her lifetime. After Bess moved in to her New Hardwick Hall in 1597 the Old Hall became an annex and, from the evidence of the inventory, a warehouse to store her furnishings removed from Chatsworth. Discomfort apart, the Old Hall had the attraction of two roof walks: one over the Hill Great Chamber and the other over the Forest Great Chamber, both giving breathtaking views over Derbyshire.

Top: Old Hardwick Hall from the south; drawing by S.H. Grimm (1734–94)
Above: The south front of Old Hardwick Hall today

Although Bess was using the Old Hall, it was not finished and work continued. The building was not completely glassed until August 1591.[60] In 1595
work was still going on in the Forest Great Chamber and in the Old Gallery,
and as late as January 1597 the walls of the tower over the west stairs were being
plastered.[61] Balusters over the little gallery were made by Nayll and Malorye

in May 1598.[62] The Forest Great Chamber was panelled in December and January 1595–6,[63] and the chimney-piece was put in place in February 1596 by the very skilled mason William Gryffen,[64] who had come to Hardwick in May 1594.

There are thirteen surviving plaster overmantels in the Old Hall. Of these the most significant is that in the Hill Great Chamber, which has been identified by Anthony Wells-Cole as possibly the clue to the whole programme of decoration in both Old and New Hardwick.[65] The lively, winged figure in the centre of the overmantel is Desire, who, in the woodcut from which it is modelled, is pulling a triumphal car carrying Patience. What this signified to the few educated Tudors who would have seen it will be discussed in Chapter 6 on New Hardwick Hall where images of Patience appear several times more. The woodcut is from the first of an eight-part suite called *Patience* produced by Dutch printmaker Dirk Coornhert from the work of Dutch artist Maarten van Heemskerck in 1559.[66]

Other subjects on the overmantels include the 'Elements', taken from prints by Dutch engraver Crispijn de Passe the Elder after the work of the Flemish painter Maarten de Vos;[67] among the elements only Earth is missing. On the second storey, more obscurely, the overmantel shows Nepthali riding a stag; this comes from a woodcut after another work by Maarten van Heemskerck from *The Twelve Patriarchs* (the twelve sons of Jacob) published in 1550.[68] The same source is used again in the overmantel on the third-storey north side next to the stairs, which (now damaged) shows Aser alone, milking a goat, but accompanied by a reclining Ceres in the woodcut. Only one of an unidentified suite of the *Four Winds* survives: in the complete series there would have been North, South, East and West; it is not clear which one this overmantel represents. The final identified overmantel is on the second storey in a chamber in the north-west corner, above the kitchen; this, more comprehensibly, depicts the *Departure of Tobias and the Angel* by an unidentified engraver after Maarten van Heemskerck.[69] We shall encounter Tobias again in the New Hall.

The overmantel in the Hill Great Chamber of Old Hardwick Hall; the central figure is Desire, who, taken from the print below, is pulling the triumphal car of Patience.

A print from a suite called *Patience*, by Dirk Coornhert after Maarten van Heemskerck, published in 1559

As at Chatsworth, the decoration was cast *in situ* by a plasterer from wooden moulds made by a master plasterer – a person such as Abraham Smith or Thomas Accres, two very skilled and unusually gifted craftsmen. Accres does not appear in the building accounts until April 1595 so can have had no hand in the Old Hall. There are no payments for this work in the building accounts, which indicates that they were made by a skilled crafts-man on a yearly wage and paid out of the household accounts. The only candidate for this is Abraham Smith.

Smith began his work in the quarterly wages account for December 1589 – his name but not his payment was noted.[70] By Christmas 1592 the household accounts record that he received a annual wage of £13. 6s. 8d., together with a rent-free farm at Ashford, Derbyshire, conveniently near the blackstone quarries.[71] How he found time to do his courting is anyone's guess, but he married in September 1592 and was given 40s. by Bess as a wedding gift.[72] It is very likely that the lively panels in the west wing are his work – the figures in these panels are filled with movement and with three exceptions there is nothing like this in the New Hall, where the plaster figures are wooden by comparison. These overmantels were made on wooden frames, modelled by hand and copied from published woodcuts; there were no life classes then. Nevertheless, the sculptor has caught his subjects vividly, and the images are better than the originals – he improved on the original figure as he patiently built up the figures with layer on layer of wet plaster. When set firmly they were fixed to the walls with 'hicks' (hooks). Stallybrass reports in his 1913 article that the overmantel in what he called 'Mr Wm Cavendishes chamber,' the corner room above the low larder, was even then fixed with hooks, as was the hall overmantel.[73] It represented a male figure riding a deer.

Who would have supplied the woodcuts used as a source? It was unlikely to have been Abraham Smith himself. A near-certain guess is John Balechous, sometimes called John Painter. Painter first entered Bess's employment at Chatsworth, where he was paid in the household accounts for May 1578. He was valued enough to be paid a yearly wage of

£2 with keep.[74] Painter first appeared at Old Hardwick on 22 November 1589 when he was paid 2s. for 'on weeck bord wadges'.[75] Later, like Accres and Smith, he was rewarded with a farm at Bolsover, four miles (six kilometres) from Hardwick, so board wages were no longer needed. As mentioned in the Introduction, he was called 'Painter' because that was his calling, but he was more than that: when clerk of the works David Flood was paid off in November 1591[76] and one of Bess's tame priests (Sir Henry Jenkinson) took over, Painter was given responsibility for paying the carpenters cutting joists. The reason for Flood's departure cannot be known for certain. His shaky addition may have become tiresome to Bess. More significantly, however, the building site now included the New Hall, the winter shutdown was coming and Bess was leaving with Arbella Stuart and her household for what proved to be a ten-month visit to the royal court in London. The building of the New Hall had become a far bigger project than previously, with a responsibility possibly beyond Flood's capabilities. The site now contained only carpenters, joiners and masons cutting stone for the New Hall ready for Bess's return.

Later, at the New Hall, we shall see Painter making a major decision to heighten the six towers without Bess visiting the site. Clearly he knew what he was about, and no doubt he and Bess – together with Abraham Smith and, after 1595, Thomas Accres – discussed and decided on the major points of the interior decoration. We do not know if Bess's favoured son, William, was included in these consultations, but it was likely, as he was her heir; neither should contributions from Charles Cavendish be overlooked. As a further measure of Painter's position, an entry in the building accounts for 6 November 1591 records that a joiner was paid for wainscoting a little chamber in the Old Hall 'next to John Paynter's chamber'.[77] Painter's chamber was probably some sort of site office with a bed in the corner; he would have kept plans, drawings, details, notes, prints and pattern books there.

Given that John Painter had considerable and increasing responsibility it is safe to say that he had influence on the choice of subject for the overmantels. Did he arrive with the woodcuts or were they acquired by Bess during her year-long London visit? We shall never know for sure.

Construction of the brewhouse court – the range of buildings lined up north and south about a hundred yards (ninety metres) to the south of the Old Hall – was started early in 1589. The masons, Harry Nayll and Richard Mallory, were paid for hewing three windows on 12 March 1589. Then Thomas Hollingworth and his wallers were paid in the building accounts on 16 August of that year 'for the wallinge of Fortty and three Roods of wall of the bruhouse and the Rest ther at 2s. the Rood £4. 6. 0'.[78] The 'Rest ther' included bakehouse, stable, washhouse and dairy.

The brewhouse was at the north end of the range and is now (together with the rest of the range of adjoining buildings) accommodation for the National Trust. The range was completed and the wallers paid off on 11 September 1591 when Bess generously rewarded them with an extra 10s.[79] That was not the complete accommodation: in addition the inventory lists slaughterhouse, chaundlers (chandler) house, still house, Mr Cavendish's stable and smithy. None of these is accounted for in the building accounts. A smithy occupied the far south-east corner; judging by the bottle-mould decoration of the windows, it was built in 1588 when the west wing of the Old Hall was going up. In 1609, the year after Bess died, William Senior carried out a complete survey with maps of all William Cavendish's lands. If that survey is accurate, then by that date only the brewhouse range and smithy had been built in the area. Although the work on this range began in 1589 the stable was not roofed until June 1593.[80] The 1601 inventory has as its last item: 'In the smithie a Slithie [possibly a scythe], a payre of bellows'. A later bellows was, until recently, still there.

Beer was an important addition to household wages. At least two types would have been brewed – strong beer and small beer. Strong beer was made from the first brew of freshly malted barley and was kept for the senior men of the household, while small beer was drunk instead of water.

Small beer had a lower alcoholic content and was not fully fermented, with a resulting high sugar content producing a refreshing beverage unlikely to intoxicate. Some idea of its importance can be gleaned from the beer cellar accounts. In March 1857, for example, 158 gallons (748 litres) were brewed.

The inventory gives the contents of the brewhouse in 1601: 'In the brewhouse three great Fates [open containers], a little fatt, a bowling lead [a lead container for boiling], a Cooler, eight hogsheads [barrels containing about fifty-two gallons/246 litres], a tun dishe [tunn is a fermenting vat], two skopes [scoops], too firkins [small barrels holding about nine gallons/forty-three litres]'. Brewing continued until 1857 when, in March, 108 gallons (511 litres) of strong-brewed ale, and 158 gallons (748 litres) of weaker beer were brewed.[81] The building was converted to a gardener's house in 1872: wood floors were laid and additional windows inserted.

On the west side of the brewhouse an external staircase runs up to the roof with a hoist shaft: this was used to take the fresh barley up to a drying floor measuring 175 square yards (145 square metres) in the roof space over the adjoining buildings. These buildings were the bakehouse (conveniently placed for brewer's yeast, also used for raising bread), the washhouse, a stable (approximately in the centre of the range, with nine stalls for horses and later converted for use as a garage). Was this Bess's stable? Two double-door entries are modern; the coach entrance was eighteen feet (5.5 metres) south from the southernmost double door, past four steps leading up to a cottage door. Adjoining the door is a comparatively modern four-light window thirteen feet (four metres) wide, with the wall below the sill infilled: this fills in a gap that would have been wide enough for a coach. The section is now a cottage with nineteenth-century brick partition walls and a wooden floor raised three feet (one metre) above ground level. The inventory, which did not include livestock, listed only the following contents in the stable: 'a bedstead, a featherbed, too bolsters, a blanket, too coverlets, three Coshes [coaches], a Lytter [Bess's preferred means of travel], too payre of Lytter saddles with furniture to them, & poles for the Lytters, too gentlewomens saddles, three saddle clothes, three brydells, too pillions, too great buff saddles, a sumpter saddle [for a pack animal], too trunk saddles'. This does not seem a great deal, but then the stable was used only for Bess's needs; visitors' horses – even those of her immediate family – were boarded out at Bess's expense, and her son William had his own stable. It may seem surprising that the stabling was so modest, but this was in line with many other great houses; only those that entertained the monarch were equipped with large stabling. Had Queen Elizabeth or King James I decided to stay with Bess she would no doubt have built suitable accommodation for the royal horses.

During the autumn of 1590 there was a large increase in the employment of labour; there is no indication what these people were working on. It had been usual for the number of labourers hired to increase when building restarted after the frosts; indeed in 1589, when the west wing of the Old Hall was being heightened and enlarged, mid September was the peak of labour employment. By 1590 all the major building work on the Old Hall was complete, yet in September there was a large increase in the number of labourers employed. For the fortnight ending 14 September only four were employed (as in the preceding months), but this figure increased to ten by the end of the month. For the fortnight ending 12 October this had gone up to thirty and remained at that number for four whole weeks until forty labourers were paid for the two weeks ending 23 November. There was also the purchase for 2s. of a dozen spades and shovels. By the following fortnight they were reduced to the usual average of four labourers.[82] Clearly there was major work in progress. The most likely cause was the 'New Foundations' of the New Hardwick.

After the death of Bess of Hardwick in February 1608 the properties at Hardwick came into Sir William Cavendish's possession exactly as his mother had willed. He continued to maintain the Old Hardwick Hall. In 1620, £111. 12. 9d. was spent on 'pulling down and building up the east end of the old house before the 12 of February'.[83] This referred to rebuilding part of the east wing, and the work was undertaken by John Painter. A little over a decade earlier (from March to August 1608) Painter had built the New Inn (now the Hardwick Inn) at the entrance to the park; he was now the landlord of this establishment.[84] Subsequently the inn was taken over by his son, another John, in 1618 – probably after John Painter senior's death, so this work at Old Hardwick was likely to have been supervised by John Painter the son. In 1620 a further £239. 10s. 2d. was expended 'about Hardwick building'.[85] The following year £101. 17s. was spent, making a total over the two years of one penny under £453. On 27 August 1621 'Sir Wm Cavendishes Surveyor' was paid 22s.;[86] this was likely to have been paid to Smythson's son John for advising on the repairs. In 1622 a further £120 was spent on the Old Hall. This fits in neatly with tree-ring dating taken from the roof timbers of the East Lodge in the north-east corner of the forecourt giving dates of 1622–45. Tree-ring dating from the stairs of the West Lodge in the north-west corner of the forecourt gives 1625. A survey map of Hardwick dated 1628 shows the East Lodge in place but not the West Lodge. The work on the Old Hall itself involving John Painter was concerned with rebuilding the north bays of the east wing and adding a porch to the great hall entrance. The quality of the work at the Old Hall is called into question by the necessity for this rebuilding. Between 1660 and 1661 eighteen chimney stacks had to be replaced,[87] the following year ten chimneys were removed, and in December that same year two more were taken down over the Hill Great Chamber.[88] By then it was a matter of removing decayed and unsafe stonework in preference to maintenance.

The now-vanished north side of the east wing may have provided the rubble used in the construction of the Great Pond and Miller's Pond below Bess's Fish Ponds, which post-date the Senior Survey of 1609. What is certain is that at various dates between 1745 and 1767 parts were taken down and materials sold. It has been suggested that the 1st Duke of Devonshire used the stone for rebuiding Chatsworth in 1700–7. That is hardly likely because the walls of the Old Hall are built of rough stone and not the ashlar blocks used at Chatsworth, but if it is true, we should be grateful that he took no more than he did.

*

On the death of his father in 1950 the 11th Duke of Devonshire was faced with an immense tax bill, which threatened the future of the Devonshire estates. The Old Hall was passed to the Ministry of Works in lieu of taxation, which in turn gave it to the care of the Department of the Environment (on its formation in 1972) and then to English Heritage in 1984.

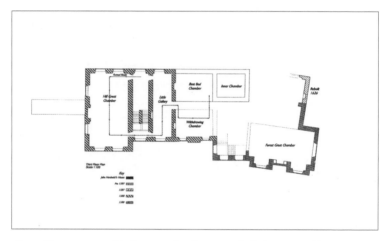

Above: The top storey with the processional route marked; the rooms without cross-hatched walls have now gone but have been reconstructed from the 1601 inventory. Below: The third storey, showing the heightened east wing of 1589

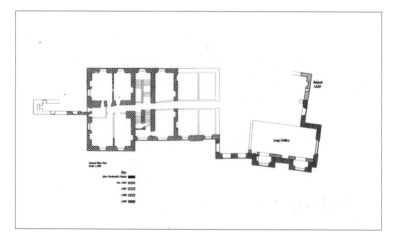

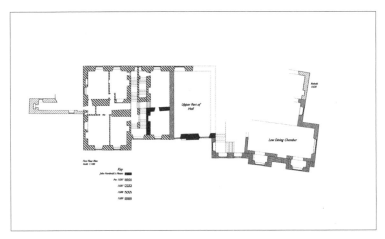

Above: The second storey, showing the west wing of 1588
Below: The ground floor, where the angled building of the east wing can clearly be seen; John Hardwick's hall was sited east–west at the south end of Bess's north–south hall. The rooms to the west of the hall are part of John Hardwick's house.

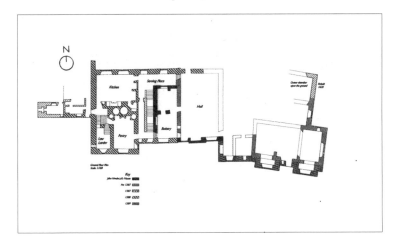

133

An aerial view of New Hardwick Hall from the west

6

NEW HARDWICK HALL
IN THE CARE OF THE NATIONAL TRUST

New Hardwick Hall was a statement of dynastic aspiration: Bess of Hardwick's intention was to build a power base for her heirs. She created a suite of magnificent state apartments in order to provide accommodation suitable for entertaining a monarch; by the time she had built the New Hall in the 1590s Bess knew that Queen Elizabeth would never travel as far as Hardwick, but she intended the house to be available for her descendants in case they were ever to host a royal visit. As it happened, although the Prince of Wales visited in 1619, the only monarch ever to sleep at Hardwick was King George V, who spent a night in the state bedchamber in the 1930s. Hardwick was a huge investment – estimated to be £5,000 – for little return.[1]

According to some authorities, in constructing the grand new hall Bess was inspired by the possibility that her granddaughter Arbella Stuart, born in 1575, might succeed Queen Elizabeth on the throne. Mary, Queen of Scots certainly believed that Arbella's succession was possible, but that spirited woman used every means within her power to cause trouble. I have never believed that Bess envisaged Arbella becoming queen and inhabiting Hardwick: Bess was dynastic and built Hardwick for her assigned heir William Cavendish and his descendants.

If Arbella should have been named as Queen Elizabeth's heir, the queen, always parsimonious, would have expected Bess to provide funds to support a queen. Bess knew Elizabeth well and knew her duty: apart from giving Arbella the loan to the Willoughbys she provided just over £1,000 more for Arbella to buy lands in Lincolnshire. The income was sufficient to catch a wealthy husband but far below that befitting royal status – although the queen did pay Arbella £200 annually. I believe that Bess never seriously entertained the idea of Arbella succeeding Elizabeth as queen, despite the fact that Arbella was second in the line of succession.

The background to the story of Arbella Stuart is as follows. In 1574 a secret marriage for Bess's daughter Elizabeth Cavendish was arranged by Bess and Margaret Douglas, Countess of Lennox. Margaret Douglas was the mother of Charles Stuart, 5th Earl of Lennox, grandson of King James IV of Scotland and great-grandson of King Henry VII of England – a young man of nineteen with a double dose of royal blood in his veins. In mid October 1574 the countess and her son were travelling north and stopped at Newark, Nottinghamshire, when Bess and her daughter Elizabeth were staying at Rufford Abbey, Nottinghamshire – one of the Talbot properties and only a short journey from Newark. Bess sent a message inviting the party to Rufford, which was gratefully accepted. The countess, exhausted by the journey and complaining of feeling sick, took to her room for four or five days, leaving Bess in full charge of what followed. The only matter Bess could not fix was the affection of the young couple, but Elizabeth did not let her mother down – she and Charles fell in love. The Earl of Shrewsbury, unwillingly drawn into the matter, wrote to Queen Elizabeth on 5 November: 'The young man, her son, fell into liking my wife's daughter . . . and such liking was between them as my wife tells me she makes no doubt of a match . . . The young man is so far in love, that belike he is sick without her.'[2]

The young couple married. Margaret Douglas was ordered back to London and shut up in the Tower for the third time in her life. Bess, on the other hand, escaped serious retribution because she was needed to attend to the captive Mary, Queen of Scots – and also because her loyalty to Queen Elizabeth was understood. A daughter, Arbella Stuart, was born to the young Stuarts in the year following their marriage, and Charles Stuart died

New Hardwick Hall west entrance front; to the right, on the ground-floor level, can be seen where the cornice is missing and the colonading was never put in place – one of the rare occasions when Bess of Hardwick paid for something she did not use.

a year later in 1576. After Bess's daughter Elizabeth died on 21 January 1582 Bess was left with the upbringing of her granddaughter; Margaret was subsequently pardoned.

By 1586 Bess of Hardwick had managed to get her own money back from her estranged husband, the 6th Earl of Shrewsbury, and on his death in November 1590 she was entitled to a one-third share of the income from his estate for her lifetime. There were problems: his heir Gilbert Talbot (who was married to Bess's daughter Mary) did not pay up the money to which Bess was entitled. Lord Burghley was a supervisor of Shrewsbury's will and Bess wrote to Burghley in April 1591 reporting that she was not getting her dowry from Gilbert; a court case followed before the matter was finally settled. The total was about £3,000 annually, worth many millions today; it is no wonder that Gilbert was slow in parting with the money. With that settled Bess, taking Arbella her granddaughter with her, set off in November 1591 for what proved to be a ten-month visit to the royal court in London. The party did not return to Hardwick until early August the following year.

By this date building work on the New Hall had been under way for more than eighteen months. 'New foundations' are mentioned in the building accounts for the first time on 5 December 1590 in connection with a job in one of the top-floor chambers in the east wing of the Old Hall: 'T[owards] the new Foundacion'.[3] The subsequent year the information was more definite: on 22 May 1591 William Carpenter (a carpenter, as it happens) was paid on a reckoning for his bargain-in-great for the 'newe foundacion Floors'.[4] A further pointer is that from the fortnight ending 12 October and that ending 26 October 1590, thirty labourers were employed; by the fortnight ending 9 November there were forty labourers and a dozen shovels and spades were paid for.[5] Carpenter was paid 41s. on that date and had so far been paid £5. 6s. 8d. By 19 June he was halfway through his bargain, having received £6. 13s. 4d. From this it is clear that the foundations had been dug out and laid to sufficient height for wooden ground floors to be put in and that Carpenter was halfway through his job by 19 June; by 28 August there remained 33s. 4d. to be earned.[6] Thereafter William Carpenter vanishes from the accounts.

This evidence indicates that work must have started on New Hardwick in the autumn of 1590 to be sufficiently advanced for Carpenter to work out his bargain. Obviously the planning must have taken place before building began: Robert Smythson would have visited the site with Bess and likely enough William Cavendish (her son and heir) and his brother Charles, who, according to his son, was a good amateur architect. Their input, although supposed, should not be ignored – even if, as we shall shortly see, Charles's later relationship with his mother was not good because he took Gilbert Talbot's part in the dispute over payment due from the will. The site of the new building was decided – not too close to the old building but not too far away either, because the old building was to be in continuous use as an annexe. This consultation must have taken place in about 1588 at the latest, and we can imagine that Smythson would have listened to Bess's wishes: she wanted large windows, and those on the third storey should be a repeat of the big twelve-light windows in the two top-storey great chambers of the Old Hall; she wanted the kitchens on the north side and her own bedchamber on the warmer south side; and she wanted her New Hardwick to be placed on sufficiently high ground to be seen from afar. Smythson would have drawn up plans and elevations, bringing them over from Wollaton to Hardwick for further consultation. Finally the plans were approved and the work started in the autumn of 1590.

The site, in fact, has a thin layer of topsoil lying on a convenient sandstone bed – ideal foundations for the new building. In addition to foundations excavated to support the exterior and interior walls, a beer cellar, wine cellar and storage cellar were excavated and the kitchen floor was dug out by about three feet (one metre) to give height without interrupting the level of the second storey. In the centre of the site was a large smooth level of natural rock on which the great hall would stand. This matched exactly what Smythson had done at Wollaton.

The beer and wine cellars ran beneath the east side of the building. Barrels were moved in and out through wide doors in the north end of the house (the back door). They were laid out as one would expect: the beer cellar was accessed by a stair from the buttery, the butler's department; the wine cellar was accessed by a stair from the pantry, the pantler's department. The wine cellar was enlarged, probably in 1785–91 when the York architect John Carr did a great deal of work at Hardwick. Visiting Hardwick in 1789, John Byng (subsequently 5th Viscount Torrington) commented on some of the repairs in progress.[7] This narrow cellar, which stopped at the foundations of the interior wall of the southwest turret, accommodated twenty-seven wine bins for storage of wine bottles – which were coming into use by the late eighteenth century. A new cellar was necessary because the Elizabethan wine cellar could not be securely locked by the butler (by the late eighteenth century the pantler's position had been completely usurped by the butler). Beneath the raised pastry kitchen was the cool cellar for the storage of meat, pies and the like. This was accessed by a short stair near the back door; it is now the boiler house.

The clerk of works responsible for paying the workforce fortnightly on Saturdays was the family priest, Sir Henry Jenkinson, who carried on from the same job at Old Hardwick. Smythson was unable to fulfil the responsibility of surveyor, as he had at Wollaton, because he was now employed by the Willoughbys, and his days of being a mason were over. However, he

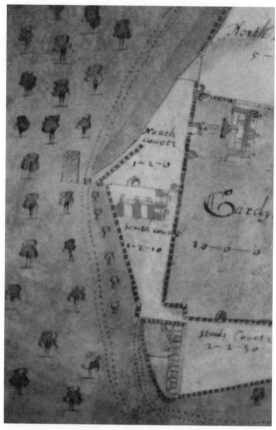

Detail taken from William Senior's Survey of 1609; New Hardwick is at top right with Old Hardwick at the centre and the stable court due south.

provided plans in his spare time. John Balechous was the surveyor. It will be clear from what follows that Bess was in charge and knew exactly what was going on. She signed off Jenkinson's accounts at the end of each fortnight, often querying an entry. Painter was responsible for paying the carpenters from December 1591 to August 1592, the period when Bess was in London for ten months. When Bess was away the responsibility for the work often fell to Painter. He made decisions himself when her permission was not needed. For example, in the margin of the payments to masons for 22 January 1597, the number of balusters needed for the completion of a roof balustrade is discussed: 'one hundredth fifty and three balasters Sr Henry [clerk of works] sayth John Paynter thinks about 10 more will serve'.[8] On one occasion when it was clear that the turrets were too short he went to see Bess at South Wingfield Manor to discuss the problem; the turrets were heightened by six feet (two metres).

Accidents are not mentioned in the building accounts. These are found in Hardwick MS 7, and although there are many payments to workmen who may have suffered injuries, only one specifies an accident, on 5 September 1596: 'to Hollingworth 1s and when he was hurt 2s. 6d.'[9] Since there were five Hollingworths employed at that time – four rough-wallers and one mason – it is impossible to identify which one was involved.

The basic plan for New Hardwick is a rectangle sited north and south with the walls pierced by huge windows. It is an unfortunate fact that when Bess decided to have large areas of glass in the walls she was weakening their structure – and this is a design fault that has plagued succeeding generations of Cavendishes. Medieval church-builders understood the weakness caused by large windows and supported their walls with buttresses. At Hardwick, Smythson did the same: the buttresses take the form of rectangular turrets. Unfortunately Bess's demand for large windows in the turrets as well weakened those structures because the window piers proved too slender to take the stress.

The walls around these turrets have been moving for centuries. In the late 1780s the 5th Duke of Devonshire called in the architect John Carr of York and spent £1,226 on repairs to the building;[10] new beams and iron cramps were put in to hold the walls in place. Some of this work is still visible: the south-west turret still has the end plates of tie bars showing, although the bars themselves have been removed; these may have been inserted by Carr or they could be nineteenth-century repairs. The fact is that the building has survived far longer than its builders even hoped. In any event, recent remedial work on all six turrets has at last corrected the problem.

In fairness to Smythson, he had seen at Longleat the same structure of window bays in the exterior walls on all four façades. He might have reasoned that the design had worked at Longleat; however, the design was different there in important ways. The window piers at Longleat are narrower than those at Hardwick, but at Longleat the bays are much shallower and of only three storeys, and there is nothing in Longleat like the masses of glass at Hardwick. Aso at Longleat there are interior walls acting as supporting buttresses, except in the north-west corner where the outer wall is thicker than elsewhere. The prototype plan of Hardwick (see page 149) shows the turrets all supported by interior walls, but the final plan takes these away, and the turrets in the long gallery and high great chamber have no interior supporting walls – none of the four turrets supporting the main body of the building has the support of interior walls throughout their entire height; here is a weakness in the design caused, almost certainly, by Bess's insistence on having large windows.

Another feature that was new in the Hardwick plan was the placing of the transverse great hall. This repeats what Bess had already done at Old Hardwick Hall, where she was restricted by the site and buildings already in place, so making a transverse great hall the only means on that site to accommodate a countess's large household. The great hall in New Hardwick is only slightly larger than that in the old building. The convenience of a transverse hall meant that a balanced front to the building could be designed; windows on the left could exactly balance those on the right. This was a revolutionary design. Previously, great halls had always run parallel to the façade of a building, meaning that the big window to light the high table was not balanced outside by a similar window to the far side of the central entrance. In any event, by the time Hardwick was built great halls served as dining-rooms for the household and visiting servants, with the upper servants occupying the high table once used by their masters. The Elizabethan great hall was a noisy, smelly and crowded place; Bess would have processed through it only when arriving or leaving the house.

In contrast to Longleat and Wollaton, at Hardwick there were no garde-robes. The principal bedchambers all had closets off them – furnished, as in the 1601 inventory, with close-stools that would be emptied into out-side privies by servants. In 'a little roome' off Bess's bedroom was her close-stool, 'covered with blewe cloth stitcht with white, with red and black silk fringe' – blue was the Cavendish livery.[11] Also in this 'little roome' were 'three pewter basons, a little Close stoole, a great Cofer, a wood Chest, a great trunk, a little trunk'. The 'little roome' is still there and it measures just over six feet six inches by thirteen feet (two by four metres); the trunks must have been stacked, with the 'Cofer' on top of the 'wood Chest' – hardly, one would imagine, a convenient arrangement, and Bess was living there at the time. In the strong room was a silver chamber pot, no doubt intended for the state bedchamber. There was no chamber pot in Bess's bedchamber. The privies were in the north wall of the court, a row of seats set on a stone floor covered with wooden slats, a long journey from Bess's 'little roome'. The privies were sited not far from where the public toilets are today.

Slightly off-centre in the plan is a heavy supporting spine wall running north to south. It is off-centre to give width to the state apartments on the top storey and was necessary to support the floors. It is broken in the middle to allow for the space of the great hall, but it required floor timbers thirty-two feet (ten metres) long to span the floor wall to wall on the widest (west) side. To span the roof above the space of the great hall there were heavy internal central buttresses on the east and west ends of the hall. This feature may have taken Smythson some time to work out because the buttresses were placed in bays and intended to add solidity and support in order to counter the weakness caused by the bay windows. The floors in the turret bays were supported on shallow stone arches stretching across the width of the bays: one, plastered over, can be seen just outside the door to what is now called the Mary, Queen of Scots Room. (This name is a misnomer, caused by the 6th Duke's sketchy knowledge of history. Mary, Queen of Scots was beheaded in 1587, before the house was even started.)

The ground floor is given over to service and servants. The second storey is the family floor, where Bess had her withdrawing room, together with her bedchamber on the warm south side. The top storey accommodates the state apartments and is taller than the lower storeys. On the outside the storeys are marked by windows of increasing height and the floor levels by a ledged string course – in the accounts correctly called a cornice. At Longleat and Wollaton pilasters of the classical orders mark the storeys in the accepted sequence – Tuscan, then Ionic and, finally, Corinthian on the turrets. At Hardwick, however, there is no more than a nod to the classical orders. The east and west porticos are supported on Tuscan columns that were originally intended to fill the four corners made by the turrets as well. The entablatures (cornices) marking the floors correctly follow the orders except that the top floor is not Corinthian; they do not have the supporting classical columns found at Longleat and Wollaton. The front door is correctly framed by the Ionic order of pilasters (and decorated with a design borrowed from the works of Italian architect Sebastiano Serlio); the capitals are Ionic – and also, correctly, the entablature and cornice. Further classical touches are the consoles beneath the windows and the roof balustrade. Aside from this, Smythson and/or Bess made no great display of classical rules.

On one of the Tuscan columns near the front door is carefully carved Latin graffiti: *Hic locus est quem si verbis audatia detur haud timeam magni dixisse Palatia caeli*. This was obviously put there by an educated hand; the line comes from the *Metamorphoses* of the Roman poet Ovid and translates as 'This is the place which, if boldness were given to my utterance, I should not hesitate to call the palace of the sky.' The date, at a guess, is late sixteenth to early seventeenth century.

There is nothing in the building accounts that says which masons laid the foundations of the New Hall. By May 1591 the walls were high enough for William Carpenter and his man or men to begin laying his floors. However, in the records for November 1591 John Rhodes, who had worked at Wollaton, is mentioned as being paid for hewing ashlar (smooth-faced stonework) and windows for the second storey of the New Hall.[12] He arrived just a few weeks before Bess left for her visit to the court in London; when she departed, Rhodes and his men were left to hew ashlar, make window and door jambs and the like, in preparation for her return, but they did no actual building. The building work was mainly put on hold, although during April and June 1591 six chimney-pieces were set. After Bess returned, in August 1592, Rhodes and his team were setting the stonework; building had restarted.

Carpenters and joiners worked out their bargains in the building accounts; for example, Peter and William Yates completed their bargain for the whole roof of the New Hall, including the turrets, between May and November 1593 for a total of £50. In their case the job could be accurately assessed, but this was not the case for other trades: sawyers (who were engaged to cut up tree trunks into joists) were paid by measure because it could not be known what quantity would be needed.

The largest quantity of building work fell to John Rhodes (called Roods in the accounts) for all the walls of the New Hardwick. This was a massive job of work, requiring expert management – yet he marked his payments with an 'X', as he couldn't write. Yet although the cost could not easily be assessed Rhodes was paid by a bargain-in-great: in the accounts a margin note for December 1591 reads 'delivered unto Roods 120 foot ashlar which was List before he [made] his bargayne which is to Reckoning for'. This is recording that while paying Rhodes for hewing ashlar there was already 120 feet (thirty-seven metres) of ashlar hewn and paid for before Rhodes arrived.[13] The first oblique reference to John Rhodes was in late October 1591: 'To Rods his man for hewing fyve foots of the great cormish that stand over the pastery at 6d. the foot 2s. 6d.'[14] The cornice was marking the floor of the second storey of the north turret – the north end of the building was further advanced than the rest. Rhodes himself does not feature in the accounts until 11 December 1591. On this date the documents record the enlargement of Rhodes's own house: 'Payd to Drabble and Gibson in full payment of their bargayn for settinge upp tow bays of houssing at Roods house';[15] Drabble and Gibson were carpenters, and they were adding two timber-framed bays to a house allocated to Rhodes.

For a time Rhodes's brother Christopher (sometimes called 'Rhodes Junior') was working with him. Christopher's name rarely appears in the accounts; neither do the names of the under-masons working for his brother nor the names of John's labourers, who were used for fetching and carrying stone and mortar for Rhodes and whom he would have paid out of the sums he received. In July 1593 five of their labourers were paid 15d. by Bess for one day's work, but that is the only mention of the labourers. Labourers were usually paid 6d. a day; the 15d. among five must have been a reward payment and shows Bess's care for her employees. In the first mention of Rhodes working at Hardwick he was hewing a great deal of ashlar for the second storey; there were to be thirty windows and six blind (false) windows, both at 4d. a foot. As with so much in these accounts, the numbers do not add up: there are ten blind windows and thirty-four others. Of course some may have been cut before Rhodes arrived. In April 1592 he was paid for seventeen feet six inches (5.3 metres) of door moulding for two small rooms over the pastry (S1 and S2 on the floor plan on page 168),[16] which is in the second storey of the north turret. Nevertheless, whether or not the numbers add up, it is a very impressive amount of work to have completed the second storey in a matter of only six months. The scaffolding for the third storey was paid for in June 1592,[17] and by early August Rhodes was paid for hewing the first of the huge windows for the third storey; but he was not paid for setting them until after Bess returned.[18] Bess arrived back from London on 5 August that year and must have been pleased with Rhodes's work because only the next day she gave 30s. to him and his men, and the day after that she gave two of Rhodes's men a shilling each.[19]

From 22 April 1592 to 20 April 1593, when John Rhodes was hewing stone, building rough walling and setting windows in the walls he was building, Bess paid him, in round figures, £250, out of which he had to pay his team of men. As a top-class mason he could earn 16d. a day, which is about £20 a year; quite clearly, he was responsible for overseeing substantial amounts of work and large sums of money were passing through his hands. Also Rhodes was running a production line making windows; he was turning out a few more windows than were actually needed, and this, as it happened, was an asset. In May that same year, 1593, Rhodes's brother Christopher left Hardwick, and Bess gave him a parting gift of 10s.[20]

As with the earlier buildings discussed in this book, the walls at Hardwick are faced with smooth ashlar about ten inches (twenty-five centimetres) thick, with rough walling approximately four feet six inches (1.4 metres) deep behind it. In places where no ashlar was necessary because the walls were not usually seen – places such as the cellars and the roof space – the walls remained rough. The ashlar, both interior and exterior, carries two sets of masons' marks: one (called a bench mark) was made by the mason who cut the stone, while the other was the mark of the mason who laid the stone. Although very visible, the marks were essential – Rhodes needed to see them to work out how much to pay his men out of the staged payments due under his contract; seemingly, Bess had no objection to seeing the marks.

*

Changes were made during the course of building. The first and most obvious of these are two blocked doors at second-storey level; one on the west side of the north turret and the other on the south side of the south-west turret. These were to access the roof walks over corner porticos; rough-hewn stone courses mark the missing cornices. The doors were left open until November 1595 when they were finally blocked up. The new cornice was hewn and paid for but never put in place. There are no other blocked doors, indicating that the west front was furthest advanced when the decision was made in early 1592.

For the week ending 27 March 1597 there is an important entry in the household accounts: 'Geven to Mr Smythson the surveyour xxs and to his Sonne xs.'[21] Was Bess rewarding her 'surveyour' now that Hardwick was nearing completion, or was it for some other surveying work? His son was John Smythson, a freemason who worked at Wollaton in 1588 and was possibly in his early twenties by that time; was Robert introducing his son to Bess in the hope that she would employ him? In the event, Bess never employed John Smythson, but he went on to work for Sir Charles Cavendish, Bess's youngest son – one is left to speculate. Unfortunately the household accounts for 1590 and for most of 1591, which might have revealed more, are missing.

Bess had to wait a further seven months before she could take over her new house: she and her household moved into New Hardwick on 4 October 1597; the building was not finished and work continued for several years. Something of a rush preceded the move: the hall eclectic screen was not in place until August. (Here 'eclectic' means that the screen mixed up classical details.) William Gryffen, a mason who had come to Old Hardwick Hall in 1594 (see Chapter 5), was paid £6 on 20 August: 'In full payment of his bargane for hewing setting and lombing the Skryne in the hall at the new byilding.'[22] There is one mason's mark on the base of the southern column. The eclectic design follows some of the fundamentals of the classical orders: the frieze and fluted columns are basically Roman Doric, with strapwork panels adapted from the work of Hans Vredeman de Vries. Completed only

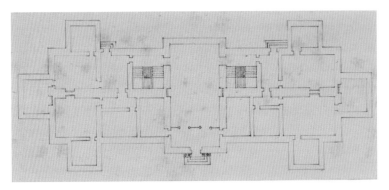

A drawing by Robert Smythson of a variant plan for the ground floor of Hardwick Hall showing the stairs; the service stair to the left was altered during the course of construction.

weeks before the grand opening, the screen was a triumphal arch through which Bess processed to the sound of music.

In the collection of Smythson's architectural drawings at the Royal Institute of British Architects library is a drawing of the ground floor of a variant plan for New Hardwick (see above). The chief difference is in the placing of the staircases, which begin where the present stairs begin and continue up in square stairwells. These would have finished in the floor of the long gallery and broken up the long and impressive vista down the room. However, from the first the main stair avoided this error by arriving at the third storey on the landing before the high great chamber. The other, the service stair, was changed only after the floor beams and joists in the long gallery were in place, and this could only have been done after the main roof was completed and leaded in September 1594. John Rhodes was hewing steps for the 'Lesr stear' on 2 November 1594, and by the 30th of that month he was hewing steps 'for the new steare that goeth by the Chapel'[23] and the paved room (paved because it was to have been a landing), which was called 'the new chamber'. The decision to change the route of the service stairs had then been made.

Today, beneath the lime-ash floor of the long gallery, the frames of the beams and joists still exist where the service stair was originally planned to arrive. (They use the same double tusk and tenon joint found in the south great chamber at Wollaton; see page 91.) Also, on the second flight of the stairs leading to the chapel landing, there is a cupboard door that conceals the sloping support of where the stairs were originally intended. Above this cupboard is an interior window, now covered by a hanging, to give borrowed light to the stairs; this is a cut-down second-storey window from Rhodes's production line, surplus to requirements. By this change of plan Bess won the privacy of a dining chamber for herself and her ladies off the low great chamber.

A major change already touched on was the decision to heighten the turrets. In the spring of 1594 the top of some of the turrets was reached when John Painter realized that they looked unimpressive because they were too short. As mentioned earlier, he went to South Wingfield, where Bess was staying, discussed the problem and won her agreement to heighten the turret windows by another pane, adding some six feet six inches (two metres) to the height of the turrets. On 20 April that year the accounts record: 'paid [to John Rhodes] for hewing 200 foot of window stuff for the heightening of eight windowes for tow of the turrets upon the Leads viz for every window 25 foot at 4½d. the foot £3. 15s.', which amounted to the heightening of one turret.[24] By 21 September Rhodes had been paid an extra £13. 3s. 2½d., all the heightened windows were in place and by 5 October all turrets were finished. By Christmas 1594 New Hardwick was completely roofed and work could start on the interior.

To the gifted mason Abraham Smith fell the bulk of the decorative plaster-work. He was paid an annual wage, so what he was working on is not directly accounted for, and it is only by oblique and other references that it is possible to identify his work. His annual wage was £13. 6s. 8d. plus a rent-free farm of fifty-five acres (twenty-two hectares) at Ashford, near the black-stone quarries. Stylistically, three pieces in New Hardwick can be attributed to him: *Cybele*, an overmantel in the little dining chamber, made after the end of 1594, and *Spring* and *Autumn* in the frieze of the window bay of the high great chamber. He also carved Bess's coat of arms on the roof of the east side of the building in the late summer of 1595, but the original has been renewed several times since. On 20 May 1594 a mason was paid for hewing two stones for: 'ye hall cheymney [for Abraham's work]'. A joiner named Bramley was paid on 2 October 1596 for panelling beneath the windows: '. . . in the bedchamber whear Habrahames Tearmes ar . . . '[25] – these are two figures on either side of the fireplace in Bess's bedchamber. Smith was also responsible for the carved stonework of the great hall fireplace in 1594.[26] He was by far better than any of the other plasterers. He found time to get married in September 1592 when Bess gave him a generous 40s. 'against his wedding'.

Thomas Accres (called 'a mason') was, like Smith, a highly gifted sculptor. Also like Smith, he was paid £13. 6s. 8d. a year 'besides his ferm'; it is not recorded where the farm was. The impression is that he was older than Smith because his daughter was married in 1598 when Bess gave her £1. We are told rather more about Accres than is the case with Smith: in July 1599 Accres was responsible, together with the duo of masons Nayll and Mallory, for the overmantel in the state bedchamber. Something of a mystery is a payment in April 1595 to Nayll and Mallory 'for scapeling (rough hewing) ix stones for accres for one payer of terms 17/-'.[27] A term is a half body, usually human or animal, or that of a mythical figure, merging into the top of a tapered pedestal. Judging by the cost and the number of stones, these must have been huge terms, but they have vanished. They may have been on the state withdrawing room chimney-piece and removed when the ceiling was lowered some time before 1764 or they could have been in one of the vanished rooms in the Old Hall. Accres had as his apprentice Miles Padley and, by 1595, Luke Dolphin as well. He appears to have assumed responsibility for cutting and polishing blackstone, which is used in the overmantels; in April 1595 an entry reads 'Pd unto Accres upon a bill for the makinge of an engine for the sawinge of blackstone 10/-'. In June the same year he was paid for work done 'at the mille for the sawinge of

Blackstone'.[28] Obviously the mill was water-powered. Rather charming is the entry dated May 1596: 'Geven unto Acres [*sic*] wyffe in respect of her husbands devise of sawing of blackstone to buy her a gowne withal 20/-'[29] – one can imagine Bess visiting the mill to see the new machine working at a time when Accres's wife was present in an old gown and Bess feeling the need to buy her a new one. The polishing of the blackstone was shared with John Painter; chalk was a constituent of the polish.

The only work that can firmly be attributed to Accres is the coat of arms on the roof over the west front, but his original, badly weathered, has been replaced, probably more than once. Moreover, the chimney-piece in the state bedchamber is certainly mainly his work (see page 160). On 28 January 1599 an entry gives this: 'Pd to Mallory for . . . helping Accars with hys worke in the beste bede chambar . . . ' and on the same day, 'Pd to Nayle for helping Mallory with Accareses hys worke in the Best Bede chamber 4½ days at 6d. the day 2/4d'.[30]

John Painter's first recorded entry for Old Hardwick was on 22 November 1586, when he was on board wages. Sometime along the way he married, because a payment 'To John Painters wyffe 10/-' is recorded for 28 January 1593.[31] Thereafter she received the same sum occasionally at various times, but on 5 January 1595 it was 20/-. Some payments coincide with the new year, but October and November also feature. By 1598 Painter employed a boy and then boys: 'Geven to John Painters boy 1/-' in 1598 and in 1599 'geven to his boys 5/-'.[32] His eldest son was John, of whom more later; he also had another son, William, who was old enough by 1599 to be trusted to buy paints for his father. However, it was only when the interior work began that Painter's trained skills were called into use. It will become clear that Painter was, in modern terms, the art consultant.

Two plasterers, John Marcer (who had been at Hardwick since July 1590) and Richard Orton (newly arrived in July 1595), had their scaffolding up in the high great chamber by 25 August that year.[33] They were preparing to make the great frieze but strangely are never mentioned as having been paid for the work in the building accounts or in the household accounts, unlike Smith and Accres. (Beside Accres's work their figures appear stiff and lifeless.) Orton was at Hardwick from November 1594 to June 1596, and the only payments recorded in his name are in the Hardwick household accounts, MS 7, chiefly concerning work in the high great chamber, where there are four payments totalling 13s.;[34] payments to John Marcer (or Marker) are scattered through MS 8 in similar small sums of 6d. a day, but he had been at Chatsworth in August 1579 and was already known to Bess.

Over a year earlier in April 1594 John Painter was paid for twenty-four pounds (eleven kilograms) of white lead 'for the great chamber',[35] likely enough for the ceiling, but he also had four pounds (1.8 kilograms) of yellow ochre and 4 pounds of red lead.[36] As the frieze was not then in place what was he painting? It may have been the two plasterworks of *Summer* and *Winter* attributed to Abraham Smith. Also there are no payments recorded to anyone for painting the frieze. Judging by the amount of coloured paints bought up to 1601 by Painter, he was responsible for much of the decoration, but the only certain attribution is that he painted the swagged frieze in the long gallery.

A set of painted cloths hanging in the chapel are certainly by Painter and show his art at its best. In February 1600 200 tenter hooks were bought by Painter to suspend hangings, and a week later an entry records 'paynting stuff for John Paynter for stayning the cloth hanging. 1lb Fernando bark 1/-, 1lb of brasil fusticle 10d. 2lb of blackwood 6d. 2lb of alloe 6d. 2lb of fusticle 10d. 1lb of copris 6d. 1lb of gumme 16d. 2lb of glewe 7d.'[37] The 'alloe' was probably alum, which was used to fix dyes. The four painted cloths tell the story of the conversion of Saul and are rare survivors; they are not mentioned in the 1601 inventory because they were still being painted at that time and were not yet ready for hanging. The figures in the paintings seem strangely elongated, which may have been deliberate if the hangings were designed to be viewed from below; unfortunately there is no way of knowing where they hung until the nearest inventory of 1764, when they were in the chapel. Painter based his scenes on woodcuts from Bernard Salomon's illustrations of the *New Testament*, published in Lyons in 1556 with an English edition that same year.[38] It is highly likely that Bess had access to a copy, perhaps belonging to her son William and that she chose the subject, but there was clearly input from Painter because detail was added from prints designed by Dutch artist Maarten van Heemskerck published in 1565, 1566, 1567 and 1572, and these were likely to have been provided by Painter. Painter did not go to London with Bess in 1591–2: he was busy with work at Hardwick. How these prints arrived in Derbyshire is yet another Hardwick mystery.

The ceilings at Hardwick are surprisingly plain: the only ceiling with any pretence of decoration is the rib-panelled long gallery ceiling. The reason is likely to be that there was a scarcity of skilled plasterers: Smith was very busy making overmantels at the Old Hall; some fifty hearths are listed in the 1601 inventory, and, of the few surviving, the majority are Smith's work. Meanwhile, Accres was fully occupied with sculpture for chimney-pieces. On the other hand, Marcer, although not in the class of Smith, is referred to obliquely in a payment to another plasterer in May 1595: 'the roof upon the Leads wheare Marcer wrought the fret of the roof '.[39] This refers to the south turret banqueting house on the roof where the 'fret' or moulding is still in place. There is another oblique reference to Marcer for May 1595: 'paid to Woodthorpe for the sawing of 400 foots of bords to make barkets [brackets] for Marcer in the galary'.[40] This is a huge number of brackets, which can only have been for the heavy cornice. Clearly, the turret ceiling was made before that of the gallery. Did Marcer make the gallery ceiling? Mark Girouard suggested that the moulded ceiling could have been part of William's mysterious expenditure on Hardwick; that could be so, but with the scaffolding there to put up the cornice and an experienced plasterer in place it could just as easily have been Marcer's work. (Girouard made this suggestion during a conversation in which he was referring to William Cavendish's account book – 'Book of Accounts of Various Stewards of William Cavendish, 1608–23' – which contains entries for sums spent on Hardwick that are not completely accounted for. Some of the expense was Painter's work at Old Hall detailed in Hardwick MS 29; the rest, Girouard suggested, could have been this moulded ceiling.)

Inlaid panelling is also scarce in New Hardwick: the only inlays were brought in from Chatsworth – an enclosure to the altar in the chapel and four framed panels on the chapel stairs. Bess was unable to find inlayers and was perfectly content with panels painted with imitation intarsia, very likely by John Painter – in August 1601 he was paid for a pound (roughly half a kilogram) of lamp black, perhaps for this work.[41]

Painter was probably responsible for painting the frieze, but there is nothing in the accounts to show this because he was paid an annual wage. We attribute the work to him because there are no other painters mentioned in the accounts. Originally the frieze would have been vibrant with colour and the tapestries beneath not the charming faded shade we see today but filled with fresh colour.

Educated Elizabethans loved an intellectual puzzle, and we have to read the frieze over the chair of state as they would. In the centre, sitting enthroned and surrounded by ladies-in-waiting is Diana the huntress, symbolizing Queen Elizabeth – who would have sat in a chair of state immediately below had she ever visited Bess. To the viewer's left in the corner are wild animals – lions, a tiger or leopard (all carnivores) and a monkey; these symbolize the dangers of the world. Between these creatures and Diana are brave Cavendish stags (stags are still the supporters in the Devonshire's coat of arms) keeping the dangers at bay. To the viewer's right are peaceful herbivores – elephants and camels, not to scale because they were copied from as yet mainly undiscovered woodcuts, and no one at Hardwick had seen these animals in the flesh. The two lions in the left corner are from woodcuts by Dutch engraver and publisher Philips Galle, published in 1578.[42]

The friezes covering the other sides of the room feature a bear hunt and a gazelle hunt, both from the same Galle publication as the two lions. In the reveals of the window are two plaster panels, which must be by Abraham Smith, depicting *Summer* and *Spring* and based on designs by Crispijn de Passe the Elder. The plaster heraldic design based on the Hardwick Saltire (cross) over the door into the high great chamber is certainly by Smith: an entry dated 20 March 1596 reads, 'by the Great Chamber door where Habraham mad the pyck . . .'[43] The work continued, and although Bess moved into her New Hardwick to the sound of music in early October 1597 the interior was certainly not finished.

The ground floor was open to all and not used by the family except for Sir William Cavendish's room in the south end furnished with a four-poster bed; the great hall chimney-piece shows Bess's arms – the Hardwick Saltire – and stag supporters with her countess's coronet on the apex of the armorial shield. This proclaimed Bess's dynasty and power, making a simple but authoritative statement. The stone surround was hewn and set in April 1597 – the year Bess moved in – by two masons, Henry Nayll (at Hardwick since 1587) and Richard Mallory (who arrived in 1589). The second storey was the family floor and follows a sequence starting with the low great chamber. These rooms were the humbler counterpart of the high great chamber, reception rooms for lesser folk such as visiting neighbours. A plaster chimney-piece dated 1597 tells the visitor 'The conclusion of all thinges is to feare God and keepe his commaundementes.' The stone surround was hewn and set in February 1596 by two masons, James Adams (who came to the site in 1594) and Leanard (who had been at Hardwick since 1589).[44] From here the more important visitor would have progressed to Bess's withdrawing room, where the chimney-piece has a more detailed repeat of Bess's arms and stag supporters; the arms are quartered with the Hardwick saltire and incorrectly repainted with what may originally have been Talbot quarterings. In Bess's bedchamber, to which almost certainly only family members would have had access, the plaster chimney-piece has had the centre removed, but the two stone terms by Thomas Accres that flank the chimney-piece remain. 'My Lord's Arms' – those of Bess's late husband the 6th Earl of Shrewsbury – were relegated to the chimney-piece of a turret chamber.

The figure of Desire in the overmantel in the Hill Great Chamber in the Old Hall (see page 125) is perhaps the clue to the decorative scheme of the two buildings. Here we shall look at the hangings in New Hardwick, and I lean here on the considerable research of Anthony Wells-Cole, to whom I owe a debt of gratitude.

It has long been recognized that the figures of Lucretia and Penelope in the hanging signify Bess, whose patience was sorely tried by her last husband, the 6th Earl of Shrewsbury. The figure of Desire in the Old Hall was taken from a print depicting the *Triumph of Patience* (see page 125); the overmantel was put up when Bess's husband was still living, and it then had meaning. In a needlework mounted in one of the glazed screens in the hall of New Hardwick, Lucretia is depicted as the virtuous wife: she is shown running herself through with a knife after a rapturous night with man she had believed to be her husband but who had turned out to be someone else. The original for this figure is an oil painting (artist and date unknown) in the Art Gallery of Beaune, France, in which Lucretia is not clothed, as she is in the needlework; the painting may well have been in the possession of Mary, Queen of Scots when she was the Shrewsburys' prisoner.

The two plaster panels of *Spring* and *Summer* in the high great chamber have no particular reference to Bess and neither does the figure of Cybele in the overmantel in the Paved Room attributed to Abraham Smith (see page 125) . Cybele, classically seen as a representation of the Earth, was at this time a common reference for Queen Elizabeth, who was credited with bringing prosperity to England. Of more significance is a small painting of the *Return of Ulysses to Penelope*, attributed to John Painter and dated 1570, which hangs in the state withdrawing room and was there in 1601. The background to the story is that Ulysses went off to the Trojan wars, leaving his devoted wife Penelope on her own, and was reported killed in action; Peneleope was then approached by suitors – and is shown in the picture giving her stock reply to one ('I will give you my answer when I have completed my needlework'). She is then seen by candlelight at night undoing her day's work, so that she would never have to give a response and consequently would remain a faithful wife. This has been interpreted in a number of ways but mainly as a message to Shrewsbury that his wife was as faithful and persevering as Penelope.

This, in addition to the image of Lucretia, seems to be overloading the message that Bess was a faithful wife, especially as when Bess moved into her New Hardwick she was eighty years old, and her husband had been dead for ten years. However, there is nothing in her new house in the way of fixed decoration even hinting at the faithful wife. What remains are the hangings, the needleworks and the picture: they were distant echoes of the scheme at Chatsworth. For her new house she simply rearranged the symbols; moreover she had triumphed. It is also important to note, however, that Bess had christened her youngest daughter Lucretia; this girl, born in 1557, died young. Bess's strong interest in the story of Lucretia goes back a long time, to before she married the 6th Earl of Shrewsbury or, indeed, before Hardwick.

The alabaster chimney-piece of the *Marriage of Tobias* in the Blue Room is another importation from Chatsworth, confirmed by the just decipherable outline on the central blackstone panel beneath the sculpture of the initials spelling out the names of Elizabeth (Bess), George (her husband the 6th Earl) and Mary (Queen of Scots); there is an octagonal needlework version of this in the Marian hangings at Oxburgh Hall, Norfolk. (The Marian hangings, now kept at Oxburgh Hall, are a set of needleworks mounted on hangings and stitched by Mary, Queen of Scots and Bess while Mary was in the Shrewsburys' captivity.)

Who was responsible for the detail of the New Hardwick? Anthony Wells-Cole speculates that it was Bess and John Painter together; but the input of Bess's son William should not be overlooked. As indicated earlier, William's younger brother Charles, who would have had some useful advice to offer,

The overmantel in the Paved Room showing Cybele – a compliment to Elizabeth I, whose reign brought relative peace and plenty to England – attributed to Abraham Smith

had supported his friend Gilbert Talbot in the row over Bess's husband's will and is unlikely to have been consulted. When all is said and done William was set to inherit Hardwick, and he could almost demand that his opinions should be heard.

The third storey contains the apartments of state. Had Queen Elizabeth visited Hardwick, the house would, in theory, have belonged to her, as all land was technically held by the Crown; consequently the first of the state rooms has the royal arms on the chimney-piece. Bess managed to weave in her initials ES into the royal motto 'Dieu ESt mon Droit'. There is no account for the carving of the stone surround, which suggests that it was done by a mason on wages – in all likelihood, Accres; the only reference is in May 1598 to Nayll providing the two stone plinths.[45] Turning to the final flights of the stairs leading to the high great chamber. It was the custom at the royal court to precede the great chamber, or what is now called the throne room, with a guardroom; Hampton Court is a perfect example of this layout. At Hardwick there is a large landing at the foot of the final

The chimney-piece in the state bedchamber on which Thomas Accres, the mason and sculptor, worked with the masons Nayall and Mallory in July 1599

The chimney-piece in the long gallery with the figure of Justice above, attributed to Thomas Accres; the other work surrounding it was done by the masons Nayall and Mallory in the summer of 1596.

flight of stairs before the high great chamber, which, in the case of a visiting monarch, would have served as the guardroom.

From the high great chamber the route progressed to the adjoining withdrawing chamber; this was originally of the same height as the great chamber and the long gallery, but the ceiling was lowered before 1764 when the chimney-piece was removed. The present fine alabaster sculpture of *Apollo and the Nine Muses* was put in by the 6th Duke in the nineteenth century and may well originally have been in the Muses Chamber at the Elizabethan Chatsworth. Behind the present tapestries, painted on the wall plaster, is imitation tapestry to cover a gap between the hangings and the chimney-piece. The 'seadog' table – a highly decorative draw-leaf table originally covered in gold leaf and paint – after designs by the French architect Jacques Androuet du Cerceau was in the room in 1601 and has a counterpart in the furnishings of the château of Chambord in France.

The state bedchamber has an intricate chimney-piece incorporating the door case, made of blackstone and alabaster, whose authorship has already been explored (see page 160). Above the architrave of the hearth is an alabaster figure of Charity, which, together with Justice and Mercy above the long gallery hearths, comes from a set of *Virtues* by Maarten de Vos (a painter from Antwerp) that were published as prints in the 1570s by Hans Collaert.[46] Mark Girouard has attributed the design of these chimney-pieces to Robert Smythson; we can carry this further – the two sculptures of Justice and Mercy are obviously carved by the same hand as Charity, attributed here to Thomas Accres. A date can be put on the building of the chimney-pieces of the long gallery: on 31 August 1596 an entry records payment '[to Nayll and Mallory] for hewing 19 footes of molding stuff that goeth alonng by the pylasters one the side of one of the chymneys in the galary at 4d. the foot for the galary in the new house paid mor for hewing 18 foots of molding that goeth betwyene the mantle stone and the arkatrave of that same chimney at 4d. the foot ... 6s. paid for hewing 7 foots of plynt that is sett under the base of the pylasters of the same chemeny at 1 ½ d. the foot ... 10 ½ d.'[47] The design is based on chimney-pieces in Book VII of

Sebastiano Serlio's *L'Architettura*. Like the hall chimney-piece, these are the work of several nameless masons. The elaborate chimney-piece in the state bedchamber was damaged and had been repaired by John Rhodes earlier in September 1594: 'Payed to John Roods . . . for mendinge the cheymneye in the bed chamber next to the great withdrawing chamber . . . 10s.'[48] There was little regard paid to hangings already in place: 'Payd the 23rd Julye (1596) to Bramleye the Joyner for making a portal in Tobias chamber . . . '[49] This is the room in the north turret on the second storey called the 'Tobias chamber' after the hangings in it and where Bramley is paid to make the doorframe regardless of the sawdust settling on the tapestries.

Bess had a household staff numbering eighty-two in 1596. Mrs Elizabeth Digby, a gentlewoman holding the place of housekeeper and the highest-paid member of the staff at £30 a year, was married to Mr John Digby, a gentleman servant in the household paid £5 a year. In fact Mrs Digby was far more than a housekeeper and much valued by her employer: she had the attentions of Bess's personal doctor when she was sick, and when Bess was ill she gave Bess her medicine; payments 'to Digby' show her buying fabrics for Bess's dresses. The Digbys left in March 1695 but they were back again by Christmas 1596 and thereafter stayed on until the end of Bess's life. They then lived at Mansfield Woodhouse in Notting-hamshire; John Digby became sheriff of the county in 1622 and was knighted in 1641. He saw no discredit in being in service to a great lady and was proud to wear her livery. William Reason, paid £10 a year, was another gentleman servant and Bess's man of business: he received the estate incomes on her behalf from the seventeen bailiffs who managed her estates. Timothy Pusey, paid the same salary as Reason, was not only the household steward but also Bess's personal secretary; he wrote most of her letters and knew her financial affairs inside out; he may have had a legal training.

*

The New Hardwick only really achieved its purpose after the death of Bess on 13 February 1608. In August 1619 the Prince of Wales came over from Welbeck Abbey and dined at Hardwick; it was a splendid affair with no expense spared. 'John Bertram the London Cook', with his workmen and a boy, were paid the huge sum of £12 – a little less than Abraham Smith's annual wages; and that was not all, for fifteen cooks were paid £15. 5s. 8d. Some £50 was tipped to the Prince's servants, and the court musicians played outside 'my Lady's Chamber window', no doubt on the front colonnade's flat roof. The costs were carefully recorded in the earl's account book in small, crabbed but just legible handwriting.

Other houses built by Bess of Hardwick included Oldcotes, sometimes called Owlcotes, which was begun in 1593 on a site only four miles (six kilometres) north-west of Hardwick and was intended as a house for Bess's son William. There was already an older Oldcotes Hall, which remained on the site until at least 1666. Oldcotes may have had a transverse hall and a thick spine wall but only two turrets – making it a smaller version of Hardwick. If the drawing in the Smythson Collection in the Royal Institute of British Architects library is of Oldcotes (see page 166), the house gained a third storey, which is shown in a tiny representation in a survey map of 1659, revised in 1688, by Browne and Bainbridge and confirmed by an inventory of 1666.

The inventory follows a logical course and begins in the hall, which – as can be seen from the bargain-in-great – had a ceiling twenty feet (six metres) from the ground. After the hall the inventory shows the expected ancillary chambers, with the main rooms of reception, including a gallery on the second storey. The inventory also notes that one turret had stairs and the other a chamber, and that the building was of three storeys. It is also known that above that height of twenty feet (six metres) the wallers were to be paid an extra 5s. per rood; this is another indication that the building was of three storeys – the two turrets above the leads and the chimneys earned them a further 30s. The Smythson drawing may have been a prototype before the decision was made for an extra storey.

On 8 March 1593 Bess and her son William signed a bargain-in-great together with four Plumtree brothers (Godfrey, Reynold, Ralph and George), Robert Ashmore and John Ward, all rough-wallers, for the building of a smaller Hardwick-type house at Oldcotes, or Owlcotes. The document is the only surviving bargain-in-great from the Hardwick building programme and gives us a very good idea of the details of these contracts (see Appendix III).

One accident at Oldcotes is reported in a letter dated 17 October 1597 from Bess's half-sister Elizabeth Wingfield to her niece, Mary Countess of Shrewsbury, in which she described the fall of a great beam bringing down two others; she does not report anyone being hurt.[50]

After Bess's death William moved into Hardwick Hall and Oldcotes was left empty; when it was sold in 1641 by the 1st Earl of Devonshire's widow to the second son of the Earl of Kingston it was referred to as being 'two messuages [dwellings] one of them called the New House and the other the Old House . . .'[51] It was demolished in the late seventeenth or early eighteenth century. Today there is little left of Oldcotes, but in the garden of the farmhouse on the site there is a stone alcove similar to the two shown in the Smythson drawing (see page 166), a few fragments of stone strapwork and some courtyard walls.

All six of the men signing the bargain-in-great had worked at both Old Hardwick and at New Hardwick; they left in May 1593 for Oldcotes. Ashmore, by then classified as a mason, was the first to return to Hardwick in the autumn of 1595; at Oldcotes his work would have consisted of hewing stone for windows, doors, cornices and strapwork decoration. The other five returned to Hardwick by the summer of 1596, their contract complete and the Oldcotes site left to joiners and carpenters – as might be guessed by the account of the accident with the beam.

Ashmore's mark on his will is a large square-topped A; on the Oldcotes bargain it is the same, only upside down. This mark does not appear on any stonework at Old and New Hardwick. In any event both he and Ward were paid in the servants' wages: 10s. for the half-year. His mason's mark would consequently not appear on stonework. In the Senior Survey for 1618 Ashmore rented a house and yard at Edensore from the Earl of Devonshire, together with five acres (two hectares) of arable land. Ashmore seems to have been very much the junior partner of the Oldcotes bargain. Reynold Plumtree, the leader, on his death in 1631 left an inventory (Appendix II) valued at the large sum of £70 and was renting a farm of sixty-six acres (twenty-six hectares); he can be said to have prospered.

Another building part financed by Bess at this time was begun in 1597 by Bess's third son, Sir Charles Cavendish, at Kirkby-in-Ashfield in Nottinghamshire, a quarter-mile (four hundred metres) from his home. It was never completed. That year Bess gave Charles £300 and another £100 in March 1599.[52] Sir Charles's relationship with his mother was strained because of his unfailing support for his friend Gilbert Talbot, with whom Bess had fallen out over the slow administration the will of his father (the 6th Earl of Shrewsbury). Sir Charles's wealth came from his second wife, Catherine Ogle, daughter of Lord Ogle – whose lands were in Northumbria. The building was abandoned after Charles, with his brother-in-law Henry Ogle, accompanied by his page Lancelot Ogle, were attacked by twenty mounted men led by Sir John Stanhope in November 1599. Swords were drawn and pistols fired. Sir Charles's horse fell, and he was shot twice, once in the thigh. Then Sir Charles, Henry and Lancelot Ogle fought back. Six attackers and two of the band were killed, causing the party to make off.

The Stanhope family was based at Shelford on the river Trent in Nottinghamshire and had quarrelled with Gilbert Talbot. The vendetta went back to 1592 when Sir Thomas Stanhope, John's father and another difficult man, was charged with having put a weir across the river Trent near Shelford to the detriment of navigation and depriving thirty-nine

Façade of an unidentified two-storey house, possibly a proposal by Robert Smythson for Oldcotes; in the garden of the farmhouse now on the site of Oldcotes there is a stone alcove similar to the two on either side of the entrance steps in this drawing.

Detail from the Browne and Bainbridge survey of Oldcotes of 1659, revised in 1688, showing a three-storey building with a similar façade to that shown on the drawing above

villages further downriver of fish.[53] Both Gilbert Talbot and his father, the 6th Earl of Shrewsbury, had earlier given Sir Thomas permission to construct the weir. By 1592 the old Earl was dead, and Gilbert now took a contrary view, which clearly irritated Stanhope. The dispute went to the Privy Council, and finally to the Star Chamber; in April 1593 the weir was destroyed.

However, there was more to the argument: Gilbert Talbot, whose father and grandfather had been Lords-Lieutenant of Nottinghamshire, expected to inherit the post, but Sir John Stanhope was shortlisted as a candidate, clearly damaging Gilbert Talbot's pride. Sir Thomas died in 1596, and his heir, Sir John Stanhope, carried on the vendetta. Sir Charles Cavendish had supported his friend Gilbert Talbot, and, at the height of the weir affair, he had felt obliged to defend Gilbert's name by challenging Sir John Stanhope to a duel with rapiers in London, at a time when Cavendish was staying with Gilbert Talbot. When Stanhope turned up wearing a heavily quilted doublet the challenge turned to farce; Stanhope claimed that he had a cold and that the padding was for warmth, and Sir Charles jokingly offered him his own doublet. The duellists' two seconds agreed that it was an unequal contest, and honour was seemingly satisfied.

The affray at Kirkby caused Sir Charles to halt his new building and shortly afterwards the house was abandoned. Whatever was there was used as a quarry in 1612 when Charles started his new house at Bolsover Castle.

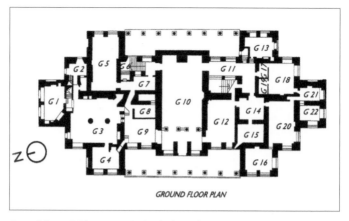

GROUND FLOOR PLAN

Ground floor: G1 The pastry; G2 Dry larder with room over.; G3 Kitchen; G4
Scullery with chamber over; G5 Low chapel; G8 Buttery; G9 Serving place; G10
Hall; G12 Pantry; G13 Low banqueting house; G14 Room whear pantler must lye;
G15 Lytle rome where plat must be; G18 Parlour next to the Evidence House; Mr
Cavendish's chamber; G19 Little room in the chamber next to the Evidence House;
G20 Room/parlour where Accres worketh; G21 and G22 Evidence houses

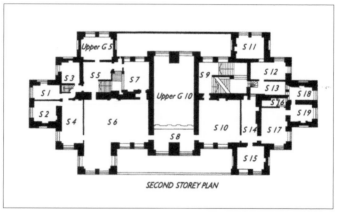

SECOND STOREY PLAN

Second storey: S2 Chamber over pastry, Tobias chamber; S3 Stair chamber,
chamber next to the foot of wooden stairs, chamber where the *Story of Jacob*
hangs; S5 Upper/over chapel, Half-pace between chapel and Weyricks Stairs;
S6 Low great chamber over kitchen; S7 Little dining chamber; S10 Square great
chamber, low great chamber, low great chamber over pantry, chamber where
my lady's arms are; S11 Chamber over low banquetting house, Ladie Arbells
chamber; S15 Chamber where my Lords Arms are, turret within square
chamber; S16 Brushing/pallett place, a little room within my Ladies Chamber;
S17 Chamber over parlour where Accres worketh, chamber where Abraham's
Terms are, my Ladies Bedchamber

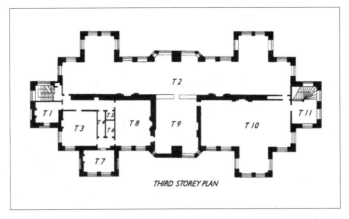

THIRD STOREY PLAN

Third storey: T2 Gallery; T3 Second chamber; Pearl bedchamber; T5 First of two stool places; T6 Second of two stool places; T8 Best bedchamber, bedchamber next to great withdrawing chamber; T9 Withdrawing chamber, great withdrawing chamber over hall; T10 High great chamber, great chamber

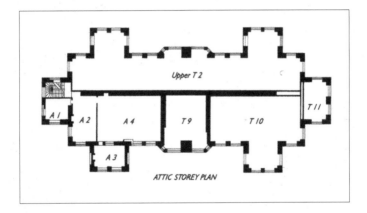

ATTIC STOREY PLAN

Attic storey ('The uppermost rooms next the leads'): A1 Room in the stairs next to the leads; A3 Room over the scullery; A4 Room next to the leads over the kitchen

Above and left: Floor plans for Hardwick Hall, based on the 1601 inventory and the building accounts; those rooms mentioned in this book – with their original descriptions from the inventory and accounts – are shown in the keys accompanying the plans. These are redrawn from plans published in *The Building of Hardwick Hall, Pt 2: The New Hall, 1591–8*, edited by David N. Durant and Philip Riden, Chesterfield: Derbyshire Record Society, 1984.

An aerial view of Bolsover Castle taken from the north-west, showing the Little Castle to left overlooking the Fountain Court and the Terrace Range in the foreground with the Riding House behind it

7

BOLSOVER CASTLE
IN THE CARE OF ENGLISH HERITAGE

Bess of Harwick's youngest son, Sir Charles Cavendish, built Bolsover Castle from 1612 onwards, first with Robert Smythson and then his son John as architects. The castle is a very impressive building – particularly when approached from the nearby M1 motorway: a three-storey square tower backed by a long range, it stands high on top of a hill surrounded by fields, with the small town of Bolsover hidden behind the castle. Bolsover was a mining town in Bess's day, but the local coal industry is no more. The building was never intended to be Sir Charles's principal residence, for he owned Welbeck Abbey just six miles (ten kilometres) distant as the crow flies: he planned Bolsover as a fantasy castle, recalling the imaginary world of knightly chivalry as described in English poet Edmund Spenser's *The Faerie Queene* (1590–6) and Italian poet Ludovico Ariosto's *Orlando Furioso* (*Roland Maddened*; 1532). Even today one's imagination can ride unbridled, conjuring an image of tournaments with armoured knights in the courtyard. It was an amazing conception and still is – we are lucky that it has survived. The mural decoration is the only complete scheme existing in England from that time.

Bolsover was not part of Bess's own estates, but by her marriage agreement she had the use of it for her lifetime. It was Talbot land, acquired in 1553 by the 5th Earl of Shrewsbury.[1] Sir Charles and Gilbert Talbot, later 7th Earl of Shrewsbury, were brought up together and had travelled abroad together, so Charles was familiar with architectural styles in Europe. On the land was a ruined Norman castle surrounded by a medieval curtain wall. Sir Charles made a legal arrangement with Gilbert under which the land was to be rented to Charles on the death of his mother. She died in 1608, and Charles took on the property's rental. Quite what he had in mind for his acquisition is not clear; nevertheless he bought the property from Gilbert before 1612. In 1597 he began renting Welbeck Abbey from Gilbert, buying it from him nine years later, when it became his principal home.[2] Charles began building what came to be called the 'Little Castle' to distinguish it from the greater part of the other, mainly later, buildings on the site.

The need for huge quantities of water in building operations was touched on in the Introduction; at Bolsover there was a problem in that even though a Norman castle was built there no source of water could be found within the walls. There was 'the dark well' at the foot of the cliff on the north side of the building, but this was probably a small pool of water around which a wall was built. Early in the surviving building accounts for Bolsover (in February 1613) there is a payment for 'Labourers taking down of the old walls and some time at the spring against the Castle'. This refers to two quite different jobs – taking down old walls and work at the spring below the castle. In the same period there is another reference: 'Pd Jo Spittellhouse for 8 days at the spring against the Castle 6s. 4d.', immediately followed by 'Pd the carpenter for fitting of punch wood for the spring 18d.'.[3] At Bolsover, springs occur where the limestone of the escarpment overlies the marls at its foot.[4] Water was carried to the building site in buckets by labourers paid 7d. a day, which must have been gruelling work. An entry for April 1613, when outside work recommenced after the winter, reads 'Pd. for two well ropes for the well for drawing water 8s.' By the end of January 1614, 'Pd. for 2 new buckets for the Castle well. 22d.'[5]

*

The building accounts for Bolsover survive from 2 November 1612 to 26 March 1614, by which time the Little Castle was up to ground-floor level.[6] By this date Robert Smythson was an old man in his late seventies; nevertheless Mark Girouard has argued convincingly that because of the compact nature of the planning Smythson must have had a hand in the design of the building.[7] The name of Robert's son, John Smythson, appears (mainly fortnightly) in the accounts, where he is paid for meals for himself and provender for his horse; he would, of course, have been paid a wage in the household accounts. He follows in his father's career: he is the 'architector and survayor' of the building. There is no indication in the accounts as to who is the clerk of works keeping the accounts and paying the workers. The accounts show only regular two-weekly payments after 23 January 1613. Before that date the accounts are written up in retrospect over longer intervals of time.

Labourers, alternating as quarrymen, were paid 7d. by the day; freemasons (the term used in the accounts) were generally paid on piecework but when paid by the day received 10–12d.; stone-layers received the same rate when paid by the day. Along with masons, stone-layers were the highest-paid workers, although this depended on the type of work: laying the vaulting in the beer cellar, for example, paid the higher rate of 12d., whereas other work, such as building a wall, was paid at 10d. a day. Carpenters were also paid on piecework, but there is no separate classification for joiners; carpenters were paid for felling trees and making doors, sawyers for cutting planks in sawpits. Twenty-four women were paid 3d. or sometimes 4d. a day and five girls 2d. a day, while boys were better rewarded with 2d., 3d. or 4d. a day. There is no indication that any of the skilled craftsmen took out bargains-in-great and consequently there are few masons' marks, the exception being in the case of special items such as alcoves on the stairs, a number of door cases and window jambs. Nine masons' marks at Bolsover are repeated at Worksop Manor Lodge (1598) and three at Charlcote Park, Warwickshire (1558).

When the accounts open masons were hewing and cutting stone at

A distant view of Bolsover Castle from the north-west

The entrance front of the Little Castle; the figure of Hercules supporting the balcony is the introduction to the interior decoration.

the principal sandstone quarry at Shuttlewood, three miles (five kilometres) north-west of the building site, ready for transporting to the castle. The freemasons working at Shuttlewood (Richard Barham and Goodwin and their 'fellows') did not do any work at the castle site. Correspondingly, Thomas Raffell and Symson (masons at the castle) never cut any stone at Shuttlewood. A second quarry in Bolsover called 'Town Quarry' was used occasionally: it produced a lower-quality stone that was used for walling. Thatched masons' lodges at Shuttlewood and the town quarry were being erected for the masons to work under. High-quality stone was obtained later from a quarry at Bolsover Moor, about a mile (1.6 kilometres) north-east of the town; oven stone was quarried there in April 1613.[8] Another source of stone was from the Kirkby-in-Ashfield site where Sir Charles had stopped work after being attacked (see Chapter 6). In December 1613 thirty loads of stone were dragged from Kirkby-in-Ashfield, and in January 1614 a further sixty-four loads were hauled from there. Payments were made in February to masons for cleaning and adapting 'window stuff' brought from Kirkby-in-Ashfield. Also in February another fifty-eight loads of ashlar were hauled from Ashfield,[9] making a total of one hundred and fifty-two loads.

Forty loads of limestone, used for making mortar and plaster, were quarried 'beyond the town'. Lime kilns were built and coal transported for firing the kilns. On 23 January 1613 there was a payment of 2s. 6d. to 'the brickman that came from Wollaton as given by my master per me'.[10] This may have been an advisory visit; however, some bricks were used at Bolsover in relieving arches over doorways and windows, and some interior walls on the top storey were made of brick of varying dates. In addition, seven labourers were paid a total of 29s. 7d. for digging foundations, work that continued until mid March, before the layers could 'cast' (lay) the foundations after the winter closedown. Meanwhile, the masons were busy at Shuttlewood hewing ashlar for sixteen arch stones in the kitchen ranges[11] of the castle – all of which can still be seen today. Additionally, corbels, quoins and paving were cut, ready to go into the kitchen when the walls were up. Erecting the vaults was a complicated business because the stone had to be supported on scaffolding and 'centres' (temporary wooden supports beneath arches and vaults) until the lime mortar was firmly set. It also required skilled carpenters, because the 'form' or mould for the centres had to be accurate – otherwise the vaulting would be uneven. However, in the kitchens at Bolsover the vaults are plastered, which covered any misalignments. Above stairs the perfect stone vaulting is clearly visible.

The accounts give no indication of what was left of the old castle or exactly what was on the site; that foundations were dug suggests that there was nothing useful left standing. However, there is a reference to 'taking down of window stuff . . . out of the old walls'.[12] In May foundations were still being dug, but this is likely to have been for the north end of the terrace range, for by that month the vaults were being built in the Little Castle kitchens.

The Norman castle at Bolsover had been besieged in 1215 during the Barons' Revolt against King John, when one of the towers in the curtain wall was breached and the castle surrendered. Thereafter it is likely that the inhabitants of the town used the castle as a quarry. Three entries in the building accounts suggest that the castle was in ruins. On 11 December 1613 an entry reads 'Labourers work at taking down of Castle wall. Pd Tho Kichen and his sons for pulling down of one part of the old Castle wall 13s. 6d.'.[13] An entry for 25 December 1613 reads 'Labourers at taking down the old walls. Pd Kichen his fellows for taking down of window stuff and ashlar out of the old walls and sorting it into loads 33s. 6d. Pd Wyldesmithe for pulling down of one part of the Castle wall at 4s. the yard 6s.'[14] (The date of the entry does not mean that the labourers were working on Christmas Day; this is only an accounting date for work done in the preceding two weeks.) Then an entry for 29 January 1614 reads 'Task work at taking down of the old wall at Castle: Pd Kichen and Rogers for their task in the taking down of the old wall at Castle 12s. Pd Wyldesmithe [labourer] in full payment of the like work 13s. 6d.'[15] Dr Richard Sheppard of Trent and Peak

The Fountain Court of Bolsover Castle with the Venus Fountain
in the foreground; the balcony marks the Elysian Room.

Archaeology at the University of Nottingham claims that the walls surrounding the Fountain Court (see above) are not medieval but that medieval
stonework was used when they were rebuilt.[16]

There are references to 'the Old House' being restored. An entry for 12
February 1614 reads, 'Work done for the old chimney: Pd Halle for working of stuff for the old chimneys of the old house 6s. 5d.'[17] Halle was a
skilled freemason and in February would have been working inside on
chimney-pieces. Another entry for 12 February 1614 records 'Pd Glossope
for digging of the way for the old larder stair 2s. 8d.' On the same date
three layers were 'paid £2 11s. 6d. for 26 days work . . . at the old house'.[18]
On 12 March 1614 the entry says 'Layers at the larder and cellar of the old
house: Pd Raffell [mason] for 8 days 8s. Pd Thos Raffell for 10 days 8s. 4d.
Pd Thos Woode for 7 days 7s.'[19] and 'Layers at the larder and cellar of the
old house' and three labourers were paid 23s. 4d. for twenty-five days
work. Also on 12 March four labourers were paid 'for serving the layers at
the old house 22s. 6d.', then followed the last payment in the accounts on

12 March 1614, 'Pd the glazier of Mannffeld for 40 foot of new for the old house and mending the rest 31s. 9d.'[20] Glass was put in only when the heavy work was completed.

Where was 'the Old House'? Dr Sheppard has pointed out that the angled building at the north end of the terrace range stands in the castle ditch and, moreover, cannot stylistically be medieval in origin. The ditch was the dry moat outside the walls of the original castle's inner bailey. Archaeological surveys commissioned by English Heritage are piecemeal. Dr Sheppard has found nothing in the Fountain Court indicating the foundations of an earlier substantial building. In the angled building a door lintel in the cellar and a fireplace in the second storey survive: each has four-centred moulded arches, an Elizabethan feature.[21] Both are in the transverse interior wall, which contains five flues – it is an original wall. Its origins probably lie after 1553, when the 5th Earl bought the land, and before 1568, when Bolsover was passed to Bess for her lifetime under her marriage agreement with the 6th Earl. The Old House was built outside the ruined castle, perhaps to accommodate a bailiff who was overseeing the estate. One thing is certain: Bess would not have spent money building a house on land that did not belong to her.

By 1614 this building could quite easily have been called 'the Old House' and have been in need of repair. However, by the time the terrace range was planned the exterior walls of the Old House did not match those of the new range and three exterior walls of the Old House were pulled down to ground level, leaving only interior walls standing. The exterior walls were rebuilt with matching string courses (projecting horizontal lines of decorative stone on the exterior, usually marking floor levels), hood moulds (dripstones above windows) and window mouldings. The rebuilding was marked by initialled and dated stubs (for the years 1629 and 1630) in the west elevation of the Old House.[22] The lower courses of the north wall, from the first string course to ground level, are built of a different grey stone and may be the base of the original walls. It was not necessary to rebuild the centre transverse wall, so it was left in place. The basement is also possibly original to the Old House. The south wall raises problems: a jamb of a door at third-storey level in the transverse wall disappears into the south wall, which has been refaced. An original south wall (then an exterior wall) may be behind the refacing.[23]

Old Robert Smythson died in 1614 aged seventy-nine and was buried in his home village of Wollaton. Sir Charles never saw the achievement of his fantasy Little Castle because he died when the building work was completed but not the interior decoration. His heir William became Viscount Mansfield in 1620 and Earl of Newcastle upon Tyne in 1628. He was appointed Governor to the Prince of Wales, later Charles II, in 1638, then became Marquess of Newcastle upon Tyne in 1643 and finally Duke of Newcastle upon Tyne in 1665. It was left to William to complete what his father had begun, and the interior of the castle is mainly William's creation.

Sir Charles Cavendish died at Welbeck Abbey on 29 March 1617, aged sixty-five, when work was still going on at the Little Castle. Before his death he had discussed with his children his monument and its details. He was buried at St Mary's Church, Bolsover, and his monument is in the Cavendish Chapel commemorating both Sir Charles and his second wife, Catherine, who died in 1627. The finer stone carving of the decoration was ordered from Southwark.[24] His epitaph is a short poem composed by Ben Jonson. In 1618 Ben Jonson walked from London to Edinburgh with a companion who kept a diary of the journey which lasted nearly two months. The diary tells of a stopover at Welbeck Abbey by Jonson and his companion in August that year, when Sir William Cavendish took Jonson over the Bolsover to meet 'one Smithsonn an excellent architect, who was to consult with Mr Jonson about the erection of a Tomb for Sir Williams father, for which my gossip [Jonson] was to make an Epitaph'. The monument was therefore designed by John Smythson.[25]

The hall chimney-piece is an example of earlier work, however: it is dated 1616 at the top and would have been Sir Charles's choice – like the others in the castle, it is based on designs by the Italian architect Sebastiano Serlio. The fireplace is Tuscan, that in the pillar parlour Doric, while in the star chamber it is correctly Ionic – all in the right classical order. In this case the orders marked not different floors, as usually, but social levels – the pillar parlour, where the family ate, was socially superior to the hall, where the servants ate, but both were on the ground floor. On the top storey a chimney-piece has the arms of Sir Charles and also his arms impaling those of his second wife Catherine Ogle. This suggests that these chimney-pieces in the hall, the star chamber and the bedchamber in the north-west corner of the top storey were in place before Sir Charles died in 1617. Additionally, paint research shows an earlier decorative scheme overpainted by William's decorative format. Obviously this was his father's work, including plain doors of a deep red colour, reflecting the taste of the early seventeenth century.

Although the building accounts stop in March 1614, two invaluable sources provide evidence of what followed. Sir Charles's heir William, by then the Marquess of Newcastle, went into exile during the Commonwealth (1651–60) following the English Civil War (1642–51) and while abroad published a best-seller in French in 1658. Called *Methode et Invention Nouvelle de Dresser les Chevaux*, the book was translated into English and published in 1743 as *A General System of Horsemanship*. Prints in the volume depict the marquess showing off his prancing horses doing astonishing caprioles, bottards and groupades (all types of leap) while sitting firmly and serenely in the saddle. These escapades are shown against background images of his houses. Drawings for Bolsover, which are the basis for the prints, are kept at Renishaw Hall, Derbyshire; they show minor variations from the prints. The drawings are attributed by Mark Girouard to Alexander Keirincx, who worked for William.[26]

The Old House is joined to the Fountain Court by an arch dating to the 1660s. There is a straight joint to ground-floor level where the north end of the terrace building abuts it, while on the side of the great court there is

Above: Plate 35 from *A General System of Horsemanship* (1743) by William Cavendish, Marquess of Newcastle, clearly shows the Terrace Range, and at the north end, behind the horse's head, is the 'Old House' rebuilt, shown with incorrect perspective. Compare the above with the photograph (left) of the Terrace Range from the north, showing the rebuilt 'Old House' in the foreground.

no straight joint. In 1947 the doorway giving on to the arch at second-storey level was reported to have the date 1633 carved above it, but this has since weathered away.[27] A print of Bolsover in 1727 by engraver and printer Samuel Buck shows the Old House as a single-gabled building detached from a four-gabled building that differs from what is there today. Was it really detached? A date after 1630 fits in with the dated stubs (see page 178) on the west elevation (the latest of these is 1630). There was then no arch connecting the Old House with the wall walk; the original arch, as we have seen, dates from 1633, therefore the drawings at Renishaw Hall can be dated to 1630–2. Plate 35 from *A General System of Horsemanship* (see page 181) shows the terrace range: if this is compared with the same view today, we see that there has been some confusion: the north end of the range shows the west façade of the Old House but facing north. However, the point of the print was not architectural accuracy but to show 'Monseigneur le Marquis acheval' ('the Marquess on horseback'), performing 'groupades' with total composure in an imposing setting.

An entry in the accounts in September 1613 records: 'Grates for the great cellar. Pd Boukett the smith for 12 grates for the great cellar 36s.'[28] However, as there is no cellar, either in the Little Castle or the Old House, big enough for twelve drains, the entry must refer to a cellar in the terrace range, which indicates that early work was carried out at the north end of this range. A later entry makes it clear that 'grates' are to cover drains in the floor.

A view of the Old House as seen from the great court in Plate 30 of *A General System of Horsemanship* shows it as an angled building of two storeys plus gabled attic, standing next to a narrow building of three storeys plus attic. Both are still there, although the narrow building was later rebuilt to match its neighbour's Dutch gable. The Old House has square stone studs projecting on the west façade, originally dated and initialled M.C. 1629, M.W. 1630, E.L. 1630, G.D. 1629, C.D. 1629, H.S. 1629; in the years since around 1980 the initials have been weathered away. (The stone has weathered quickly here, probably because of smoke emitted by a local factory.) The studs were set in what were scaffolding putt holes in 1629–30. None of the initials coincide with any of the craftsmen from fifteen years earlier in the building accounts, although it has been suggested that H.S. could refer to John Smythson's son, Huntingdon. A further suggestion is that because the studs are positioned low on the walls this was the level to which an earlier building had been demolished for

Plate 33 from the English edition of *A General System of Horsemanship*, published in 1743; the well head for the water supply, the four-storey turret on the right, was present by 1630–2.

rebuilding in 1629.[29] The prints in *A General System of Horsemanship* do not show the north end of the wing as it is today, and a print of 1698 by Dutch draughtsmen Leonard Knyff and Jan Kip is different again. Obviously some building and rebuilding has been carried out on the north end of the terrace range.

Plate 33 in *A General System of Horsemanship* shows, adjacent to the north side of the castle and near the foot of the cliff on which it stands, a small castellated building of four storeys with a pipe joining it to the kitchen in the castle (see above). The building probably contained a pump that lifted water from a well to a cistern at the top of the building. This was the water supply by 1630, and it stands on a site near the 'dark well'. The Revd Hamilton Grey, who lived with his wife in the castle from 1829 until his death in 1866, mentioned 'the remains of a well. Which was evidently another source of water supply to the Castle; it is protected by an arched stone roof. On one of the stones inside is the date 1622.'[30] Of the same date are four conduit houses built to bring water half a mile (eight hundred metres) from Spittal Green south of the Castle.

Nothing is known about the personal details of the masons, carpenters, labourers and others employed in the building of the Little Castle or of the craftsmen who completed it. Nor do we know about those who later built the long north terrace range and the riding house. The plans for the Little Castle and the later buildings are shown at the end of the chapter (see pages 200–1).

We divert here back to the building accounts that record the visit of John Smythson with two gentlemen servants from William's household – Mr Henry Luken, on two occasions, and Mr George Kellam in August and September 1613.[31] They performed much the same service in the household as Timothy Pusey and William Reason had in Bess of Hardwick's household. What service they were performing at Bolsover is never explained, but Luken was there when the 'brickman' came from Wollaton. Luken is the author of the verses on Sir Charles Cavendish's tomb, added to on the death of Lady Catherine in 1629. Over the time of the building of the Little Castle he was employed on estate business. Described in the report of 'The King and Queene's Entertainment at Bolsouer, July 1634' as a 'mathematician',[32] he was qualified as a surveyor and able to produce estate maps. He lived in the Welbeck household and would have occupied a place at the table of the upper servants in the hall. Later, possibly on retirement, he was awarded the tenancy of Sookholme Hall. He was reported to be a 'melancholy man' and is said to have committed suicide in 1630.[33]

The castle's interior was mainly the work of William Cavendish. How was it that in his twenties he was able to put together such a sophisticated scheme of decoration? He was educated at home by tutors before going on to St John's College, Cambridge, in 1608, but he would have learned nothing there to give him his later appreciation of fine art. He was made a knight of the bath in 1610 when Prince Henry was created Prince of Wales. In 1612 William, then nineteen, went to Italy with his younger brother Charles in the company of Sir Henry Wotton, who was ambassador extraordinaire to the Duke of Savoy. The point of the journey was to discuss a possible marriage between Henry, Prince of Wales, and the Duke of Savoy's daughter. It all came to nothing; Henry died that year in November. However, William went with a high-ranking party and was well received. The party left England on 18 March 1612: it comprised Wotton, William Cavendish – now Sir William – Charles Cavendish 'and some other gentlemen there are of meaner sort'.[34] Sir Robert Rich, who had studied *haute école* in Paris under the celebrated Antoine de Pluvinel, joined the party in France. (*Haute école* was the training of horses to perform, and was originally based on the maneouvres used by mounted warriors in battle.) Wotton had an abiding interest in architecture and published his influential book *Elements of Architecture* in 1624. Sir William was thus travelling with sophisticated and knowledgeable companions. Landing at Boulogne and going by way of Lyon and Turin they eventually received a royal welcome from the Duke of Savoy.

The party returned via Milan, when they may have visited Venice, but they almost certainly went to the Palazzo Te in Mantua. Circumstantial evidence indicates that Sir William visited the palazzo and used the experience to dramatic effect at Bolsover.[35] There he would have seen the Sala dei Giganti (Room of the Giants) there that contains a spectacular *trompe-l'œil* effect in which painting and architecture overrun one other, as a similar, albeit less impressive, effect is achieved in the hall at Bolsover. Did the Sala dei Cavalli (Room of the Horses), with its frescoed portraits of horses, inspire the paintings of the horses on the bosses of the vaults in the pillar parlour at Bolsover? Maybe – we shall never know. At Welbeck there were, and still are, life-size paintings of horses. Returning home, the party came through Basle and Cologne; the travellers were in Cologne on 12 July 1612 and back in England by the end of the month. It was a whirlwind visit but it must have made a great impression on the two young men.

Later in his life William showed an interest in everything. During his voluntary exile he was host in Paris when Descartes, the philosopher, and others came to dinner. He had an intimate friendship with the English philosopher Thomas Hobbes. He made amateur chemical experiments with his chaplain at Bolsover, was particularly interested in telescopes and optical instruments, and he had a love of music. None of this, except for music, was obvious before his exile. Thomas Howard, the Earl of Arundel, Sir William's first cousin by marriage, married Alathea Talbot, his brother-in-law's daughter, an association that cannot be overlooked; from the earl Sir William would have gained insight into architecture, one of Arundel's great interests. Above all was his lifelong passion for horses and the *haute école*. Yet none of this really explains how he and his brother Charles, who must have been closely involved, gained the sophisticated taste demonstrated in the castle interior.

It has already been suggested that Sir Charles Cavendish was inspired by the chivalric exploits described in Spenser's *The Faerie Queene* and Ariosto's *Orlando Furioso*. However, there is nothing of either work in the painted interior of Bolsover: whatever plans Sir Charles had had, William took his own direction and followed his own ideas. The first room in the castle, the ante-room, has lunette paintings representing the elements – Earth, Fire and Water are present, but Air is missing and the god Mercury takes its place. These are derived from engravings by Antwerp artist Pieter Jode.

What follows in the hall is a tour de force of *trompe-l'œil*: four *Labours of Hercules* (based on prints after works by Italian artist Antonio Tempesta, published in 1608) are painted in pointed wall arches that continue the lines of the ceiling vaults – as if the drama were taking place in the hall. These could be by John Balechous – the date of his death is not known, but it is known that his son John Painter succeeded him at the New Inn in 1618.[36] A John Painter was working at Old Hardwick in 1620–1, so it is more likely to have been his son who may have worked at Bolsover. Did William see himself as Hercules? Certainly the images all concern the overpowering of animal passion – his wife, in her biography of her husband, referred to him as being 'always a great master of his Passions'.[37]

The hall was where the servants ate and the pillar parlour, originally the lower dining chamber, was where William and his guests dined; the paintings in the lunettes in the pillar parlour appropriately echo this in that they depict the five senses – Sight, Touch, Hearing, Scent and Taste. The images come from prints published in 1561 by Dutch engraver Cornelis Cort. Also in the pillar parlour is a painting, dated 1619, of putti carrying symbols of Christ's Passion – judging from the style, all are by a hand other than that of Balechous. The chimney-piece can be dated by the heraldry carved on it as being between late 1618 and late 1620: it shows William's Cavendish arms impaling those of Basset, but there is no viscount's coronet – William's first wife, whom he married in 1618, was Elizabeth Basset; he became Viscount Mansfield in 1620. However, on the side of the chimney-piece are two crests surmounted by a viscount's coronet that were added after 1620.

The decoration of this room suffered badly in restorations carried out in 1970 when the original painting, graining and gilding on the panels were stripped. However, in 1999 they were restored as nearly as possible to the original conception. Before that, in 1965, the Little Castle was found to be slipping down the hill, and drastic repairs were carried out to remedy the resulting damage to the structure: steel rods were inserted through the building from each external wall, necessitating the drilling of 4½-inch (11.4-centimetre) holes through the masonry. The drilling required the use of a great deal of water, which leaked through the stonework and damaged the wall paintings.

Up on the third storey, in the south-east chamber, the chimney-piece is decorated with musical instruments – signifying William's musical passion. In the north-west chamber are the arms of his father and Catherine Ogle from before Charles's death in 1617.

Between 1618 and 1619 John Smythson was in London. He stayed at Arundel House and was probably sent by his patron – the Earl of Arundel was Sir William Cavendish's first cousin by marriage. From the drawings in the Smythson Collection at the Royal Institute of British Architects library we can see the effect this visit had on the Little Castle: the balcony over the front door of the castle and outside the Elysian Room are adapted from a balcony and gateway at Arundel House. Originally the balcony to the Elysian Room had a stone balustrade, but this was later replaced by the present iron railing. The pattern of a ceiling at Theobalds in Hertford-shire (begun by William Cecil, Lord Burghley, the queen's leading states-man, in 1564 and enlarged in the 1570s) was used for the panelling of the pillar parlour.

The star chamber was the most splendid room in the castle and was the main reception room for important guests. Its impressive chimney-piece carries not the Cavendish arms but those of Gilbert Talbot, 7th Earl of Shrews-bury, Sir Charles' great friend and brother-in-law – a sincere compliment to his friend. Both men died in 1617 within a year of each other, and it is a fair guess that the chimney-piece dates from 1616. On the south and west walls the subjects, painted on wood panels, are taken mainly from the Old and New Testaments, the exception being two men in armour. A half-panel of Moses has the date 1621 at the foot of his tablet of stone. Two panels, of saints Ursula and Catherine, are modern copies; the originals were stolen in the 1970s together with a panel originally in the north-west corner of a boy wearing a hat and carrying a cat.[38] The paintings are by no means high art and one is left to wonder why anyone would take the trouble to steal three of them. Of the painting of the *Boy with Cat* something more can be said: it was seen but not photographed and recognized as being similar to a print by the French engraver François Langlois (*Boy with Bagpipes*), which had been taken from a painting by the French artist Claude Vignon. Furthermore, there is a paint-ing of Langlois by Vignon at Althrop House, Northamptonshire. The earliest works by Vignon are from 1618 and Langlois, born in Chartres but a publisher of prints in the Netherlands, was a friend of the artist.[39]

The panels between the windows show a bearded King Solomon and a younger King David. The remaining saints and martyrs carry their attributes: Saint Catherine has her wheel, Saint Peter his keys. These are taken from prints produced by the Italian engraver Marcantonio Raimondi; there is a set of these prints at Chatsworth, but that may be pure coincidence. In the corner to the right of the fireplace are two very different figures in jousting armour, which must be likenesses of Sir Charles's son William on the left (by that time 1st Viscount Mansfield) and perhaps his younger brother Charles Cavendish.[40] We know tantalizingly little about this Charles; we are told by the Earl of Clarendon in his autobiography that he met Charles in Antwerp during their exile and found him to be 'one of the most extraordinary persons of that age'. Charles was blessed with limitless charm but suffered from the disadvantage of being a dwarf; Clarendon wrote 'He had all the disadvantages imaginable . . . which was not only of so small a size that it drew the eyes of men upon him, but with such deformity in his little person . . . that was apter to raise contempt.' Nevertheless, Clarendon went on, 'in this unhandsome or homely habitation, there was a mind and soul lodged that was very lovely and beautiful . . .'[41] It was entirely because of Charles that the marquess's estates (William was created a marquess in 1642) were kept intact until the Restoration and the marquess's eventual return. Charles was knighted in 1619 when King James I and Prince Charles stayed at Welbeck Abbey; the going rate for a knighthood was £30.

The Marble Closet off the Star Chamber was richly furnished. According to an inventory made *c.* 1676 it held '1 sett of cremsson taffetie hangings, 2 backt chares, two couches with 2 taffity quilts, 1 picttur, 2 stands & 1 table, 1 looking glas, 1 irron grate'.[42] The room today, even without furnishings, still appears luxurious and has four lunettes painted on canvas rather than directly on the plaster. Two have distinct echoes of Hardwick Hall: Justice and Prudence are represented by two nude female figures, Fortitude and Patience are again two nude figures. These are followed by Faith and Hope. The series of six comes from *The United Virtues* engraved by Dutch printmaker Hendrix Goltzius. The missing panel from this set is of Concord and Peace; in its place over the window are cherubs' heads, which have no relevance to the series. The architectural historian Timothy Raylor has suggested that the king and queen standing on the balcony of the Marble Closet symbolized the missing figures Concord and Peace.[43] The fact that the lunettes are on canvas may indicate that they are not of the same date as the rest of the interior decoration and were inserted later, and the cherubs' heads over the window, also on canvas, might be the remains of the original decoration for this closet. Their frames are decorated with 'gadrooning', a style associated with the period of the Restoration of the monarchy and therefore with a date of 1660 or later, and are not necessarily contemporary with the canvases. The subjects would have excited licentious soldiers and if left in place would certainly have been damaged; they could have been taken out of the original frames and put away for safe keeping in the early days of the English Civil War (1642–51). Margaret Cavendish in her *Life of the Thrice Noble, High and Puissant Prince William Cavendishe, Duke, Marquess and Earl of Newcastle* mentions that during the Civil War 'some few hangings and pictures' were saved by his eldest daughter.[44]

The first thing to notice about the vaulting in the Marble Closet is that it does not fit: the centred vaulting is ten by twelve feet (3.02 by 3.63 metres) and the room, although 10 feet wide is longer by seven feet (2.13 metres): to cover the gap barrel vaulting was added to each end – three feet two inches (0.96 metres) at the window end and three feet ten inches (1.17 metres) at the other. The chimney-piece is five inches (12.7 centimetres) off-centre and the boss of the vault is centred on the fireplace. The marble vaulting covers a cornice from an earlier decorative scheme; more will follow about this below.[45] A note among others referring to legal affairs concerning the 7th Earl of Shrewsbury's will (for which William was the executor) gives an indication of where William's aspirations lay: 'A note off all my businesses att London in Ester Term 1618 . . . Then for Bolsover furnesshing paynting & carving will be better though[t] off att London then heer'.[46] William was obviously planning a London visit connected with both business and the decoration of Bolsover.

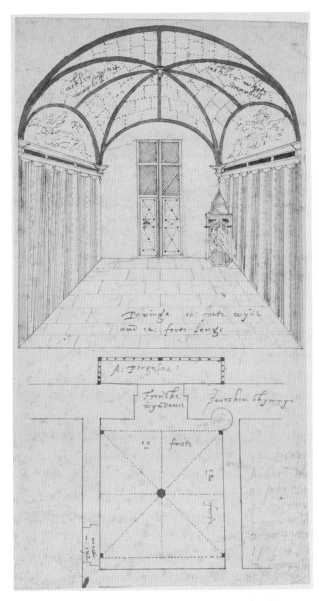

Drawing by John Smythson of the Marble Closet, now the Elysian Closet; the vaulting was re-erected in the present Marble Closet off the Star Chamber.

As part of William's redecorating scheme – which centred on two *Temptations of Hercules*, Lust or Virtue – the Elysian Closet (the original Marble Closet) was dismantled, and the vaulting re-erected in what is now the Marble Closet off the star chamber. This accounts for the cornice being hidden behind the vaulting in the present Marble Closet. There was no way in which William could have accommodated his hosts of mythological deities in that vaulting. A drawing by John Smythson of a vaulted closet with a corner fireplace correctly shows the Elysian Room as it originally was (see page 191); the corner fireplace is still there today.[47]

Because there are differing floor levels caused by different heights in the rooms beneath, one leaves the star chamber by a short flight of stone stairs leading to the principal bedchamber. The inventory of *c.* 1676 states 'In that chambar with 2 closits', which is accurate. The chamber was not luxuriously furnished according to this inventory: the bed seemingly had no hangings and colour was provided by three tapestries and a table with a carpet lying on it. As with so many of these rooms there was a garderobe turret equipped with '1 clostule and pan' (the only other close-stool was in the south-west turret off the hall). The luxury was provided by the '2 closits', which today are called the Heaven Closet and the Elysian Closet.

Taking the Heaven Closet first, the work is firmly dated 1619 above the single window. The paintings have suffered a great deal from bad restoration but were salvaged to some extent in 1999. The ceiling contains *Christ Ascending* surrounded by chubby, dancing putti, while below in the cornice are music-making putti. Two putti carry sheet music telling us that the music played is taken from 'Three Country Dances' composed by Thomas Ravenscroft in 1609; these refer to Robin Hood and Sherwood Forest, reminding guests that William was Lord Warden of Sherwood Forest, which surrounded his home Welbeck Abbey.[48] The painted work in the two closets is best described as coarse but jolly.

The Elysian Closet off the bedchamber is very different in that the subjects are taken from classical mythology: the ceiling, a version of the *Assembly of the Gods*, shows many of the Olympian gods and goddesses with their associated symbols. Anthony Wells-Cole suggests that they are based on prints from works by Italian painter Francesco Primaticcio.[49] However, that is not the last word: Venus reclining in a corner of the cornice is perhaps taken from a print of the Italian artist Titian's *Venus with the Organ Player*, the original of which was in the royal collection and would have been well known to William and others attending court; and there is a copy at Ham House in Surrey, where German painter Franz Cleyn worked. The final word is left to William Cavendish: over the window, originally a french window opening on to a balcony, two putti hold a banner with the message 'All is But Vanitie,' from the words 'All is vanity' in the Old Testament book of *Ecclesiastes*. George Vertue, visiting Bolsover in 1727, observed 'many paintings ornaments & historys. Some I judge to be the workes of Francis Cleyn . . . ' Franz Cleyn was a German painter working in London. Walpole, who may have been repeating Vertue, reported something similar; but the Bolsover ceilings are below the quality that one would expect of Cleyn,[50] for he was a highly respected and very talented artist – a contemporary described him as *il famosissimo pittore, miracolo del secolo* ('the very famous painter, miracle of the century').

Nevertheless Vertue and Walpole may have been on to something: Henry Wotton met Cleyn in Venice and was partly responsible for bringing him to England in 1624. Cleyn had been in the service of King Christian IV of Denmark, brother of Anne, wife of James I; James arranged for Cleyn to be released from the Danish court. Cleyn then worked at Holland House and Ham House and must have been known to William Cavendish. The lunettes in the Marble Closet are three of the best paintings in Bolsover and are on portable canvas so could easily have been painted in London by Cleyn. The Marble Closet could then have been redesigned around them for the visit of King Charles I in 1634.

Throughout the decorative scheme is the story of Hercules – another connection with the Palazzo Te in Mantua – and the choice between virtue and pleasure. William's second wife, Margaret, makes clear in her biography of her husband that he delighted in the company of women. One can specu-late that William's choice would be pleasure, but that choice tended to have repercussions, whereas the path of virtue brought its own rewards. This choice is obvious in the main bedchamber with two chambers off it; the Heaven Room represents the path of virtue and the other, the Elysian Closet (where Hercules, exhausted, reposes in a corner), that of pleasure. What is now a window was – as described above – a french widow opening on to a balcony, from which William/Hercules could gaze down on the buxom form of Venus on her fountain.

In 1633, while staying at Welbeck Abbey, King Charles I was sufficiently impressed to invite himself and Queen Henrietta Maria back the follow-ing year, and in 1634 the castle came into its own as the setting for a royal visit. In mid July that year the royal party went over to Bolsover for the first performance of *Love's Welcome* by Ben Jonson – an entertainment specially commissioned for the visit by William Cavendish, by then Earl of Newcastle. In the Fountain Court the figure of Venus standing on a pedestal above a round tank was in place by 1630–2, but by 1634 the fountain was in the form we see it today: it had been embellished (perhaps for the royal visit), the basin enlarged and fitted with busts of Roman emperors. At the same time the surrounding walls were repaired and small rooms inserted, heated by fireplaces, which – as with the others already there – come from designs by Sebastiano Serlio. These cosy niches were placed where, possibly, there had been towers in the medieval walls. In the cistern house in the south-east corner labourers toiled to raise water to the cistern to service the fountain.

The entertainment was not a static performance but moved into the castle and continued in the garden. Lucy Worsley, I am sure correctly, suggests that the presentation began in the Pillar Parlour with a song about the five senses, which – given the background decoration – would have been appropriate; the royal couple ate a banquet course of sweetmeats.[51]

The banquet course customarily followed a formal dinner – this would have been taken in the star chamber above.

From the castle the royal party processed to the Fountain Court, where they were further entertained by a speech given by a 'surveyour' – was this given by John Smythson, who acted as 'surveyour' for the castle? However, as he died in November that year he may have been too sick to attend. In any event, this was succeeded by a 'Dance of the Mechanickes',[52] consisting of dancers taking the parts of the craftsmen involved in the building of Bolsover – a freemason, a plumber, a glazier and others. Then, following an interlude, a second banquet course was 'set down before them from the Cloudes'.[53] This could have been lowered from the balcony of the Elysian Closet – or else, it has been suggested, the royal party were sitting in one of the wall chambers and the second banquet course was lowered from the wall overhead. However, the wall chambers are small, and the king was never alone because his courtiers flocked around him, so there may not have been space enough in these small chambers. A precedent for this was a garden seat at Kenilworth built in 1575 for Queen Elizabeth's visit. More entertainment followed; by then the fountain may have performed only fitfully. The whole diversion and visit of the royal party cost the earl a staggering £15,000 – compare this with a mason's daily rate of 10–12d. in 1613.

When King Charles arrived at Bolsover in the summer of 1634 it was still a building site and a great deal of tidying up must have been necessary. The Old House, the canted building at the north end of the terrace range, had been extended southwards by a two-storeyed, straight-gabled attic, the addition of four bays on the terrace side and by seven bays on the east side overlooking the great court, providing additional apartments and a great hall large enough to accommodate the retinue of an earl. All this was completed in 1627–30. Work that was possibly still going on at the time of the royal visit extended the terrace range southwards for a further eleven bays, creating an immensely long gallery in 1630–5 (see page 200). A building that was certainly under construction between 1635 and 1642, and at the time of the royal visit, was in the south side of the great court and comprised stables and a riding house for schooling horses, which, considering that the earl already had built a riding house at Welbeck Abbey, designed in 1622 by John Smythson, deserves comment. The marquess had a great love of horses and was a supreme master of manège (the schooling of horses), so it should be no great surprise to find riding schools at both his properties.

However, the king would not have seen the building work as his party arrived by the old, now unused entrance drive, passing before the terrace range. One can be sure that the earl would have been delighted to show his visitors the unfinished riding school had he been asked. In the circumstances the 'Dance of the Mechanickes' was appropriate.

The completion of the riding house was overtaken by the English Civil War in 1642, and the building was left unfinished until the 1660s. In the war William was given the command of four northern counties in the royalist army. After the Battle of Marston Moor, when the royalist army was routed by superior forces, the north was taken over by Cromwell's army, and William left England in 1644 together with his brother Charles and his two sons for a life in self-imposed exile. They survived on borrowed money, living first in Hamburg then in Paris at the exiled court of Queen Henrietta Maria, which was the centre for English refugees; there he met and married Margaret Lucas, maid of honour to the queen, and twenty-five years younger than he – shy, tongue-tied and bashful, she was later to write his biography. They moved on to Amsterdam, renting a house once used by the painter Rubens, and in 1658 Newcastle published his best-seller on the schooling of horses. During the Commonwealth Bolsover was sold for the value of its materials – chiefly lead from the roofs – but survived because William's brother, Charles, who returned to England before the Restoration, bought back the sequestered estates and kept them together in order to pass them to his two nephews. With the Restoration of the monarchy in 1660, Newcastle returned to England. His estates were restored to him by a bill in Parliament passed in August 1660 including 'all his honours, Manors, Lands and Tenements in England whereof he was in possession on 23 October 1642, or at any time since'.[54] Starting in 1663 the earl – acting as his own architect but with the assistance of a professional architect, Samuel Marsh – rebuilt damaged parts of Bolsover, in particular the grand rooms of the terrace range on the west side of the great court, and finished off the riding house range. Created a duke in 1665, he died at Welbeck Abbey, aged eighty-four, in 1676.

During the short period covered by the Bolsover building accounts John Smythson was living at Kirkby-in-Ashfield, and his riding charges for going over to Bolsover were paid. In 1600 he married Margaret Newton, whose family lived in Kirkby. In 1615 Sir Charles leased to him a 'mansion house' in the town called Lunnes House, with a barn, a stable and a croft, with fields in 'Kyrkby Ashfield' at an annual rent of £3; the property was known as 'Lunnes Farm'. In 1616, with Lancelot Ogle (who at the time of the fracas at Kirkby with the Stanhopes was Sir Charles's page and was a relative of his wife) Smythson received the assignment of the manor and rectory of Cotham; these may have been treated by the pair as an investment for letting, since it is unlikely that it would have been shared accommodation between the two gentlemen servants and their families.[55]

John Smythson was responsible for work at Welbeck but with the death of his father in 1614, that of Sir Charles Cavendish in 1617 and the end of the Bolsover building accounts in 1614, this account of the Smythson Circle comes to an end. John Smythson's son, Huntingdon, whose initials may or may not be those on the north end of the terrace range at Bolsover, inherited his father's connection with the dukes of Newcastle and carried out three surveys of their properties at Ogle and Moralee-in-Hayden, Northumberland, and Mansfield Park, Nottinghamshire; these form part of the great Senior Survey by William Senior of the Newcastle properties – the survey, begun in 1609, took several years to complete, but it gave

Newcastle a complete idea of what land he owned, who were his tenants and what rent they paid. On these surveys Huntingdon called himself 'Practitioner of Mathematics' and was living at Kirkby-in-Ashfield in Nottinghamshire in the same house leased to his father, who by then was living in Bolsover village. John died in the house and farm in Bolsover that had been leased to his mother, on 5 November 1634, the year of King Charles I's visit to Bolsover. Huntingdon died in November 1648 'surprised by a sickness in his intellectuals' as his non-cupative (oral) will states, and was buried in Bolsover church. His son John II continued living in Bolsover and had in his turn a son christened Huntingdon. An indication of the family's rise in the world is that John II's youngest son, Charles, born 1642, became a fellow of Christ's College, Cambridge, rector of Toft, Cambridgeshire, and a prebendary of Lincoln Cathedral. The Smythsons had become gentry.

In the Smythson drawings in the Royal Institute of British Architects library there are references to work undertaken for Sir Charles Cavendish by John Smythson on his other properties, Slingsby Castle (Yorkshire) and Ogle Castle (Northumberland); both properties came to the family by marriage. Outside the family properties, Smythson designed the stables for the Cliftons of Clifton Hall, near Nottingham, in 1632 and produced a drawing for a striking chimney-piece for the great chamber there. Further work includes: an undated floor plan for a mysterious Mr Diball; designs dated 1618 for Wyverton House, Nottinghamshire, for the Chaworth family; designs for Haughton House, dated 1618, west of Tuxford in north Nottinghamshire, for the Stanhope family; and undated designs for Grove House, south-east of Retford, north Nottinghamshire, for a 'Mr Nevelle'. All four buildings have been demolished or substantially altered. He also produced a plan 'for an orchard' at Wollaton Hall for his father's patrons, the Willoughbys. It cannot be said that he had the wide clientele of his father, as he did little work outside Sir Charles Cavendish's family. John Smythson's will survives dated 5 November 1634; in it, he calls himself 'Architecter'.[56] Huntingdon was left land leased from the Willoughbys at Twyford and Gadsby in Leicestershire, a farm leased in Skegby, Nottinghamshire, a farm in Kirkby leased to him by Sir Charles in 1615 and the house and farm in Bolsover at his mother's death.

Only eight years after his father's death Huntingdon's architectural career was cut short by the English Civil War and the Commonwealth, as Newcastle's building operations were obviously halted. Huntingdon died in 1648 and was buried in Bolsover Church. He would have lived well from the farms he controlled, and he was bailiff for the Cavendish estate in the Kirkby-in-Ashfield area, but he never lived to see the Restoration of the monarchy and the return of the Duke of Newcastle.

The Duke of Newcastle was a very grand man indeed who lived extravagantly, as was expected of a duke, maintaining a household of forty-five. He far outstripped his cousin at Hardwick, who was a mere earl. His first wife, Elizabeth Basset, came to him with £3,000 a year and £7,000 in cash. They had ten children, but five died in infancy; she died in 1643. His second wife was Margaret Lucas, whom he married in 1645; they had no children, and he outlived her – she died in December 1673.

His father, Sir Charles, also married twice. First in 1581 he married Margaret Kitson, the daughter of a rich London merchant; Margaret's father died, leaving his fortune to be divided between his two daughters, so that Sir Charles inherited the half-share of his late father-in-law's fortune. Margaret died in 1582, leaving an only son, who died in infancy. Sir Charles then married Catherine Ogle, daughter of Lord Ogle, who owned estates in Northumberland, and these also came to Sir Charles. William Cavendish had been lucky in that both he and his father had married wealthy wives. When he regained his estates at the Restoration of the monarchy he was a wealthy man once more.

As a general in the English Civil War he is often blamed for the royalist defeat at the Battle of Marston Moor in Yorkshire in 1644. This is somewhat unjust. Created marquess in 1643, Newcastle received command of the four northern counties of England and had some military successes, which –

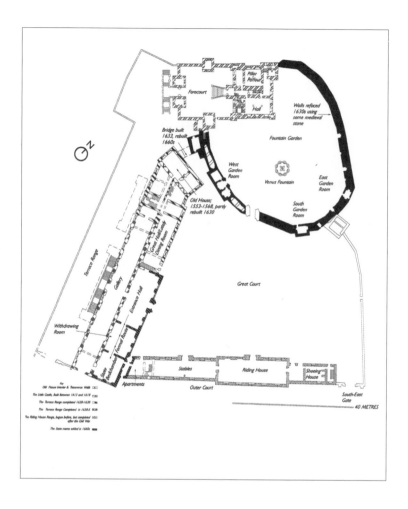

considering his lack of experience of warfare – might be considered surprising. He then joined forces with the king's cousin, Prince Rupert, and there was some friction between them. At Marston Moor, under Prince Rupert, their army was outnumbered and faced a professional army of Roundheads and Scottish forces combined, totalling 20,000 infantry against the royalists' 11,000; in cavalry they were evenly matched with 7,000 each. It was Prince Rupert's decision to attack. Newcastle

THIRD STOREY

SECOND STOREY

BASEMENT

25 Metres

Opposite: The full plan of Bolsover Castle as it was completed in the 1660s; the 'Old House' is in the north-east corner of the great court.

Left and above: Floor plans of the Little Castle and the later buildings at Bolsover

knew better but conceded to the royal prince. The defeat was the end of royalist resistance in the north, and Newcastle went into voluntary exile – sailing for the Continent from Scarborough, against King Charles's wishes, with his two sons and their tutor, his brother, his steward and personal servants but with only £90! Bolsover Castle was far away and uncompleted; the terrace range with gallery was complete, a new great hall at the north end of the terrace range overlooking the great court had been added, but the riding house and stable had been started but not finished. Garrisoned by the royalists, it was surrendered on 12 August; Welbeck Abbey had yielded ten days earlier. In exile, Newcastle was cut off from his revenues, and there was little chance he would be repaid the money he had loaned to the king. Fortunately his credit was good, and he survived on borrowed money and what money could be smuggled out of England.

He returned to England in 1660 at the Restoration of the monarchy. His wife claimed that her husband's losses in the war were the staggering sum of £941,503. However, his estates were restored to him, he was invested with the Order of the Garter in 1661 and created Duke of Newcastle in March 1665. But he had had enough of public life and retired to Welbeck Abbey, occupying himself with his horses and their schooling. In his later years he suffered from Parkinson's disease, and he regretfully gave up riding. The sudden death of his wife Margaret, in December 1673, when he was in his eightieth year, was a blow from which he never recovered. He lingered on for another three years, dying in 1676, leaving his only surviving child, Henry, to inherit the dukedom. The title died with Henry in 1691, but it was recreated in 1694 for John Holles, the Earl of Clare, who was married to Margaret, Henry's only daughter. From Margaret descended the dukes of Portland who, until the twentieth century, continued to live at Welbeck and maintained Bolsover Castle. The 7th Duke gifted Bolsover to the Nation in 1945, and it came into the care of the Ministry of Public Building and Works. In 1970 the Ministry of Public Building and Works merged with the Department of the Environment until 1983, when English Heritage was formed, and Bolsover has been in their care from that year.

APPENDIX I

WARDSHIP AND THE COURT OF WARDS

Although it became to be regarded as one of the most iniquitous impositions of the Crown on landed proprietors, wardship was a logical enough process in the feudal system under which it developed. If the male heir to land held of the Crown by feudal right of knight service was under the age of twenty-one, and thus ineligible for knight service, the estate was taken into wardship by the Crown until the heir came of age (or if a girl until she was old enough to marry – at the age of fourteen). As knight service came to be commuted to a money payment of rent, the Crown took to selling wardships to the highest bidder. If the estate were taken over by a relative, there might be little exploitation. However, it often went to a complete stranger who did not hesitate to make what he could out of the estate during the years it was in his wardship.

King Henry VIII saw the ancient laws of wardship as a means of control and a source of revenue and in 1540 created the Court of Wards, which became the Court of Wards and Liveries in 1542. The old feudal rights thus revived were very strictly enforced. Early marriage was one means employed by Tudor landowners to avoid the possibilities of wardship – tax avoidance is not by any means a modern obsession alone. Bess of Hardwick was married to Robert Barlow over his father's deathbed in 1542, when she was fifteen at the time and he was only thirteen. For a married heir there would be no question of wardship, but as Robert lived only a year after his marriage the plan failed, and after a post-mortem inquiry the Barlow estate was taken into wardship. On the death of Bess's own father in 1528 she, with her mother, brother and three sisters, lost control of the Hardwick lands to wardship until the heir, James Hardwick, became twenty-one in 1547 – although since the family continued living in Old Hardwick it is likely that Bess's mother was able to rent back part of the estate from wardship. Wardship was abolished by the Long Parliament in 1645. Robert Cecil, under Queen Elizabeth I, was master of the Court of Wards for thirty-seven years, and under his influence the court became more considerate of the circumstances of its victims.

APPENDIX II

WILLS

Will of John Hills, freemason of Worksop, Nottinghamshire (part-damaged).
He was buried in 1592. (Nottinghamshire Archives, PRNW)

I John Hills Freemason [of Willington] Street in the County of Kent . . . In
Worksop in the County of Nottinghamshire in the diocese of York . . . [The
customary preamble follows.]

ITM [Item]. I give unto the repair of the church of Maidstone the sum
of ten shillings. Item I give unto the poor of the same parish the sum of
twenty shillings to be dealt amongst them. ITM. I give to the said town of
Maidstone for ever to the use of the poor five pounds. ITM. I give and
bequeath unto Catherine Fisher my sister two old angels of gold. ITM. I give
and bequeath unto my brother Peter Hills his children every one of them
five pounds. ITM. I give and bequeath unto my nephew Walter Rooke and
his heirs for ever one messuage in Willington Street aforesaid with all the
lands to the same belonging now in the tenure of William Horndon freemason. ITM. I give and bequeath all my messuages lands tenements and
hereditaments whatsoever lying and being in the parish of Maidstone aforesaid and Ottome in the county of Kent unto Thomas Everndon George
Everndon James Stace Henry Stace and Gabriel Stace being the children of
her former two husbands and their heirs for ever. ITM. I will and my mind
is that all implements and household stuff as are now in my chief house in
Willington Street shall remain as heirlooms therein. ITM. I give unto my
nephew William Everndon the sum of ten pounds of lawfull English money.

ITM. I give and bequeath unto my said nephew William Everndon one feather bed one bolster one bedstead with valence and curtains thereunto belonging one covering of tapestry work one pair of large flaxen sheets and one carpet all which is now in Chilwell Hall that I had off William Styles in the county of Nottinghamshire. ITM. I give further unto the above Walter Rooke and his wife all the linen cloths which is in Chilwell Hall that I brought out of the West Country. ITM. Furthermore I give unto the said Walter Rooke my annuity and sum of money which is due to me by Richard Crispin as well as that which the said Walter that he hath received to be paid by the said Richard Crispin towards the bringing up of his children. ITM. I give and bequeath unto the children of the said Walter Rooke the sum of twenty pounds of lawful English money to be divided equally amongst them. ITM. I give unto George Everndon a bolster of a bed of white linen cloth and two diaper napkins. ITM. I give unto every one of my godchildren five shillings a piece. ITM. I give unto John Smithson ten shillings. ITM. I give unto Mary Smithson ten shillings. ITM. I give unto Mr Smithson's daughters all the brass and pewter that is mine at Chilwell Hall to be divided equally amongst them. ITM. I give unto William Brise and his mother either of them ten shillings. ITM. I give and bequeath unto that place unto the use of the poor thereof for ever and whenever it shall please God that I die and be buried the sum of five pounds. ITM. I make executors of this my last will and testament the aforesaid Walter Rooke George Everndon and William Everndon to whom I (bequeath) all the residue of my goods. ITM. I do make supervisor hereof Mr Robert Smithson I give him (for his) pains twenty shillings. In witness whereof I have hereunder set my hand and seal the day and [date] first above written. Signed John Hills.

Sealed and subscribed In the presence of Edward Smythe.

Probate certificate [attached]. Will of John Hills of Willington Street in the County of Kent formerly emigrated from there unto the town of Worksop in the diocese of York. George Everndon and William Everndon executors Walter Rooke executor.

Notes

Hills, or Hilles, worked as a mason at Longleat from 1568 onwards and then at Wollaton; he did not go on to Hardwick. In the 1550s he seems to have worked for the Duke of Somerset. The Worksop Parish Register says he was buried on 3 October 1592.

Richard Crispin was a carpenter at Longleat and Wollaton Hall.

The will of Catherine Fisher of Boughton Monchelsea, Kent, widow, was proved on 23 July 1605. She was Hills's sister and beneficiary under his will. Her beneficiaries were James and Henry Stace, Jane and Anne Stace, daughters of Gabriel Stace, William Everndon, and Susan the daughter of Thomas Everndon. (Kent County Archives, PRC 17/54 f. 319)

William and George Everndon both worked at Wollaton, as did William Styles as a mason. Gabriel Stace appears in Nicholas Stone's notebook.[1] He acted as clerk of the works under Stone during building works at Oxford Botanical Gardens and Cornbury House, Oxfordshire in 1631–2 and later was engaged on mason's work at Somerset House and Greenwich.[2]

⟨≋⟩

Will of Thomas Plumtree of Moorhall in the parish of Dronfield, Derbyshire, dated 16 March 1612. (Joint Record Office, Public Library, Lichfield)

[The customary preamble, occupation husbandman, 'sicke in body, but of good and pfecte memory'. His body to be buried in Dronfield churchyard.]

Also I geve and bequeath and my will anmynde is That Dorothy Plumtree my wife shall have all my goods and Chattells moveable and unmoveable quicke and deade, of what kinde or Condition soever they bee; to dispose of att her will and pleasure reposing my full trust in her, that shee will prove a natural and kind mother to my two small children. Item I will and desire that all such debts as I owe of Right and of Consience to any pson, be well and truly paid by my Executrix hearafter named. And I make the said Dorothie Plumtree my wife sole and full Executrix of this my last will and Testament. And I make Raphe my brother And Thomas Quicksall of Cold-aston, husband, supervisors hereof. And I give unto either of them for their paynes xijd. In witness whereof I have hereunto putt my hand and seale the day and yeare abovesaid 1612.

These being witnesses George [his mark] Plumtree.

Debts owing by the above William Mowes [his mark] named Testator to Richard Taylor xxs.

Sign preds Thome [his mark] Plumtree. [Signed by]

Inventory of Thomas

The 4th Daye of April 1613/

A full and pfecte Inventory of all the goods and Chattells of Thomas of More-hall in the pishe of dronfield late deceased praysed by Robert Cooke, Renald Plumtrye, George Plumtrye, Will Wigall

Iprimis his apparel and money in his purse . . . . xxs.

Itm his Cattell . . . . x li

Itm his sheep . . . . xl s.

Itm his corne of the grounde . . . . xxs.

Itm his pewter and brasse . . . . xvjs.

Itm his bedding and Cushings . . . . xxiiijs.

Itm his woodware and handirons . . . . vs.

Sma . . . . xvj li. vs.

Will of Thomas Roberts, freemason, of Wollaton, Nottinghamshire. (Borth-wick Institute, York Probate Registry: Vol. 35 f. 523 & f. 523v. The original, but badly perished, is in the Nottingham County Record Office.)

IN THE NAME OF GOD AMEN The two and twentieth day of January 1614 in the reigne of our sovereigne Lord James by the grace of god king of England ffrance and Ireland fender of the faythe etc, And of Scotland the eight & fortieth. I Thomas Roberts of Wollaton in the Countie of Nottingham freemason beinge sicke in bodie yet in good and perfect rememberance praysed be the Almightie for the same doe make my last will & Testament in manner and forme following FIRST I give and bequeath my soule into the hands of allmightie god my Maker hoping that by the pretious deathe and passion of our Lord and saviour Jesus Christe my sins shall be forgiven mee and my bodie to be buried in the Churche of Wollaton aforesaid so neare my seate or deske as may bee. And for the setting and disposing of that small estate wch it hath pleased god to bestowe of mee in this world and for the avoiding of all further strife wch may happen amongste my friends or the Children after my decease I GIVE to my fower daughters viz Margaret, Jane, Olive and Bridgett one hundredth powndes amonst them that is to eche of them five and twentie powndes a peece which saide hundredth pounds is nowe forthe in the handes of Mr John Smithson and others. And my will is that my Executors and Supervisors hereafter named shalbee careful to get the same in, And then to put it forth foir tenne yeares next after the same shalbee recyived for the benefit of my saide foure daughters and their childeren wch they now have or hereafter shall have before the end of the said tenne yeares equally amongst them. And after the saied tenne yeares is expired then my will is, and it is my full meaning that my said fowre daughters shall have the same hundredth pounds equallie divided amongst them in fower equall parts and if anie of my said daughters shall dye before the said tenne yeares be expired then I will that her Children then livinge shall have the said xxv li amongst them, ITM I GIVE to my two sisters Margerie and Olive five pounds betweene them to be equallie payed wthn six monthes after my decease, ITM I give to Henerie Hooley daughter Janes sonne one Bowe in Janes keeping. ITM I give to Elizabeth Bestocke fowre poudes in monie and my greene Rugge which now lyeth upon my bed the saied fowre poundes to bee paid within one month after my decease. ITM I give my seaven god childeren whose names I have given to my executors hereafter named, to each of them five shillings of lawefull monie ITM I give to my worshipfull good Master Sr ffrances Willoughbie knight three poundes and to Mr Thomas Willoughby his brother one peece of golde of xxijs ITM I give to eche of my daughters aforesaid xxijs All the rest of my goods and Chattells not hereby bequeathed after my debts and Funeralls payd I give to James Walker my sonne in Lawe whome I make sole executor of this my last will and testament And I desire my loving friends John Roberts and Robertt Greaves to bee supervisors of this my will giving to eche of them for their paynes herrin Tenne shillings of lawful money. These being wytnesses Stephen Hill, John Roberts, Robert Greeaves.

Notes

The inclusion of Sir Francis Willoughby and his brother Thomas is puzzling, because by 1614 they were both dead – the former died in 1596 and the latter in 1558. The heir Percival, who succeeded Francis, died later in 1643.

Roberts was churchwarden at Wollaton Church in 1576 – the reference to being buried near to 'my seate or deske' indicates that he was still a churchwarden when he died. He was buried at Wollaton, as he requested, on 28 January 1614.

Roberts worked at Wollaton as a mason from 1582 to 1588, paid at the higher rate of 12d. a day. He is mentioned by Basil Stallybrass in his article 'Bess of Hardwick's Buildings and Building Accounts': 'Itm geven by yo La commandment to Thoms Roberts 1/-' on 21 January 1579 at Chatsworth.[3] He is not recorded as having worked at Hardwick. Surviving evidence gives little account of his association with Smythson, yet – apart from Smythson himself – he was the most prosperous of the Smythson circle. The John Roberts whom he appointed a supervisor of his will was probably the John Roberts who married Smythson's youngest daughter, Elizabeth, in 1602. Robert Greaves, his other supervisor, worked as a mason at Chatsworth in 1560.

Will of Thomas Beane of Wighill, freemason, proved 8 March 1614/5.
(Borthwick Institute, York Probate Registry 348, f. 456)

I Thomas Beane of Wighell within the county of the Citty of yorke
ffreeMason make this my last will and testament in manner and form
following . . . [The usual preamble follows, he wishes to be buried in
Wighill churchyard.]

ITM I give to Xpafer Beanes children Every one of them Twelve pence
Itm I give to my daughter Jane Rawlinge one Matterisse one Blanekett and
one Coveringe and the rest of all my goodes and Chattells moveable and
unmoveable my debts beinge paide my legacies and funeral expenses discharged I doe give and bequeath to my sonne Thomas Beane whome I make
my sole executor of this my last will and testament Witnesses hereof Robert
Potter James Wilkinson Bartholomew Agau, Charles Wilson and Anthony
Cunpley with others; debtes oweing by Thomas Beane Thelder deceased
IMPRIMIS. to Mr John Hammond of Wighell Seaventene Shillinges and
fower pence Itm to William Gregges of York Sixteen shillings Debts oweinge
to the said Thomas Beane, IMPRIMIS. the lord Sheffield oweth Three
pounde Sixtene shillings and Eight pence Itm Stephen Potter of Cawood
Webster oweth Three Pounde, Memorandum that all the rest of my children
are fully satisfies of their porcons and some of them a great deale more.

Notes

Thomas Beane first worked as a mason at Hardwick in July 1591 and was
paid 7d. a day. His son Christopher also worked at Hardwick as a freemason
in the same year at 12d. a day.

The note that 'the lord Sheffield oweth Three pounde Sixtene shillings
and Eight pence' suggests that Beane had worked for Lord Sheffield and
was still owed money. In the collection of Smythson drawings in the Royal
Institute of British Architects library there are floor plans for a central-
courtyard house 'for my Lord Sheffield', which may have been built at

Normanby Park but which was demolished and rebuilt between 1825 and 1830. Normanby Park is in Lincolnshire, five miles (eight kilometres) north of Scunthorpe, quite a way from Wighill in Yorkshire.

Will of Robert Smithson of Woollerton in the Countie of Nottingham, dated 1 August 1614. (Borthwick Institute York, Probate Registery Vol. 334. f. 405v. and f. 406)

[The customary preamble followed by his wish to be buried in the church or churchyard.] I give and bequeath unto my oldest daughter Marie Johnson £30 also I give unto my second daughter Barbara Berry £20 and to her children to be divided amongst them in equal portion amongst them £10 and to be paid at first tyme as he my executor shall think most fitting also I give and bequeath unto Elizabeth Roberts my youngest daughter £30 and her eldest son John Robertes £20 Conditionally that what goods I have already Reconed to be his own which was given him by me that shall be part of the said £20 and further my will is that his uncle John Smithson my executor shall have the tuition and government of the said John Robertes until he be 21 years of age and the said £20 remaining in the hands of the said John Smithson until the time of 21 years be expired and if it Chance that the said John Roberts should die before the said time of 21 years then my will is that the said £20 shall be equally divided amongst the rest of daughter Elizabeth Children by equal and even portions and further I give and bequeath unto Elizabeth Bestwicke my servant in regard of her service done unto me £10 of which I have of her own money in my hands 25 shillings which is part of the former sum of £10 and to conclude my debts being paid my legacies discharged I give unto my son John Smithson all other of my goods and chattels whatsoever whom I do make and ordain my sole executor to see this my will performed in witness whereof to this my last will I have in the presence of those hereunder written sett to my hand and seal the first of August Anno Dom 1614.

Notes

Smythson died on 15 October 1614, and was buried at Wollaton church on 26 October 1614. His wall plaque, inside the church on the south wall, records him as 'Architector and Surveyor unto the most worthy house of Wollaton with divers others of account'. His daughter Elizabeth married John Roberts on 18 May 1602 at Wollaton. There were two baptisms: Robert Roberts, son of John Roberts, on 3 May 1612 and Elizabeth, daughter of John Roberts, on 25 September 1614. There is no record of her son John in the Wollaton registry nor of her two sisters, Mary and Barbara.

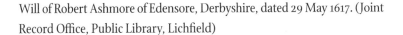

Will of Robert Ashmore of Edensore, Derbyshire, dated 29 May 1617. (Joint Record Office, Public Library, Lichfield)

[The usual preamble gives his occupation as Husbandman and he is 'sick in bodie but pfect in mynde'. He asks to be buried in Edensore churchyard (not the present church; the village was moved by the 1st Duke to its present position).]

IMPRIMIS. I give unto Margaret White daughter of Katherine my wife one Ewe and lambe after they have been shorne.

ITEM I give unto Jane Hollingworth my Goddaughter two shillinge

ITEM I give to Robert Ripton brother in lawe to my wife my Blacke Suite and blewe Coate.

ITEM I give unto John Howard my ould servant two yards of Russet cloath with all my toales with all my apparrall whatsoever.

ITEM I give unto Roger Ribben my wifes kinsman five shillings

The residue of all my goods moveable and unmoveable wth all debts due unto me I give and bequeath unto Katherine my welbeloved wife and John Heward before mentioned my servant, equally to be divided betwixt them paying and discharging all legacies funeral expenses debts and all other demands whatsoever out of the whole betwixt them. Appoynting my wife whole and full executrix of this my last will and testamt not doubting her honest care for the due pformance hereof. And for my overseers of this my will doe appoint and ordaine my welbeloved in Christ Tristram Daintrie and John Marple of Edensore aforesaid, written and delivered as my last will and testamt the twentie ninth of may and the fifteenth year of the Raigne of our Sovraigne Lord James by the grace of god kinge of England ffrance and Ireland and of Scotland fiftieth nyght Anno Dm 1617 I ye psence of these

    Robt Ashmore his marke

    Witnesses Robt Birley his marke

    John Marples marke

    James Troughton.

The Inventory of all the goods and Chattells moveable and immovable whereof Roberte Ashmore late of the pishe of Edensouer husbandman were possessed of att his death iustly and truly valued by these three honest and of ye most sufficient men of the same pishe : Viz /

    Richard Allen Theleer

    John Norton and

    Richard Hibbard.

IMPRIMIS. one Cowe and Calfe and one heifer . . . . . . foure pownds

Item one mare and foale . . . . . . fiftie three shillings and foure pence

Item twelve sheep . . . . . . fortie foure shillings

Item beddinge wt furniture herunto . . . . . . fortie shillings

Item potts pans and pewter . . . . . . three poundes

Item one Cupboard, tables stooles and other wooden ware . . . . . . twentie shillings

Item six Cushions . . . . . . three shillings

Item Corne and haie . . . . . . foure pounds

Item three hives . . . . . . six shillings eyght pence

    Summa Totalis £19-6-8.

Notes

Robert Ashmore worked at Chatsworth and both Old and New Hardwick Halls as a waller. He was not a rough-waller but a worker who built walls with cut stone blocks called ashlar. He worked also on Oldcotes, where he was classified as 'mason'. His mark on his will is a large A; on the Oldcotes bargain it is the same upside down (see discussion in Chapter Six, page 164).

According to the Senior Survey for 1618, he rented a house and yard at Edensore from the Earl of Devonshire, together with five acres (two hectares) of arable. Ashmore seems to have been very much the junior partner of the Oldcotes bargain-in-great, but, nevertheless, he had sufficient assets to cover the cost of making a will. In the Hardwick servants' wage accounts he was paid 20s. a year from 1594 to 1601.[4] One of the overseers of his will, Tristram Daintre, rented a house and garden of nine acres (a little under four hectares) in Hatton, Derbyshire, from the Earl of Devonshire, where he was a freeholder of fifteen acres (six hectares), but he also rented 106 acres (forty-three hectares) at Edensore and was therefore a neighbour of Ashmore, as was Richard Hibbard (one of the makers of the inventory of Ashmore's property), renting five acres (two hectares), and Richard Allin or Allen (another of the makers of the inventory), renting sixty-three acres (twenty-five hectares). A Richard Allen was a carpenter at Chatsworth in 1578; if this is the same man, he would have been in his sixties at the time of Ashmore's death.

Will of Renould Plumtree of Hardstafffe in the parish of Ault Hucknall, Derbyshire, dated 7 January 1630. (Joint Record Office, Public Library, Lichfield)

[The customary preamble; he wishing to be buried as his executors shall think fitting.] IMPRIMIS. I do give and bequease unto William Plumtree my eldest sonne the summe of five poundes of good and lawful monie of England. ITEM I do give and bequease unto Adam Plumtree my youngest sonne the somme of five poundes of like lawful English mony to be paid to them both within one whole yeare next after my decease. ITEM all the rest of my goodes Cattles and Chattels moveable and unmoveable living and dead I give and bequease Unto Ann Plumtree my wife towards the bringing up of my younger children and raising them some portions as god shall enable her and as shee in her discretion shall thinke fitting. Also I do make and ordaine the aforesaid Ann Plumtree my wife my sole executore of this my last will and Testament hoping that shee will see all thinges herein Contained honestly and Concionablely performed according to the true meaning hereof. In Wittness whereof I the said Renould have here unto sett my hand and seal the seventh day of January in the sixt yeare of the reign of our sovereigne Lord Charles by the grace of god of England scottland ffrance King defendoure of the faith etc Anno Dm 1630.

Sealed subscribed and
Delivered in the psence of
John Ouldham
Weenefreed Ouldam
John Ludlam
John Reason

Inventory of Renould

December 19 Anno Dm 1631
An inventorye of the all the goods and Cattell of Reynould Plumtree of Harstaffe in the parishe of halt hucknall taken and prysed by James Balechouse, John Ouldham, Adam Ufton and George Cooper the day and date above written.

IMPRIMIS. his purse and his apparel 02-00-00

Item one oxe 04-10-00

Item eyght kine and heifers 18-13-04

Item tow younger hyfers 02-06-08

Item three calves 02-00-00

Item one ould Mare and a fyllye 03-00-00

Item fowrteene sheepe 02-16-00

Item A hogge and tow pigs 01-14-00

Item Corn and hay in the barnes 12-00-00

Item Corn on the ground 05-00-00

Item In the upper Chamber a bedsteedd 00-10-00

Item tow trundle beds a chist a kimnell and woodin ware in the chamber 00-10-00

Item Materis and tow chasse beds 00-06-08

Item five cowlitts and tow ould blancketts 01-00-00

Item three boulsters and five pillows 00-10-00

Item Three peare of Lining sheets one peare of hempin Sheetes six pillow
beares 01-14-00

Item a bed in the parler 00-10-00

Ite[m] A cubbard foure Coaffers and tow kimnells 01-00-00

Ite[m] Tow barrels two loomes a churne and kytts and piggins 00-06-08

Item A table and a frame a cubbard. three chers a form

Item A wooden safe a dysh bord and tow joint stooles 01-06-08

Item fowre brase post three pans and a kettle 03-00-00

Item tow and twentie pewter dyshes 01-02-00

Item five kandlesticks a chaffindysh tow salts a malter and a pestle and a
pewter cup and Can 00-10-00

Item Cobbards and a spit and other Iron ware belonging to the fyer 00-06-08

Item Goods in the nether chamber 00-10-00

Item Husbandry ware as waynes harrows plows yokes and teames 02-13-04

Item tow frying pans And kushons 00-02-00

Item tow geese a gander five hens and a cocke 00-06-00 70-04-0

    James Balechous

John Ouldam
Adam Ufton
George Cooper

Notes

Renould with his three brothers and with John Ward and Robert Ashmore took the bargain-in-great in 1593 to build Oldcotes. By the time of this will another generation had grown up; James Balechous is the son of John.

That he left as much as £70 indicates that he was a prosperous farmer, although his will does not give his occupation; the livestock, along with his 'corn and hay in the barnes', represented a big capital investment of £52, of which £35 was in livestock. His house had three bedchambers and a parlour; the table and frame, three chairs, a form and a cupboard were probably in the hall. All in all, this was quite a large home. There is no mention of his old tools of trade, and we may assume that was all in the past.

The Senior Survey of 1609 shows Renould as renting sixty-six acres (twenty-seven hectares) in Harstoft and Ault Hucknall, both villages near to Hardwick Hall, from Bess's son Lord Cavendish. Oldham, who rented thirty-five acres (fourteen hectares), and Ufton, who rented ninety-three acres (thirty-eight hectares), were both neighbours.

⬛

Noncupative will of John Johnson, freemason of Kirkby-in-Ashfield, Nottinghamshire, dated 3 September 1631. (Nottinghamshire Archives PR/NW)

[The customary preamble; occupation freemason of Kirkby-in-Ashfield, Nottinghamshire 'lying sore sicke under the hands of Almightie god but yet in whole mind and good and pfecte remembrance'. His body to be buried in Kirkby churchyard.]

IMPRIMIS. I give to Margaret my deare and loving wyffe the third part of all my goods and also the whole use and profit and Commodity of my ffarme whereon I dwell with all the housing thereunto belonging and appertaining during her naturall life and no longer, the use of which ffarme I bequeath unto her in Consideracon of the education and bringing up of my three youngest daughters, Margaret Elizabeth and Sarai. ITEM I give and bequeath unto my sonne John the somme of three pounds six shillings eight pence of good and Lawful mony of England to be paid unto him at the expiracon of his Apprentiship. And also I give unto him my ffarme with the lease thereof after the decease of Margaret my wiffe. ITEM I give and bequeath unto my two Daughters Mary and Isabell for their child porcions ether of them the full and just somme of ten pounds of good and lawfull money of England to be payd unto each of them upon the dayes of their severall marriages. ITEM I give and bequeath unto my three youngest daughters Margaret Elizabeth and Sarai for their Childs portione the full and just somme of fifteen pounds a piece of good and lawful money of England to be payd unto them at such time and times as each of them shall accomplish the age of twenty and one yeares severally without any further delay. ITEM I give to my daughter Anna the wiffe of John Breedon the somme of ten shillings in Lue of her Childs pt and portion. PROVIDED alwayes and my will and mind is that if the Inventory of all my goods will not extend so farre as to pay all these portions and Legacyes [proportionally] so that my Loving wiffe my Executrix be not overcharged therewith Lastly I give unto Mr ffrancis Linley Cleric the somme of two shillings six pence. And of this my Last will and testament I make institute and ordayne my deare and Loving wiffe Margaret my full and sole Executrix. In witness whereof I have set to my hand and ffeale the iij th day of September above sayd in the seaventh yr of the Raigne of our Soverayne Lord Charles of England, Scotland and ffrance and Ireland King deffendor of the ffaith etc.

Sealed and subscribed in

The psence of

Fran Linby jurat (Juror)

Clrec. (Clark)

Elisbeth Hollingworth

Anthony Farnsworth jurat

Notes

This will was discovered by Dr Lucy Worsley and quoted in her unpublished work *The Building and Furnishing of the Little Castle at Bolsover*, June 2000. Dr Worsley points out that John Johnson was witness to a document dated 4 October 1615 in which Sir Charles Cavendish leased to John Smythson a mansion house known as Lunnes House in Kirkby-in-Ashfield. There is no John Johnson in the Bolsover building accounts, but there is Thomas Johnson, a freemason, and a man named simply as Johnson, who was a labourer. Neither of these would appear to be our man. However, the building accounts cover only the period from November 1612 to March 1613/14, when the Little Castle was up to ground-floor level. It is very unlikely that John Johnson, close enough to Smythson to witness his lease and living in Kirkby, was not involved in the building of Bolsover Castle after 1614. His wife was Margaret Stubbing; they married at Mansfield in 1620. Our John Johnson had achieved the freemason's ambition of having 'a small farm' to leave him independent during periods of unemployment, and he was wealthy enough to make a will leaving the large sum of £15 apiece to three daughters and £10 each to two younger daughters.

APPENDIX III

FROM WILLIAM DICKENSON'S NOTE-BOOK

(Sheffield Central Libraries, MD192 f. 76v)

MD [Memorandum]. Yt is covenanted and agreed between Willm Deken-
son Srvant unto the Right honourable Erle of Shrewsburye of thone partie
and Peter Sympson of Skagram nere unto Aplrtreeweke in ye County of
yorke and James Hellywell of haslington wthin ye County of Lancastr
masones of thother partie that the said Peter and James shall serve the said
Erle one whole yeare for iiij mrks wages to either of them & a Coate also to
either of them ye said masones fyndeinge them selfes all manr of toyles
[tools] to worke wth ptayning to yer Scyence of their owne Costs & chardgs./
my L gyveing them towards yeir toyles ij stone of yron in wyttnes whereof
they have sette their hands ye xxvth of Januarye 1574/5.

[Signed by two marks, one of which appears at Shireoaks Hall, a Smythson house of 1600.]

Notes

The contract is interesting because of its rarity; very few survive. It
records the agreement that Sympson and Hellywell, both masons, are to
work for the Earl of Shrewsbury for a year and then gives the conditions
of their employment. What the document does not reveal is where this
work was carried out. That year, 1574, Shrewsbury was building at
Sheffield Lodge: no building accounts survive, but the following can be
extrapolated from other records, and it is fair to assume that Sympson

and Hellywell were engaged to work on Sheffield Lodge. Two other masons, named Roodes and Turner, certainly did work there and were paid between them 40s. 5d. for building the 'Tyrrett' and other details of work at Sheffield Lodge,[1] with a further £3 to be paid when the job was completed; they had already been paid £5. 3s. 8d. Roodes and Turner would have had a team of men working for them. Nevertheless, the cost, at 10d. a rood, represents a great deal of work and consequent organization. James Wigfull in his article 'Extracts from the Note-book of William Dickenson' states that the measurements of the walls and windows for which they were paid exactly coincide with those of the turret and enclosing walls still existing at Sheffield Lodge.[2] Roodes and Turner appear again in the same note-book in 1576 when they were paid 2s. and were 'casting earth' for three-and-a-half days 'gayttinge of basing stone'.[3] No Christian name is given for Roodes: therefore he may not be the same as John or Christopher Rhodes – both masons who worked at Wollaton and New Hardwick.

Oldcotes Agreement 1593. (Item no. 115 of vol. 242 of Leeds University MS295, Wilson Collection)

Articles of agreement Indented and Concluded the eight daye of March In the xxxvth yere if the Raigne of our Soveraigne Ladie Elizabeth (1593) Betwene the Right Honorable Elizabeth Countess of Shourewsbury and William Cavendish of Hardwick in the Countie of Derby Esquire on theone part and Godfry Plumtree Reynold Plumtree Raufe Plumtree George Plumtree Robert Ashmore and John Wade on the other part.

First the sayde Godfrey Reynolde Raufe and George Plumtrees Robert Ashmore and Jon Warde doe for themselves theyre executors and assignes Covenant promise and graunt to and with the saide Countess and William Cavendish theyre executors and assignes by theise presents viz to wale and make all wales belonging to one house ment and appoynted by the said Countess to be erected and built at Owlcotes in the Countie of Derby from the bottome of the Celler to the top of the roufe and too Tyrrets above the roufe according to a plat thereof alreddy drawne whereunto the saide Godfry Reynoulde Raufe and George Plumtree Robert Ashmore and John Warde have set theyre hands.

The utter wales of which house they Covenant to make too foote Eight inches thick till it comes to the highest height, and then to be too foote and a halfe thick and to put seven through stones in everie rode and well and workmanlike to skappell the outside of all the saide wales and Coynes according and like unto the best of the wales of that house which is already built at Owlcotes aforesaid and likewise to skappell the insides of all the wales in the kychin and to make the particon wales too foote thick or less as it shalbe thought needful by the saide Countess and William Cavendish or theyre officers. And the myddle wale to be fowre foote thick and to make all the Rannge boyling plave too ovins Chymneys dores and steps which rise within the grounde the saide Countess and William Cavendish fynding all the stone which shalbe by them or theyre offivers appointed to be geven eyther for foores windowes or Chymneys and causing the same to be set at the Costs and Chardges of the said Countess and William Cavendish and of which too ovins aforesaid must be fowre foote wide and the other three foote wide.

Item the sayde Godfry [*etc.*] doe Covenant and promise by these presents after the Parrells in the Chymneys of the said house ar sett to bring up all the Chymney Conduits to the top of the saide wales reddy to set on the shafts and to parget the Conduits of the sayde Chymneys and to make the backs of the said Chymneys of fyre stone and to make good and sufficient arches over all the doors windows and Chymneys or in any other place that shall happen in the side wales and to bring up and work all the wales of the saide house strayte well and workmanlike.

Itm the said Countess and William Cavendish doe Covenant to cause so much stone Lyme sande and water to be brought and layde forwarde to the said house as shalbe needful and Covenyent for the making of the said wales at the costs of the said Countess and William Cavendish and the said Plumtrees Warde and Ashmore doe Covenant to make all the mortar and scaffolds at theyre owne Costs having twentie dozen of hurdells and poles layde by somany as shalbe needful.

Item the said Plumtrees Warde and Ashmore doe Covenant to doe what they can well and workmanlike to worke skappell and finish all the sayde wales before allhallautide next and that they will all Contynually worke the said works until they have done and finished the same and will doe theyre best to get fowre walers more to help them until they have finished and done all the saide wales.

Item the sayde Countess and William Cavendish doe Covenant to paye unto the saide Plumtrees Warde and Ashmore for everie rode of wale aswell the utter wales as Inner wales till they come the height of twentie foote above the ground which wilbe to the top of the hale roofe threes shillings fowre pence for every rode of wale and everie rode of wale above the sayde height five shillings measuring all the Dores windowes and Chymneys in the sayde wale and in Consideration of the too Turrets above the leads to give them xxxs more then theyre work shall amount to by measure after the sayde rates and for making of the too Ovins twentie shillings more and to paye them at the end of every fortnight somuch as theyre work shall amount to by measure after the rates aforesayde and to measure the utter wales on the outsides thereof. And to lende them the sayde Plumtrees Warde and Ashmore sixe beds so long as they salbe in the sayde works and likewise to lend them three kyne from Maye Daye next until Martilmas next and to gyve them a quarter if Rye and a strike of Otemeal.

In wytnes whereof the saide parties to theise articles have set theyre hands and Seals the daye and yere first abovewritten.

Marks of Robert Ashmore, John Warde, Raffe Plumtree, George Plumtree, Godfry Plumtree, Reynold Pluntre.[4]

Notes

For biographical notes on Renould Plumtree and Robert Ashmore, see their wills in Appendix II. John Ward is first recorded working as a waller at Old Hardwick in July 1587 at 4d. a day;[5] he was paid 10s. for a half year in the Hardwick servants' wages account from 1593 to 1601.[6] He was working with cut stone blocks and was not a rough-waller – see also notes on the will of Robert Ashmore in Appendix II. In the Senior Survey he is listed as a free-holder living in a house in Beighton, Derbyshire, and farming twelve acres (five hectares). Stallybrass states that Ward was at Chatsworth in December 1578, when he was paid for repairing an orchard wall. He is usually paired with Robert Ashmore and the two of them had labourers working for them.[7] Stallybrass records Ashmore working at Chatsworth in February 1597,[8] and like his friend Ward he was paid 10s. for the half year from 1594 to 1601 in the household wage accounts. Also like Ward he achieved some security: in the Senior Survey he occupies a house with four acres (around one and a half hectares) at Chatsworth and some ten acres (four hectares) in Winster, Derbyshire. By the terms of the contract it can be seen that Bess was very much in charge and that she kept to the letter of her bargain we can be sure: in April 1594 there is a record 'Pd to Tho Ocle for the halffe yeares joyst of 3 kyne for 3 of the Plumtrees at Owlcotes 12/-.', which was repeated in October, exactly as the bargain stipulates.

None of the Plumtree brothers achieved the promotion required to be paid from the household wages, but in the Senior Survey for the year 1609 Reynold has a house and croft at Heath, Derbyshire, and a house with sixty-six acres (twenty-seven hectares) at Harstoft.

APPENDIX IV

MASONS' MARKS

These are a small selection of the masons' marks to be found on the buildings referred to in this book, along with those also found at the contemporary houses of Kirby Hall in Northamptonshire and Temple Newsam House in Yorkshire.

It can be seen from these that at least four under-masons using the same marks went on from Longleat House (4) Burghley House (4), Shireoaks Hall and Kirby Hall (8) to New Hardwick Hall, and at least three others went on to Bolsover Castle after working at New Hardwick Hall. However, although the same marks appear in different buildings that does not necessarily mean that the same under-mason was involved; they may have used a particular mark for one building – a simple mark such as (1), which appears at seven buildings, makes it seem unlikely that it was the same mason.

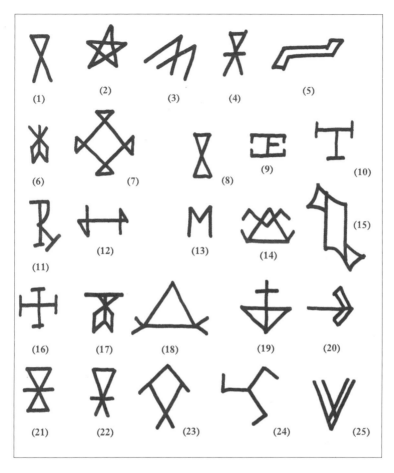

(1) Found at New Hardwick Hall, Bolsover Castle, Burghley House, Kirby Hall, Charlcote Park, Worksop Manor Lodge, Shireoaks Hall; (2) Found at New Hardwick Hall, Shireoaks Hall, Burghley House; (3) Found at New Hardwick Hall, Grimsthorpe Castle, Lyvedon New Build; (4) Found at New Hardwick Hall, Longleat House; (5) Found at New Hardwick Hall, Longleat House, Burghley House, Shireoaks Hall, Bolsover Castle; (6) Found exclusively at New Hardwick Hall; (7) Found at New Hardwick Hall, Temple Newsam House, Bolsover Castle; (8) Found at New Hardwick Hall, Burghley House, Longleat House, Kirby Hall, Shireoaks Hall; (9) Found exclusively at Old Hardwick Hall; (10) Found at Old Hardwick Hall, Lyvedon New Build; (11–19) Selection of marks from the High Great Chamber, New Hardwick Hall; (20–22) Selection of marks from the Little Keep, Bolsover Castle; (23) Found at Longleat House, Bolsover Castle, Kirby Hall; (24) Found at Longleat House, New Hardwick Hall; (25) Found at Longleat House, Burghley House

APPENDIX V

THE BEST BEDCHAMBER AT
HARDWICK OLD HALL

Old Hardwick Hall was not unusual in having two sets of state apartments; Wollaton Hall also had two. However, these sets of apartments evolved indifferent ways: at Wollaton Hall they were conceived as part of the original plan, but at Old Hardwick they were built at separate times for no clear reason.

As discussed in Chapter 5, it is not clear exactly what structures were standing at Old Hardwick Hall before the building accounts begin in 1587. Something was already built in the east wing, and Bess, as a countess, would have needed the facilities of state apartments. The building accounts are useful in this case only to establish what was being built and not as a record of what was already there; the 1601 inventory is only a record of what was there at that date.

The state apartments in the east wing belonging to the Forest Great Chamber were listed in sequence in the 1601 inventory, as one would expect: great chamber, bedchamber and a fully panelled withdrawing chamber. This seemingly marked the end of that session of work for the clerks making the inventory. Then they embarked upon a new listing, 'In the bed chamber in the best lodging . . . ', indicating that they were beginning on another range of state apartments that were better than those of the Forest Great Chamber. The contents were listed, but there was no heavy wood panelling, with hangings taking its place. This may be important, because if the bedchamber occupied the space above the hall some of the interior walls were not supported on load-bearing walls and so panelling –

so obvious in other rooms over the hall – would have been dispensed with to save weight. The inventory continued with 'Withdrawing Chamber' (no panelling), an 'Inner Chamber' to the best bedchamber (with full panelling) and the (fully panelled) 'Gallerie by the best lodging . . . ' before going into the 'Hill Great Chamber'.

In the plan at the end of Chapter 5, I have put the best chamber on the north side and next to the gallery but it could just as easily have been where I have put the 'Inner Chamber' and, by the argument of the weight of full panelling, probably was. All this establishes is that the best lodgings were next to and included the Hill Great Chamber and would consequently have been for the use of Bess when a full state reception was called for. There is no record of the best lodgings ever being used.

Using the same argument it follows that rooms allocated in the inventory to Mr Digby, Mr Reason (both upper servants) and Mr Manners, none of which has full panelling, were in the floor below and immediately over the great hall (see floor plans on pages 132–3). (Mr Manners had an inner chamber plus a bedchamber; he was a relative of Bess's husband but had supported her in her quarrel.) The lesser state apartments in the east wing, where Sir William Cavendish had his chamber, may have been for Mr Manners's use: he was knighted in 1580, married in 1582 and became high sheriff of Derbyshire, so he would have needed state apartments.

MANUSCRIPT SOURCES

CHATSWORTH HOUSE

The method of reference for documents held in the Devonshire archives is complicated. This is an amalgamated collection: part was previously held at Hardwick Hall, where many were stored in drawers, while the main Devonshire collection was held at Chatsworth. This results in rather long reference titles, but the result is clear. The Muniment Room at Chatsworth is now open to visitors, and the Hardwick Hall drawers, now empty, are still there.

Manuscripts listed in chronological order:

Devonshire MSS, Chatsworth, Hardwick MS 1: an account book for 1551–3

Devonshire MSS, Chatsworth, Hardwick MS 3: an account book for 1557–9

Devonshire MSS, Chatsworth, Hardwick MS 2: an account book for 1559–60

Devonshire MSS, Chatsworth MS, Bess and Earls' Misc. Box 2: account book of disbursements made by William Cooche on behalf of his master, Sir William St Loe, 1560

Devonshire MSS, Chatsworth, Hardwick MS 12: James Hardwick's survey of Hardwick lands, 1570

Devonshire MSS, Chatsworth, Hardwick MS 4: an account book for 1577

Devonshire MSS, Chatsworth, Hardwick MS 5: an account book for 1579–84

Devonshire MSS, Chatsworth, Hardwick MS 6: the Hardwick Building accounts, 1587–99

Devonshire MSS, Chatsworth, Hardwick MS 7: an account book for 1591–8

Devonshire MSS, Chatsworth, Hardwick MS 9a: an account book for 1592–3

Devonshire MSS, Chatsworth, Hardwick MS 10: an account book for 1593–4

Devonshire MSS, Chatsworth, Hardwick MS 9: an account book for 1593–8

Devonshire MSS, Chatsworth, Hardwick MS 8: an account book for 1598–1601

Devonshire MSS, Chatsworth, MS 29: book of accounts of various stewards of William Cavendish, 1608–23

Devonshire MSS, Chatsworth, Hardwick Drawers 143, 144, 145 and 367 contain leases, and so on

Devonshire MSS, Chatsworth, Hardwick Charters: concerns Hardwick family charters

Devonshire MSS, Chatsworth MS, Brief Day Book 1655–68, Michaelmas 1660 to Lady Day 1661

Devonshire MSS, Chatsworth MS L/60/22. Inventory of the beer cellar taken 25 March 1858

BRITISH LIBRARY

Harleian MS 4955, 'The King and Queene's Entertainment at Boulsouer, July 1634'

FOLGER SHAKESPEARE LIBRARY, WASHINGTON, DC
Phillips Collection

Over time some of the Hardwick MSS have been taken and sometimes auctioned. Fortunately the Folger Shakespeare Library in Washington, DC, bought many of these.

Xd 486: The earliest of Bess's account books to survive, covering the years 1548–50

Vb 308: London account book of Bess's expenditure kept by Richard Whaley, 1589–92

Xd 428: Cavendish/Talbot letters

(Xd 486 (Phillipps 4865), and Vb 308 (Phillipps 14784) were both acquired
by the Folger Library from the sale at Sotheby's of the Bibliotheca
Phillippica on 6 June 1967. These were Lots 734 and 735. At that time,
the Phillipps Library was the property of the Trustees of the Robinson
Trust who were selling it off. Xd 428 is part of the Cavendish Talbot
Papers.

LONGLEAT HOUSE

R.O.B. Records of the Building of Longleat

Vol. I: Up to 1550

Vol. II: 1550–70

Vol. III: After 1567

L.P. Longleat Papers.

Box LXVIII

Book 59: Building accounts January 1568–December 1570. This includes
some payments made in 1567 after the fire.

Book 60: Building accounts 1571–5

Book 61 (a): This includes some money paid out on building in 1568 but
mainly the expenditure of Lady Thynne in 1567–8

Box LXXXV

Book 141: General accounts 1550–2

Book 143: General accounts 1554–5

Book 144: General accounts 1555–6

Book 145: General accounts 1558–9

Box LXXVI

Book 146: General accounts 1559–60

Book 147: General accounts 1561–2, November–June only

Book 148: General accounts 1565–6

Box LXXXVIII

Book 159: General accounts but also gives total of building expenditure for
October 1578–December 1579

Book 160: Many miscellaneous costs, but includes some for building 1576–9

Book 161: Building accounts for May–December 1580

T.P. Thynne Papers

Vols. I–IV: Bound in leather and mostly Thynne correspondence.

Vols. XLVIII (Box I), XLVIII (Box II), Vol. L (Box III): Contain papers
concerning John Thynne Senior and dated Box I: pre-1561, Box II:
1561–76, Box III: 1577–81.

The Big Account Book

Contains a copy of the first half of Book 59 and the building accounts from
the fire in April 1567–November 1568

UNIVERSITY OF NOTTINGHAM
Department of Manuscripts

Middleton Manuscripts

A huge collection concerning the Willoughby family. For our purposes, the
most important are the Wollaton Hall building accounts:

Mi A 60/2 for 1583

Mi A 60/3 for 1584

Mi A 60/4 for 1584–5

Mi A 60/5 for 1596

Mi A 60/6 for 1587

Mi A 60/7 for 1588

Inventories for the period covering this book:

Mi I 9. 12 October 1596

Mi I 8i. 10 December 1596

Mi I 811. 7 October 1599

Mi I 15a/6. 8 October 1601 (This is the fullest of this series.)

Mi I. 16 September 1609

Mi I 17/1. Mid seventeenth century 'Catalogue of the Library in the handwriting of the natural philosopher, Francis Willoughby'

Also of interest is

The Portland Welbeck Collection, 1/553

Special Collection pamphlet No. 411 D64 Wol 1925. Sale catalogue of the contents of Wollaton Hall in 1925 in which nine lots of books of dates contemporary with the life of Sir Francis Willoughby are listed.

LAMBETH PALACE LIBRARY AND THE COLLEGE OF ARMS

A collection of Talbot and Shrewsbury papers is held in the Lambeth Palace Library and the College of Arms in London. A Calendar (record) of these documents was published in two volumes by Her Majesty's Stationery Office (HMSO) – see Bibliography, under G.R. Batho (ed.) and E.G.W. Bill (ed.). In these books each document is given a reference number, and there is a précis of what the document contains. The books can be purchased from the HMSO or ordered through public libraries. Most of the references in the footnotes are to these two volumes. The manuscripts may be consulted at Lambeth Palace Library or the College of Arms by appointment.

BRITISH MUSEUM

British Museum Manuscript Room, Cavendish Papers 1661–95. Loan 29/236: 756c

NOTES

INTRODUCTION

1 These are my figures, interpolated from Devonshire MSS, Chatsworth, Hardwick MS 6.

2 G.R. Batho (ed.), *A Calendar of the Shrewsbury and Talbot Papers in the Lambeth Palace Library and the College of Arms*, Vol. II, London: Her Majesty's Stationery Office, 1971, MS 706 f.35. (See note in Manuscript Sources on Lambeth Palace Library and the College of Arms, which explains how the manuscripts are listed and summarized in this Calendar but can be called up and inspected at the Lambeth Palace Library or the College of Arms.)

3 Devonshire MSS, Chatsworth, Hardwick MS 7, f. 35.

4 Devonshire MSS, Chatsworth, Hardwick MS 7, f. 170v.

5 Malcolm Airs, *The Tudor and Jacobean Country House: A Building History*, Godalming: Bramley Books, 1995, p. 57.

6 Airs, *The Tudor and Jacobean Country House*, p. 57.

7 David N. Durant and Philip Riden, *The Building of Hardwick Hall*, Chesterfield: Derbyshire Record Society, 1980/4, p. 245. (The two volumes of this work were published in 1980 and 1984; the pagination runs consecutively through the two volumes.)

8 Douglas Knoop and G.P. Jones, 'The Bolsover Building Accounts', *Ars Quarter Coronatorum*, Vol. XLIX, Part 1, 1936, p. 21.

9 Folger Shakespeare Library, Washington, DC, Xd 428 (104).

10 William Dickenson's Note-book, Sheffield Central Libraries, Local History Department, MD 192, f. 69.

11 Mark Girouard, *Robert Smythson and the Elizabethan Country House*, New Haven and London: Yale University Press, 1983, pp. 113–14. The reference to the 'Platte' being sent to Giles Greaves is in a letter from the Earl of Shrewsbury dated 5 August 1577 (G.R. Batho (ed.), f. 837); Greaves was working at Worksop in 1585 (E.G.W. Bill (ed.), *A Calendar of the Shrewsbury Papers in the Lambeth Palace Library*, Vol. I, London: Her Majesty's Stationery Office, 1966, Vol. 698, f. 87.

12 Batho (ed.), Vol. G, f. 225.

13 Batho (ed.), Vol. F, f. 403.

14 Nicolaus Pevsner and Elizabeth Williamson, *Buildings of England: Nottinghamshire*, Harmondsworth: Penguin Books, 1951, p. 390.

15 Girouard, *Robert Smythson and the Elizabethan Country House*, p. 115.

16 Batho (ed.), Vol. G, f. 308.

17 Bill (ed.), MS 707, f. 189.

18 I discussed this building work in an exchange of correspondence with Mark Girouard in 2009–10. Smythson's arrival in the Midlands was almost certainly the result of a call from Sir Francis Willoughby to work on Wollaton Hall. However, Shrewsbury was rebuilding Worksop Manor from 1580, and it is tempting to assume that Smythson was involved, if only from the evidence of the drawing of the screen. Mark has convinced me that this was not the case and that Smythson was involved only in adding the top floor and the hall screen, and I am happy with that!

19 Chatsworth, Hardwick Box, Chatsworth Archivist's Office.

20 Basil Stallybrass, 'Bess of Hardwick's Buildings and Building Accounts', *Archaeologia*, Vol. 64, 1912–13, pp. 347–398.

21 Knoop and Jones, p. 30.

22 Girouard, *Robert Smythson and the Elizabethan Country House*, pp. 131–3.

23 John Holland, *The History, Antiquities and Description of the Town and Parish of Worksop in the County of Nottingham*, Sheffield: J. Blackwell, 1826.

24 Holland, p. 133.

CHAPTER 1. ROBERT SMYTHSON

1   Mark Girouard, 'Robert Smythson and the Architecture of the Elizabethan Era', *Country Life*, 1966, p. 50.
2   Adrian Woodhouse, 'In Search of Robert Smythson' and 'Smythson Revisited', *Country Life*, 19 and 26 December 1991.
3   Girouard, *Robert Smythson and the Elizabethan Country House*, p. 40.

CHAPTER 2. LONGLEAT HOUSE

1   I am deeply indebted to Professor Malcolm Airs, who generously photocopied the notes he used for *The Making of the English Country House 1500–1640*, London: Architectural Press, 1975, and *The Tudor and Jacobean Country House: A Building History*, Godalming: Bramley Books, 1995.
2   Airs, *The Tudor and Jacobean Country House*, pp. 42–3.
3   Girouard, *Robert Smythson and the Elizabethan Country House*, p. 50.
4   Girouard, *Robert Smythson and the Elizabethan Country House*, p. 44.
5   Girouard, *Robert Smythson and the Elizabethan Country House*, p. 49. Girouard speculates that John Hills may have worked for the Duke of Somerset and for Thynne at Brentford in 1550.
6   Airs, *The Tudor and Jacobean Country House*, p. 114.
7   Professor Airs's notes on Longleat – see note 1 above.
8   Girouard, *Robert Smythson and the Elizabethan Country House*, p. 46.
9   Girouard, *Robert Smythson and the Elizabethan Country House*, p. 49.
10 Girouard, *Robert Smythson and the Elizabethan Country House*, p. 62.
11 Girouard, *Robert Smythson and the Elizabethan Country House*, p. 62.
12 Girouard, *Robert Smythson and the Elizabethan Country House*, p. 62.
13 Mark Girouard, 'Robert Smythson and the Architecture of the Elizabethan Era', pp. 68–9.

14 Girouard, 'Robert Smythson and the Architecture of the Elizabethan Era', pp. 60–1.

15 Girouard, 'Robert Smythson and the Architecture of the Elizabethan Era', Appendix 1.

16 Girouard, *Robert Smythson and the Elizabethan Country House*, pp. 65–6.

17 Airs, *The Making of the English Country House 1500–1640*, p. 101.

18 Girouard, *Robert Smythson and the Elizabethan Country House*, pp. 78 and 80.

19 Anthony Wells-Cole, *Art and Decoration in Elizabethan and Jacobean England*, New Haven and London: Yale University Press, 1997, p. 138.

20 Wells-Cole, pp. 137–9.

CHAPTER 3. CHATSWORTH HOUSE

1 Devonshire MSS, Chatsworth, Hardwick MS 1, f. 10.

2 John Summerson, *Architecture in Britain 1530–1830*, Harmondsworth: Penguin Books, 1970, p. 47.

3 Devonshire MSS, Chatsworth, Hardwick MS 2, f. 156v.

4 Folger Shakespeare Library, Washington, DC, Xd 428 (84).

5 Devonshire MSS, Chatsworth MS, Bess and Earl's Misc. Box 2: account book of disbursements made by William Cooche on behalf of his master, Sir William St Loe, 1560, p. 64.

6 Folger Shakespeare Library, Washington, DC, Xd 426 (78).

7 Devonshire MSS, Chatsworth, Hardwick MS 4, f. 114.

8 Stallybrass, p. 356. Stallybrass gives the year as 1576, but he was not allowing for the year change in March; 1576 in the accounts is 1577 by our reckoning.

9 Stallybrass, p. 356.

10 Stallybrass, p. 355.

11 Stallybrass, p. 376.

12 There is no mention of 'the Stand' in Devonshire MSS, Chatsworth, Hardwick MS 4 (1577–80). In the 1601 inventory there are 'turrets in the mount', which is a different building from the Stand. Nevertheless the surviving plasterwork is a tribute to the master-plasterer, and the date of 1581 would fit.

13 Devonshire MSS, Chatsworth, Hardwick MS 4.

14 Wells-Cole, p. 252.

CHAPTER 4. WOLLATON HALL

1 Richard Smith, *Sir Francis Willoughby of Wollaton Hall*, Nottingham: City of Nottingham Arts Department, 1988, p. 2.

2 Smith, p. 11.

3 Historical Manuscripts Commission, *Report on the Manuscripts of Lord Middleton*, London: Her Majesty's Stationery Office, 1911, p. 521.

4 HMC, *Middleton*, p. 522.

5 Smith, p. 8.

6 Girouard, *Robert Smythson and the Elizabethan Country House*, p. 83.

7 University of Nottingham Department of Manuscripts, Middleton Collection, Mi A 60/5.

8 University of Nottingham Department of Manuscripts, Mi A 60/2.

9 Smith, p. 23.

10 Smith, p. 34

11 HMC, *Middleton*, p. 429.

12 Mark Girouard, 'The Smythson Collection', *Architectural History*, Vol. 5, 1962, pp. 89–90.

13 Girouard, *Robert Smythson and the Elizabethan Country House*, p. 101.

14 Mark Girouard, *Elizabethan Architecture: Its Rise and Fall*, New Haven and London: Yale University Press, 2009, pp. 244–5.

15 Girouard, *Robert Smythson and the Elizabethan Country House*, pp. 99–101.

16 David N. Durant, 'Wollaton Hall – A Rejected Plan', *Transactions of*

the Thoroton Society, Vol. LXXVI, 1972, pp. 13–16

17 David Thomson, 'France's Earliest Illustrated Printed Architectural Pattern Book', in Jean Guillaume (ed.), *Architecture et vie sociale: L'organisation interior de grandes demeures à la Moyen Age et la Renaissance*. Paris: Picard, 1994, pp. 221–34.

18 Wells-Cole, p. 68.

19 Pamela Marshall, *Wollaton: An Archaeological Survey*, Nottingham: Nottingham Civic Society, 1996, pp. 81–7.

20 Letter from Mark Girouard to the author dated 30 September 1988. Girouard states that he has photographs of the four alabaster statuettes, which he thinks represented the Four Seasons.

21 Marshall, p. 144.

22 University of Nottingham Department of Manuscripts, Mi A 60/2, p. 8.

23 Marshall, p. 48.

24 Rosalys Coope, 'The Byron Family and their Building Works at Newstead Abbey, Nottinghamshire (1540–1640)', *The Transactions of the Thoroton Society*, Vol. 111, 2007, p. 105. (Compare note 16 from same source – after Vol. 100 the journal changed the format from Roman numerals, so this is Vol. 111.)

25 University of Nottingham Department of Manuscripts, Mi A 60/5.

26 University of Nottingham Department of Manuscripts, Mi A 60/6.

27 University of Nottingham Department of Manuscripts, Mi A 60/7.

28 University of Nottingham Department of Manuscripts, Mi A 60/3.

29 I am indebted for this information to Rodney Melville, the architect responsible for Hardwick Hall over many years.

30 William Dickenson's Note-book, f. 76v.

31 Devonshire MSS, Chatsworth, Hardwick MS 8, f. 35v. and MS 7, f. 154.

32 University of Nottingham Department of Manuscripts, Mi A 60/5, p. 45

33 Lichfield Probate Registry, held at Lichfield Joint Record Office, Lichfield, Staffordshire. Probate means that the will has been proved

and is lawful. The Lichfield registry runs up to 1858, after which wills were proved by the probate division of the High Court and kept at Somerset House, London.

34 Devonshire MSS, Chatsworth, Hardwick MS 7.

35 Chatsworth: William Cavendish's Account Book for March 1607. I am indebted to Mark Girouard for this reference.

36 The receipt for 1588 was on a loose piece of paper, which has since gone missing but which was described by Philip Rossall in 'The Building of Wollaton Hall', master's degree thesis, University of Sheffield, 1957. The law case is in the Public Record Office (1600–1), E.1., 34/43.

37 Smith, p. 20.

38 University of Nottingham Department of Manuscripts, Mi C 30 (2) and (3), Mi D 165/76, Mi D 169/20 and the valuation in Her Majesty's Stationery Office (HMSO), *Calendars of State Papers (Domestic)*, Vol. CCLXV, No. 83, at the Public Records Office in Kew.

CHAPTER 5. OLD HARDWICK HALL

1 Devonshire MSS, Chatsworth, Hardwick MS 6.

2 Lindsay Boynton and Peter Thornton, *The Hardwick Hall Inventories of 1601*, London: Furniture History Society, 1971.

3 Batho (ed.), Vol. G, f. 308.

4 Details of John Hardwick's will and his widow's problems with the Office of Wards are at Public Record Office, Kew (PRO): (IPM) C/142/50/102; PRO: (IPM) C/142/47/25; PRO Wards Books 149 and 50; Star Chamber Hen. VIII, Vol. VII, ff. 15–16. (An Inquisition Post-Mortem or IPM is a legal enquiry into the financial affairs of the deceased to discover if the estate could be taken in the Court of Wards.)

5 Sarah Gristwood, *Arbella – England's Lost Queen*, London: Bantam Press, 2003, p. 40.

6 Devonshire MSS, Chatsworth, Hardwick MS 12.

7 PRO, (IPM) C/142/147/25. (See note 4 for explanation of IPM.)

8 PRO, Extents for Debts 21 Elizabeth C 230/45.

9 Folger Shakespeare Library, Washington, DC, Xd 428 (35) and (48).

10 Devonshire MSS, Chatsworth, Hardwick Drawer 278, Item 1.

11 Indenture dated 22 April 1572. Chatsworth, Cupboard No. 2, Shelf 3.

12 Folger Shakespeare Library, Washington, DC, Xd 428 (50).

13 Batho (ed.), Vol. O, f. 66.

14 Durant and Riden (eds), p. 42.

15 Devonshire MSS, Chatsworth, Hardwick MS 7.

16 Her Majesty's Stationery Office (HMSO), *Calendars of State Papers (Domestic), Edward VI, Mary I, Elizabeth I and James I.*

17 HMSO, *Calendars of State Papers (Domestic)*, Vol. CLXXXV, Nos. 10 and 11.

18 English Heritage: Report No. 56/2002. Series CfA Reports.

19 Devonshire MSS, Chatsworth, Hardwick Drawer 393, Bundle A, p. 248.

20 Chatsworth, Handbook to Hardwick Charters, p. 340.

21 'The barne' was paved in June 1590: Durant and Riden (eds), 'Hardwick Building Accounts', p. 117.

22 Durant and Riden (eds), pp. 212–13.

23 Durant and Riden (eds), pp. 120 and 141.

24 Stallybrass, p. 361. Stallybrass suggested the east–west layout of the hall. More than one hundred years later I arrived at the same conclusion – we used different routes to achieve the same result!

25 HMSO, *Calendars of State Papers (Domestic)*, 1581–90, p. 453.

26 Devonshire MSS, Chatsworth, Hardwick Drawer 143: f. 165v.

27 Durant and Riden (eds), pp. 94, 95, 97, 99, 100, 107.

28 Durant and Riden (eds), p.119.

29 William Dickenson's Note-book.

30 William Dickenson's Note-book, f. 49.

31 William Dickenson's Note-book, f. 50.

32 William Dickenson's Note-book, f. 121.

33 Devonshire MSS, Chatsworth, Hardwick MS 6, f. x18.

34 Durant and Riden (eds), pp. 133 and 135.

35 Devonshire MSS, Chatsworth, Hardwick MS 7, f. 62; Hardwick MS 10, f. 16v; Folger Shakespeare Lib, Washington, DC, Xd 428 (1450).

36 Both Robert Ashmore and Hollingworth, wallers, worked at Chatsworth from 1577 to 1580. Two wallers with the same names worked at Hardwick.

37 Durant and Riden (eds), p. 33.

38 Durant and Riden (eds), p. 58.

39 Durant and Riden (eds), p. 121.

40 Devonshire MSS, Chatsworth, Hardwick Drawer 143, f. 13v (9/10/1591).

41 Durant and Riden (eds), pp. 85–6.

42 Durant and Riden (eds), p. 10.

43 Durant and Riden (eds), p. 11.

44 Durant and Riden (eds), p. 18.

45 Durant and Riden (eds), p. 45.

46 Durant and Riden (eds), pp. 45–52.

47 Durant and Riden (eds), p. 58.

48 Devonshire MSS, Chatsworth, Hardwick MS 29: pp. 650, 672 and 705.

49 Durant and Riden (eds), p. 59.

50 Durant and Riden (eds), p. 72.

51 Bagshaw's Derbyshire Directory 1846: 'One room remained floored with terras (plaster).' Plaster was made from the lime-ash residue left at the bottom of the lime kilns after firing; mixed with water, the lime ash sets very hard. The floor joists were covered with split-oak laths on which a layer of straw was laid before pouring on the lime ash mixture. The flooring was heavy and needed substantial joists and beams. It was common flooring in Derbyshire and Nottinghamshire and was cheaper than using timber. Bagshaw's Derbyshire Directory is a mine of information for the county in 1846, and includes the names of

householders, tradesmen and much else; occasionally it diverts into other comment, as in this case.

52 Durant and Riden (eds), pp. 74, 76, 77, 79, 80 and 83.

53 Devonshire MSS, Chatsworth, Hardwick Drawer, 143: f. 18.

54 Devonshire MSS, Chatsworth, Hardwick MS 6, f. 238.

55 Archaeological Recording March 1998, Trent and Peak Archaeological Trust. This is one of a series of reports prepared by the Peak Archaeological Trust for English Heritage and the National Trust. They are held in the Registrar's Department of the University of Nottingham in Nottingham.

56 Durant and Riden (eds), pp. 64.

57 Durant and Riden (eds), p. 149.

58 In the published inventory it is room 49 in the Old Hall.

59 Durant and Riden (eds), p. 234.

60 Durant and Riden (eds), p. 146.

61 Durant and Riden (eds), p. 235.

62 Durant and Riden (eds), p. 245.

63 Durant and Riden (eds), p. 221.

64 Durant and Riden (eds), p. 185.

65 Wells-Cole, p. 264.

66 Wells-Cole, p. 266.

67 Wells-Cole, p. 264.

68 Wells-Cole, pp. 263–4.

69 Wells-Cole, pp. 263–5.

70 Durant and Riden (eds), p. 53.

71 Devonshire MSS, Chatsworth, Hardwick MS 7, f. 48.

72 Devonshire MSS, Chatsworth, Hardwick MS 7, f. 37.

73 Stallybrass, p. 376.

74 Devonshire MSS, Chatsworth, Hardwick MS 7, f. 48.

75 Devonshire MSS, Chatsworth, Hardwick MS 6, f. 59.

76 Durant and Riden (eds), p. 134.

77 Durant and Riden (eds), p. 152.

78 Durant and Riden (eds), p. 60.

79 Durant and Riden (eds), p. 148.

80 Durant and Riden (eds), p. 208.

81 Devonshire MSS, Chatsworth MS L/60/22. Inventory of the beer cellar taken 25 March 1858. This is a single sheet of paper with the beer figures on one side and a list of silver plate on the other.

82 Devonshire MSS, Chatsworth, Hardwick MS 6 ff. 68, 68v. and 69.

83 Devonshire MSS, Chatsworth, Hardwick MS 29, f. 650.

84 Pamela Kettle, *A History of the Hardwick Inn*, Sutton Scarsdale, Derbyshire: self-published, 1991, p. 11.

85 Devonshire MSS, Chatsworth, Hardwick MS 29, f. 672.

86 Devonshire MSS, Chatsworth, Hardwick MS 29, f. 581

87 Devonshire MSS, Chatsworth: Brief Day Book 1655–68, Michaelmas 1660 to Lady Day 1661.

88 Kristian Kaminski, *Hardwick Old Hall: A History of Preservation 1608–1998*, London: English Heritage, 2006, p. 7.

CHAPTER 6. HARDWICK NEW HALL

1 David N. Durant, *Bess of Hardwick: Portrait of an Elizabethan Dynast*, London: Peter Owen, 1999, p.193. This sum was just over half her gross income in 1601.

2 Agnes Strickland, *Mary Queen of Scots*, London: George Bell and Sons, 1888, pp. 346 and 347.

3 Durant and Riden (eds), p. 114.

4 Devonshire MSS, Chatsworth, Hardwick MS 6, ff. x67r, x67v, x68v.

5 Durant and Riden (eds), p. 141.

6 Durant and Riden (eds), p. 145–6.

7 Hon John Byng, *Torrington Diaries*, London: Eyre and Spottiswood, 1934, Vol. 2, pp. 30–3.

8 Durant and Riden (eds), p. 195.

9 Devonshire MSS, Chatsworth, Hardwick MS 7, f. 35

10 Brian Wragg, *The Life and Works of John Carr of York*, York: Oblong, 2000.

11 Lindsay Boynton and P. Thornton, *The Hardwick Hall Inventory of 1601*, London: Furniture History Society, 1971, p. 32.

12 Durant and Riden (eds), p. 154.

13 Durant and Riden (eds), p. 154.

14 Durant and Riden (eds), p. 130.

15 Durant and Riden (eds), p. 135.

16 Durant and Riden (eds), p. 155.

17 Durant and Riden (eds), p. 158.

18 Durant and Riden (eds), p. 159.

19 Devonshire MSS, Chatsworth, Hardwick MS 7, f. 33v. and f. 35v.

20 Devonshire MSS, Chatsworth, Hardwick MS 7, f. 60.

21 Devonshire MSS, Chatsworth, Hardwick MS 7, f. 189.

22 Durant and Riden (eds), p. 263.

23 Durant and Riden (eds), p. 174 and p. 175.

24 Durant and Riden (eds), p. 169.

25 Durant and Riden (eds), p. 221

26 Devonshire MSS, Chatsworth, Hardwick MS 6, f. 64.

27 Devonshire MSS, Chatsworth, Hardwick MS 6 f. 77v. and Devonshire MSS, Chatsworth, Hardwick MS 8, f. 57v.

28 Devonshire MSS, Chatsworth, Hardwick MS 7, f. 119v., f. 120v. and f. 125v.

29 Devonshire MSS, Chatsworth, Hardwick MS 7, f. 152v.

30 Devonshire MSS, Chatsworth, Hardwick MS 8, f. 57v.

31 Devonshire MSS, Chatsworth, Hardwick MS 7, f.136.

32 Hardwick MS 8, f. 25v., 26 May 1598. and f. 56v., 19 July 1599.

33 Devonshire MSS, Chatsworth, Hardwick MS 6, f. 86.

34 Devonshire MSS, Chatsworth, Hardwick MS 7, f. 107v., f. 128v., f. 129v., f. 130v. and f. 134v.

35 Devonshire MSS, Chatsworth, Hardwick Drawer 143, f. 8v., 16 April 1594.

36 Devonshire MSS, Chatsworth, Hardwick Drawer 143, f. 8v.

37 Devonshire MSS, Chatsworth, Hardwick MS 8, f. 82.

38 Wells-Cole, pp. 276–7.

39 Durant and Riden (eds), p. 227.

40 Durant and Riden (eds), p. 215.

41 Devonshire MSS, Chatsworth, Hardwick MS 8, f. 118v, June–August 1601.

42 Wells-Cole, p. 270.

43 Durant and Riden (eds), p. 231.

44 Durant and Riden (eds), p. 184.

45 Durant and Riden (eds), 27 May 1598 f. 245-6.

46 Wells-Cole, p. 266.

47 Durant and Riden (eds), p. 191.

48 Durant and Riden (eds), p. 258.

49 Durant and Riden (eds), p. 223.

50 Batho (ed.), MS 706 f. 35.

51 Pamela Kettle, *Oldcotes: The Last Mansion Built by Bess of Hardwick*, Cardiff: Merton Priory Press, 2000, p. 40.

52 Devonshire MSS, Chatsworth, Hardwick MS 7, f. 188 and f. 196v. and MS 8, f. 48v.

53 Stanley Revill, 'A 16th-century map of the river Trent near Shelford', *Transactions of the Thoroton Society of Nottinghamshire*, Vol. LXXV, 1971, pp. 81–90.

CHAPTER 7. BOLSOVER CASTLE

1 P. Currey, 'Bolsover Castle', *Derbyshire Archaeological and Natural History Society*, Vol. 38, 1916.

2 David Durant, *Bess of Hardwick*, Peter Owen, London, 1999, p. 186.

3 D. Knoop and D.P. Jones, 'The Bolsover Castle Building Accounts, 1613', *Ars Quatuor Coronatorum* XLIX, Part 1, 1936, p. 21.

4 Lucy Worsley, unpublished draft of *Bolsover Castle Conservation Plan*, Vol. 2, p. 52.

5 Worsley, p. 52.

6 Knoop and Jones, p. 18.

7 Girouard, 'Robert Smythson and the Architecture of the Elizabethan Era', p. 177.

8 Knoop and Jones, p.27.

9 Knoop and Jones, pp. 49, 51 and 54.

10 Knoop and Jones, p. 19.

11 Knoop and Jones, p. 27.

12 Knoop and Jones, p. 49.

13 Knoop and Jones, p. 47.

14 Knoop and Jones, p. 49.

15 Knoop and Jones, p. 51.

16 Information given in conversation with Dr Sheppard.

17 Knoop and Jones, p. 51.

18 Knoop and Jones, p. 53.

19 Knoop and Jones, p. 55.

20 Knoop and Jones, p. 55.

21 Mark K. Askey, 'A Discourse on the Building Accounts for Bolsover Castle – 2 November 1612 to 26 March 1614', 1999. This is a paper Dr Askey wrote for private circulation.

22 I am indebted to Dr Mark Askey, Conservation Officer of Derbyshire Dales District Council, who pointed out the two centre arches.

23 Dr Askey suggested that the building was refaced on three sides in 1629–30. He may well be right, but the jury is still out on this one.

24 Dr Lucy Worsley, *Cavalier*, London: Faber and Faber, 2007, p. 36.

25 Dr James Loxley, 'My Gossip's Foot Voyage', *The Times Literary Supplement*, 11 September 2009. I am deeply indebted to Dr Jennifer Alexander of University of Warwick for bringing this to my attention.

26 Mark Girouard, 'Early Drawings of Bolsover Castle', *Architectual History*, Vol. 27, 1984, pp. 510–18.

27 F.W.C. Gregory, 'Bolsover Castle', *Transactions of the Thoroton Society of Nottinghamshire*, 1947, Vol. LI, p. 29.

28 Gregory, p. 41.

29 F.W.C. Gregory, 'Bolsover Castle: A Review of the Seventeenth-Century Buildings', a typed manuscript prepared for publication in *The British Architect* and in the possession of the author, p. 24, and also by Gregory in 'Bolsover Castle', *The British Architect*, February 1903.

30 Revd Hamilton Grey, *Bolsover Castle,* Chesterfield: unnamed publisher, 1894, p. 38.

31 Knoop and Jones, pp. 40 and 41.

32 British Library, Harleian MS 4955, 'The King and Queene's Entertainment at Bolsouer, July 1634.' This source is sometimes referred to as 'the Newcastle manuscript'.

33 For the information on Luken and Kellam I am deeply indebted to Dr Lucy Worsley, who looked out background research on these two gentlemen in her invaluable *The Building and Furnishing of the Little Castle at Bolsover,* an unpublished report dated June 2000, pp. 28–9.

34 Geoffrey Trease, *Portrait of a Cavalier,* London: Macmillan, 1979, p. 31.

35 Timothy Raylor, 'Pleasure Reconciled to Virtue', *Renaissance Quarterly,* Vol. 52, 1999, p. 402.

36 Pamela Kettle, *A History of the Hardwick Inn*, p. 13.

37 Margaret, Duchess of Newcastle (Margaret Cavendish), *The Cavalier in Exile, Being the Lives of the First Duke and Duchess of Newcastle,* London: George Newnes, 1903, p. 143.

38 I am indebted to my friend of many years Dr Rosalys Coope for a copy of her unpublished notes 'The iconography of the Bolsover decorations', dated 1980. Her research covers the sources used in the Pillar Parlour, as well as those of the other rooms discussed here.

39 I am further indebted to Dr Coope, who asked the late Sir Anthony Blunt if he could throw any light on the *Boy with Cat*: the information he provided is condensed here. However, for readers who would like to go further, Sir Anthony referred Dr Coope to an article in German

by Wolfgang Fischer, 'Claude Vignon (1593–1670)', published in the *Netherlands Year-Book for History of Art*, 1962. To travel even further down this esoteric path, a portrait by Anthony Van Dyck of François Langlois holding bagpipes, formerly in the possession of Lord Cowdray, is now in the National Gallery, London. One is left to wonder how the *Boy with Bagpipes* of *c.* 1618 became the *Boy with a Cat* at Bolsover by 1621.

40 The Duchess of Newcastle in her biography of her husband, *The Cavalier in Exile, Being the Lives of the First Duke and Duchess of Newcastle* (see note 35 and Bibliography), mentions this brother Charles, but nothing much is known about him. More can be said of her husband William, Duke of Newcastle; three copies of an original portrait by Anthony Van Dyck exist, all painted about the same time as the panel at Bolsover, and in all the features are similar. At Bolsover the portrait on the left, which is likely to be that of Newcastle, has hair of the same colour as his grandmother Bess and her long Hardwick nose. The other shows a younger man with hair of the same colour. Of course, that is supposition, but for the present all we have to go on.

41 Girouard, *Robert Smythson and the Elizabethan Country House*, p. 258–9.

42 British Museum Manuscript Room, Cavendish Papers 1661–95, Loan 29/236: 756c, pp. 387–8.

43 Raylor, pp. 402–39.

44 Margaret, Duchess of Newcastle, *The Cavalier in Exile*, p. 90.

45 Worsley, unpublished draft of *Bolsover Castle Conservation Plan*, Vol. 2, pp. 47–8.

46 University of Nottingham Dept of Manuscripts, Portand Welbeck Collection, 1/553.

47 Mark Girouard touches on this with the same suggestion in his notes on 'The Smythson Collection of the RIBA', *Architectural History*, 1961, Vol. 5, p. 48. It is not a subject repeated in his two subsequent books on Robert Smythson, published in 1966 and 1983 (see Bibliography).

48 Lucy Worsley, *Bolsover Castle*, London: English Heritage, 2000, p. 24.

49 Wells-Cole, p. 213.

50 G. Vertue, 'Notebooks', 11, *Walpole Society*, Vol. XX, Oxford: Oxford University Press, 1932, p. 32, and Horace Walpole, *Anecdotes of Painting in England*, Twickenham: self-published at his Strawberry Hill Press, 1762, p. 372.

51 She made the statement in a private email to the author: 'Ben Jonson's masque *Love's Welcome* kicks off with the song about a banquet of the senses, which would seem to match the pictures of the senses in that room.'

52 British Library, Harleian MS 4955, 'The King and Queene's Entertainment at Bolsouer, July 1634'.

53 Harleian MS 4955.

54 Quoted in Trease, p. 182.

55 Lucy Worsley, *The Building and Furnishing of the Little Castle at Bolsover*, an unpublished report dated June 2000, pp. 30–1.

56 Public Record Office, PCC, Seager 110.

APPENDIX II. WILLS

1 W.L.Spiers (ed.), 'Nicholas Stone's notebook', *Archaeologia*, Vol. VII, 1918–19, p. H31.

2 Airs, *The Making of the English Country House 1500–1641*, p. 193.

3 Stallybrass, p. 356.

4 Devonshire MSS, Chatsworth MSS 6 and 7.

APPENDIX III. FROM WILLIAM DICKENSON'S NOTE-BOOK

1 Sheffield Central Libraries, MD 192, f. 68.

2 James R. Wigfull, 'Extracts from the Note-book of William Dickenson', *Transactions of the Hunter Archaeology Society*, Vol. II, 1924, pp. 189–200.

3   Sheffield Central Libraries, MD 192, f. 68. and f. 44v.

4   Wilson Collection, Vol. 242, Leeds University Library. Compare another copy in the Bemrose Collection, Vol. 121, in Derby Central Library, printed in *Derbyshire Archaeological Journal*, Vol. LXXXVI, 1966, pp. 121–2 and published in David N. Durant and Philip Riden (eds), *The Building of Hardwick Hall*, Chesterfield: Derbyshire Record Society, Vol. 2, 1984, pp. lxxvi and lxxvii.

5   Stallybrass, p. 356.

6   Devonshire MSS, Chatsworth MSS 7 and 8.

7   Devonshire MSS, Chatsworth MS 7, f. 54. 16 March 1593 'to Warde and Ashmore and their labourers ijs.vjd.'.

8   Stallybrass, p. 356.

BIBLIOGRAPHY

Airs, Malcolm, *The Making of the English Country House 1500–1640*,
   London: Architectural Press, 1975

Airs, Malcolm, *The Tudor and Jacobean Country House: A Building History*,
   Godalming: Bramley Books, 1995

Batho, G.R. (ed.), *A Calendar of the Shrewsbury and Talbot Papers in the
   Lambeth Palace Library and the College of Arms*, London: Her
   Majesty's Stationery Office, 1971

Bill, E.G.W. (ed.), *A Calendar of Shrewsbury Papers in the Lambeth Palace
   Library*, London: Her Majesty's Stationery Office, 1966

Boynton, L. and Thornton, P., *The Hardwick Hall Inventories of 1601*,
   London: Furniture History Society, 1971

Coope, Rosalys, 'The Byron Family and Their Building Works at
   Newstead Abbey, Nottinghamshire (1540–1640)', *Transactions of the
   Thoroton Society*, Vol. 111, 2007

Devonshire, the Duchess of (Deborah Cavendish), *The House: A Portrait of
   Chatsworth*, London: Papermac, 1982

Durant, David N., *Bess of Hardwick: Portrait of an Elizabethan Dynast*,
   London: Peter Owen, 1999

Durant, David N., 'Wollaton Hall – A Rejected Plan', *Transactions of the
   Thoroton Society*, Vol. LXXVI, 1972, pp. 13–16

Durant, David N. and Riden, Philip, *The Building of Hardwick Hall*, Parts 1
   and 2, Chesterfield: Derbyshire Record Society, 1980 and 1984

Fowkes, D. V. and Potter, G.R. (eds), 'William Senior's Survey of the

Estates of the First and Second Earls of Devonshire, *c.* 1600–28',
Derbyshire Record Society, Vol. XIII, 1988

Girouard, Mark, 'Early Drawings of Bolsover Castle', *Architectural History,*
Vol. 27, 1984, pp. 510–18

Girouard, Mark, *Elizabethan Architecture: Its Rise and Fall,* New Haven
and London: Yale University Press, 2009

Girouard, Mark, 'Elizabethan Chatsworth', *Country Life,* 22 November
1973, pp. 1668–72

Girouard, Mark, *Hardwick Hall,* London: National Trust, 1989

Girouard, Mark, *Life in the English Country House,* New Haven and
London: Yale University Press, 1978

Girouard, Mark, *Robert Smythson and the Architecture of the Elizabethan
Era,* London: Country Life, 1966

Girouard, Mark, *Robert Smythson and the Elizabethan Country House,* New
Haven and London: Yale University Press, 1983

Girouard, Mark, 'Solomon in Nottingham', *Country Life,* 3 October 1991,
pp. 64–7

Girouard, Mark, 'The Development of Longleat House', *Royal Archaeological
Institute,* Vol. CXVI, 1961, pp. 200–22

Girouard, Mark, 'The Smythson Collection', *Architectural History,* Vol. 5,
1962

Her Majesty's Stationery Office, *Calendars of State Papers (Domestic),
Edward VI, Mary I, Elizabeth I and James I,* Vols. 1–12 and addenda,
various dates of publication, held at the Public Record Office, Kew
(PRO)

Gristwood, Sarah, *Arbella – England's Lost Queen,* London: Bantam Press
2003

Kettle, Pamela, *Oldcotes,* Cardiff: Merton Priory Press, 2000

Kettle, Pamela, *A History of the Hardwick Inn,* Sutton Scarsdale, Derbyshire:
self-published, 1991

Knoop, D. and Jones, D.P., 'The Bolsover Castle Building Accounts, 1613',
Ars Quatuor Coronatum, XLIX, Part 1, 1936

Levey, M. Santina, *Of Household Stuff: The 1601 Inventories of Bess of Hardwick*, London: National Trust, 2001

Lovell, Mary, S., *Bess of Hardwick: First Lady of Chatsworth*, London: Little, Brown, 2005

Marshall, Pamela, *Wollaton Hall: An Architectural Survey*, Nottingham: Nottingham Civic Society, 1996

Meredith, Rosamund (ed.), *A Catalogue of the Arundel Castle Manuscripts Relating to Yorkshire, Nottingham and Derbyshire Estates with an Appendix Consisting of the Talbot Letters, Part of the Bacon Franks Collection*, Sheffield: Sheffield City Libraries, 1965

Newcastle, Margaret, Duchess of (Margaret Cavendish), *The Cavalier in Exile, Being the Lives of the first Duke and Duchess of Newcastle*, London: George Newnes, 1903

Revill, Stanley, 'A 16th-century Map of the River Trent near Shelford', *Transactions of the Thoroton Society of Nottinghamshire*, Vol. LXXV, 1971, pp. 81–90

Smith, Richard S., *Sir Francis Willoughby of Wollaton Hall*, Nottingham: City of Nottingham Arts Department, 1988

Stallybrass, Basil, 'Bess of Hardwick's Buildings and Building Accounts', *Archaeologia*, Vol. 64, 1912–13, pp. 346–98

Stephenson, W. H. (ed.), *Report on the Manuscripts of Lord Middleton Preserved at Wollaton Hall, Nottinghamshire*, London: His Majesty's Stationery Office, 1911

Wells-Cole, Anthony, *Art and Decoration in Elizabethan and Jacobean England*, New Haven and London: Yale University Press, 1997

Woodhouse, Adrian, 'In Search of Robert Smythson' and 'Smythson Revisited', *Country Life*, 19 and 26 December 1991

Worsley, Lucy, *Bolsover Castle*, London: English Heritage, 2000

Worsley, Lucy, *Hardwick Old Hall*, London: English Heritage, 1998

INDEX